COMPUTER SCIENCE, TECHNOLOGY AND APPLICATIONS

RECENT ADVANCES IN AD HOC NETWORKS RESEARCH

COMPUTER SCIENCE, TECHNOLOGY AND APPLICATIONS

Additional books in this series can be found on Nova's website under the Series tab.

Additional e-books in this series can be found on Nova's website under the e-book tab.

COMPUTER SCIENCE, TECHNOLOGY AND APPLICATIONS

RECENT ADVANCES IN AD HOC NETWORKS RESEARCH

NATARAJAN MEGHANATHAN
EDITOR

New York

Library of Congress Cataloging-in-Publication Data

Recent advances in ad hoc networks research / editor, Natarajan Meghanathan (Department of Computer Science, Jackson State University, Jackson, MS, US).
pages cm. -- (Computer science, technology, and applications)
Includes bibliographical references and index.
ISBN 978-1-63321-337-1 (hardcover)
1. Ad hoc networks (Computer networks) I. Meghanathan, Natarajan, 1977-
TK5105.77.R43 2014
004.6--dc23

2014022553

Published by Nova Science Publishers, Inc. † New York

CONTENTS

PREFACE

Ad Hoc Networks has been an extensively studied research area for the last two decades. Due to the diversity of this Ad Hoc Networks and its complex constraints, there are still several open-ended problems of both theoretical and practical interests that need to be addressed. This edited book presents a collection of several such research problems as well as their solutions and comprehensive analysis. The mission of this book is to integrate both theoretical as well as practical research across diverse areas of ad hoc networks and their applications in such a manner that it can be used both as a good reference book for graduate-level courses (in wireless networks) and as a guide for researchers to solve the open research problems in this area.

The chapters included in the book have been written by eminent researchers in diverse areas of ad hoc networks, spanning Mobile Ad hoc Networks, Vehicular Ad hoc Networks, Cognitive Radio Networks, Static and Mobile Sensor Networks and Underwater Sensor Networks. Though written by different authors, there will be continuity among the chapters; the editor has ensured that the chapters are written in such a way that the flow of contents across the chapters is logical and easy to understand. The chapters have been organized systematically such that the readers do not get lost with the complexity of the materials presented in the individual chapters.

The chapters cover a broad range of issues in ad hoc networks, ranging from protocol design and performance evaluation/comparison, asymptotic analysis of network topologies for wireless networks, secure data aggregation in mobile sensor networks, target coverage in static and mobile sensor networks, localization in underwater sensor networks, energy-efficient communication in vehicular ad hoc networks and cloud-based implementation of cognitive radio ad hoc networks. Most of the chapters illustrate the close proximity between theory and applications. The solutions presented for the research problems have a strong theoretical foundation and are well-justified and evaluated. The authors present comprehensive evaluation studies (qualitative analysis, simulations, real-time experiments or a combination of these) of their proposed solution along with comparative analysis with existing solutions. The solutions and their approach presented in each of the chapters could serve as a model framework for researchers to adopt in their studies.

Chapters 1 through 4 focus on mobile ad hoc networks and vehicular ad hoc networks. Chapters 5 through 8 focus on wireless static, mobile and underwater sensor networks. Chapter 9 presents an asymptotic analysis of wireless network topologies (analyzing the scalability and connectivity measures) and Chapter 10 presents a cloud-based implementation of cognitive radio ad hoc networks. In addition to presenting a detailed analysis of the proposed solution for problems in the above topics, each chapter presents an exhaustive coverage of the background literature work on the chosen topic as well as the open-ended research problems in the subject area.

Dr. Natarajan Meghanathan
Associate Professor
Department of Computer Science
Jackson State University
Jackson, MS, US
Phone: 601-979-3661; Fax: 601-979-2478
Email: nmeghanathan@jsums.edu

In: Recent Advances in Ad Hoc Networks Research
Editor: Natarajan Meghanathan
ISBN: 978-1-63321-337-1

Chapter 1

A SIMULATION-BASED COMPARISON STUDY OF CONNECTED DOMINATING SETS FOR MOBILE AD HOC NETWORKS UNDER DIFFERENT MOBILITY MODELS

Natarajan Meghanathan[1]
Jackson State University, Jackson MS, US

ABSTRACT

The high-level contribution of this chapter is an exhaustive simulation-based comparison study of three categories (density, node id and stability-based) of algorithms to determine connected dominating sets (CDS) for mobile ad hoc networks and evaluate their performance under two categories (random node mobility and grid-based vehicular ad hoc network) of mobility models. The CDS algorithms studied are the maximum density-based (MaxD-CDS), node ID-based (ID-CDS) and the minimum velocity-based (MinV-CDS) algorithms representing the density, node id and stability categories respectively. The node mobility models used are the Random Waypoint model (representing random node mobility) and the City Section and Manhattan mobility models (representing the grid-based vehicular ad hoc networks). The three CDS algorithms under the three mobility models are evaluated with respect to two critical performance metrics: the effective CDS lifetime (calculated taking into consideration the CDS connectivity and absolute CDS lifetime) and the CDS node size. Simulations are conducted under a diverse set of conditions representing low, moderate and high network density, coupled with low, moderate and high node mobility scenarios. For each CDS, the chapter identifies the mobility model that can be employed to simultaneously maximize the lifetime and minimize the node size with minimal tradeoff. For the two vehicular ad hoc network mobility models, the impact of the grid block length on the CDS lifetime and node size is also evaluated.

Keywords: Connected Dominating Sets, Mobile Ad hoc Networks, Algorithms, Mobility Models, Stability, Simulations

---

[1] Mailbox 18839, Jackson State University, Jackson, MS 39217, USA Email: natarajan.meghanathan@jsums.edu

INTRODUCTION

A Mobile ad hoc network (MANET) is a category of wireless networks in which the topology changes dynamically with time due to arbitrary node movement. The MANET nodes have limited battery charge and hence operate with a restricted transmission range to conserve energy as well as avoid interference and collisions that may result from transmitting over longer distances. As a result, MANET routes are often multi-hop in nature and also temporally change depending on node mobility and availability. MANET routing protocols (for unicasting, multicasting and broadcasting) have been predominantly designed to be on-demand in nature rather than using a proactive strategy of determining the routes irrespective of the need [1, 2].

MANET on-demand routing protocols typically use a network-wide broadcast route-reply cycle (called flooding) to discover the appropriate communication topology (path, tree or mesh) [3]. A source node initiates the flooding of the Route-Request (RREQ) packets that propagate through several paths and reach the targeted destination (for unicasting) or receiver nodes (for multicasting). These nodes choose the path that best satisfies the principles of the routing protocol in use and respond with a Route-Reply (RREP) packet to the source on the selected route. With flooding, every node in the network is required to broadcast the RREQ packet exactly once in its neighborhood. Nevertheless, the redundancy of retransmissions and the resulting control overhead incurred with flooding is still too high, as every node spends energy and bandwidth to receive the RREQ packet from each of its neighbors.

Vehicular ad hoc networks (VANETs) are one of the most promising application areas of MANETs. VANET communication is normally accomplished through special electronic devices placed inside each vehicle so that an ad hoc network of the vehicles is formed on the road. A vehicle equipped with a VANET device should be able to receive and relay messages to other VANET-device equipped vehicles in its neighborhood. VANET applications can be broadly classified into two categories: safety applications and comfort applications [3]. An example of a safety application is on-board active safety systems to assist drivers with information (like accidents, road surface conditions, intersections, highway entries and etc.) about the road ahead. Comfort applications are those applications that can provide non-critical services like weather information, gas station or restaurant locations, mobile e-commerce, Internet access, music downloads and etc.

VANETs resemble MANETs with respect to the dynamically and rapidly changing network topologies due to fast moving vehicles. However, the mobility of the vehicles is normally constrained by predefined roads and speed limitations. Mobility of the vehicles is also affected due to traffic congestion in the roads and the traffic control mechanisms (like stop signs and traffic lights). Route stability is an important design criterion to be considered in the design of MANET and VANET routing protocols.

A Connected Dominating Set (CDS) of a network graph comprises of a subset of the nodes such that every node in the network is either in the CDS or is a neighbor of a node in the CDS. Recent studies (e.g., [4, 5, 6, 7, 8]) have shown the CDS to be a viable backbone for network-wide broadcasting of a message (such as the RREQ message), initiated from one node. The message is broadcast only by the CDS nodes (nodes constituting the CDS) and the non-CDS nodes (who are neighbors of the CDS nodes) merely receive the message, once from each of their neighboring CDS nodes. The efficiency of broadcasting depends on the

CDS Node Size that directly influences the number of redundant retransmissions. One category of CDS algorithms for MANETs aim to determine CDSs with reduced Node Size (i.e., constituent nodes) such that whole network could be covered as fewer nodes as possible. However, as observed in this chapter and previous work [9], such minimum node size-driven CDS have been observed to be unstable (i.e., have a limited lifetime). The other two categories of CDS algorithms are those based on node ids and those based on stability. The node-id based algorithms prefers to include nodes with lower id (the neighbor nodes of a CDS node are covered by the CDS node) until all the nodes in the network are covered. The stability-based category of CDS algorithms focus on maximizing the CDS Lifetime such that the control overhead incurred in frequently reconfiguring a CDS is reduced. The chapter identifies any potential CDS lifetime-tradeoff existing for the three categories of CDS algorithms.

The maximum density-based CDS (MaxD-CDS) [10] and ID-based CDS (ID-CDS) [11] are picked to be representatives of the minimum node size and node id-based CDS algorithms respectively; the minimum velocity-based CDS (MinV-CDS) [12] algorithm is chosen to be the representative for the stability-driven CDS. The MaxD-CDS algorithm prefers to include nodes with the largest number of uncovered neighbors into the CDS; the ID-CDS algorithm prefers to include nodes with a larger node ID and having at least one uncovered neighbor into the CDS; and the MinV-CDS algorithm opts for slow moving nodes to be part of the CDS. The chapter evaluates the three CDS algorithms under diverse conditions of network density and node mobility with respect to four metrics: CDS Lifetime, CDS Node Size, CDS Edge Size and the Hop Count per Path, and under three different mobility models. The mobility models considered are the Random Waypoint model [13] that is often used to simulate the mobility of nodes in classical mobile ad hoc networks; and the City Section [14] and Manhattan [15] mobility models that are used to simulate the mobility of nodes in vehicular ad hoc networks. This is the first such comprehensive comparison study of the CDS algorithms for ad hoc networks under different mobility models.

The following significant observation is made in this chapter about the overall performance of the three CDS algorithms, across all the mobility models: The MinV-CDS incurs a significantly larger lifetime compared to the MaxD-CDS and ID-CDS. However, the MinV-CDS requires relatively more nodes to be part of the CDS to provide stability. Nevertheless, the Node Size-Lifetime tradeoff ratio is observed to be the lowest for the MinV-CDS for a majority of the scenarios.

The rest of the chapter is organized as follows: Section 2 presents a generic CDS algorithm that can be used to study each of the three CDS algorithms (MaxD-CDS, ID-CDS and MinV-CDS) that will be analyzed in the simulations. Section 3 presents the algorithm used to validate the existence of a currently known CDS at a particular time instant and decide on the need to determine a new CDS. Section 4 presents examples to illustrate the construction of the ID-CDS and MaxD-CDS. Section 5 presents examples to illustrate the construction of the MinV-CDS. Section 6 describes the three mobility models that have been used in this research for comparative studies and presents related work. Section 7 outlines the simulation environment and presents the simulation results observed for the three CDS algorithms under the three mobility models. Section 8 presents the conclusions by outlining the significant observations and contributions of this chapter. Throughout the report, the terms 'vertex' and 'node', 'edge' and 'link', 'path' and 'route', 'packet' and 'message' are used interchangeably. They mean the same.

Generic Algorithm to Construct the Different Connected Dominating Sets

In this section, we present a generic algorithm that can be used to construct the four different CDSs, with appropriate changes in the data structure (Priority-Queue) used to store the list of covered nodes that could be the candidate CDS nodes and the use of the appropriate criteria in each of the iterations of the algorithm to evolve the particular CDS of interest. The advantage with proposing a generic algorithm is that all the four CDSs can be constructed with virtually the same time complexity.

Network Model

The network model used in this research is described as follows:

- We assume a homogeneous network of wireless nodes, each operating at a fixed transmission range, *R*.
- We use the unit-disk graph model [16] according to which there exists a link between any two nodes *i* and *j* at (X_i, Y_i) and (X_j, Y_j) in the network as long as the Euclidean distance is less than or equal to the transmission range per node.
- The set of neighbors of a node *i*, *Neighbors*(*i*), comprises of nodes that are connected to vertex *i* in the unit-disk graph model.
- A node learns about its own location through location service schemes such as the Global Positioning System (GPS) [17] or any other scheme (e.g., [18]).
- A node learns the location and mobility parameters (velocity and direction of movement – measured as the angle subscribed with respect to the positive X-axis) of its neighbor nodes through the beacon messages periodically broadcast by their nodes in the neighborhood.

Data Structures

The data structures used by the CDS algorithm are as follows:

- ***CDS-Nodes-List***: This list includes all the nodes that are part of the CDS
- ***Covered-Nodes-List***: This list includes all the nodes that are either part of the CDS or is at least a neighbor node of a node in the CDS.
- ***Priority-Queue***: This list includes all the nodes that are in the *Covered-Nodes-List* (but not in the *CDS-Nodes-List*) and are considered the candidate nodes for the next node to be selected for inclusion in the *CDS-Nodes-List*. The order in which the vertices are stored in the *Priority-Queue* varies with the CDS algorithms as described below. Any tie between the nodes is broken based on the node IDs (the contending node with a relatively larger ID is placed ahead of the other contending nodes).
    - For the MaxD-CDS algorithm, the *Priority-Queue* stores the covered non-CDS nodes in the decreasing order of the node density (number of uncovered

neighbors); the node with the largest number of uncovered neighbors is in the front of the queue.

- For the ID-CDS algorithm, the *Priority-Queue* stores the covered non-CDS nodes in the decreasing order of their node IDs and have at least one uncovered neighbor node; the node with the largest ID and has at least one uncovered neighbor node is in the front of the queue.
- For the MinV-CDS algorithm, the *Priority-Queue* stores the covered non-CDS nodes in the increasing order of the node velocities and have at least one uncovered neighbor node; the node with the lowest velocity and having at least one uncovered neighbor node is in the front of the queue.

Auxiliary Variables

- ***CDS-Select-node***: For every iteration, the candidate node (node *s* in the pseudo code for the CDS construction algorithm) selected for inclusion into the *CDS-Node-List* depends on the criteria used by each of the CDS algorithms.
  - The *CDS-Select-node* for the MaxD-CDS algorithm is the covered non-CDS node with the largest node density (i.e., the largest number of uncovered neighbors).
  - The *CDS-Select-node* for the ID-CDS algorithm is the covered non-CDS node with the largest ID and has at least one uncovered neighbor node.
  - The *CDS-Select-node* for the MinV-CDS algorithm is the covered non-CDS node with the lowest velocity and has at least one uncovered neighbor node.

Note that the values for the density (the number of uncovered neighbors) and NSI (sum of the predicted LETs of the links with uncovered neighbors) for the nodes could change after the end of a particular iteration, depending on the updates to the *CDS-Nodes-List* and *Covered-Nodes-List*; this would lead to rearrangement of the entire *Priority-Queue* at the end of each iteration of the MaxD-CDS algorithm. On the other hand, the values for the node velocity and node ID remain the same for each of the iterations of the MinV-CDS and ID-CDS construction algorithms on a particular instance of the network graph.

Description of the Generic CDS Algorithm

The algorithm forms and outputs a CDS based on a given input graph representing a snapshot of the MANET at a particular time instant. Specifically, the algorithm outputs a list (*CDS-Node-List)* of all nodes that are part of the CDS formed based on the given MANET. The generic description and pseudo code given here can be adapted for the particular CDS algorithm by appropriately incorporating the criteria for choosing the *CDS-Select-node* for each of the iterations as well as the criteria for maintaining the *Priority-Queue* during the different iterations of the CDS algorithm on a particular instance of the network graph.

The first node to be included in the *CDS-Node-List* is the *CDS-Select-node* (*s*) chosen according to the criteria discussed in Section 2.3. A CDS node is considered to be "covered", so a CDS node is additionally added to the *Covered-Nodes-List* as it is added to the *CDS-Node-List*. All nodes that are adjacent to a CDS node are also said to be covered, so the uncovered neighbors of a CDS node are also added to the *Covered-Nodes-List* and to the *Priority-Queue*, as the node is added to the *CDS-Node-List*. The *Priority-Queue* for a particular CDS algorithm is maintained according to the criteria discussed in Section 2.2. The node at the front of the *Priority-Queue* is the next candidate node to become the *CDS-Select-node*, as long as the node satisfies the criteria mentioned in Section 2.3.

If the *Covered-Nodes-List* does not contain all the vertices of the input graph and the *Priority-Queue* is not empty, we dequeue the *Priority-Queue* to extract a *CDS-Select-node s* that is not yet in the *CDS-Node-List*. All the uncovered neighbor nodes of node *s* are added to the *Covered-Nodes-List* and to the *Priority-Queue*; node *s* is also added to the *CDS-Node-List*. The above procedure is repeated until the *Covered-Nodes-List* contains all the vertices of the graph or the *Priority-Queue* becomes empty. If the *Priority-Queue* becomes empty and the *Covered-Nodes-List* does not have at least one node that is present in the network graph, then the underlying network is considered to be disconnected.

The time complexity of the generic CDS algorithm can be given as: $\Theta((|E| + |V|)*\log|V|)$ on a network graph of $|V|$ nodes and $|E|$ edges – each of the $|V|$ nodes and their associated edges have to be explored for inclusion in the CDS. If the *Priority-Queue* is implemented as a binary heap, it takes $\Theta(\log|V|)$ time to reorganize the heap after each dequeue and enqueue operation. There could be a total of $|V|$ dequeue operations, one for each of the iterations and a total of $|E|$ enqueue operations, one for every edge that is traversed across all the iterations.

Generic Pseudo Code for CDS Construction

Input: Snapshot of the Network Graph $G = (V, E)$, where V is the set of vertices and E is the set of edges *CDS-Select-node s* – vertex chosen according to the selection criteria

Auxiliary Variables and Functions:

CDS-Node-List, Covered-Nodes-List, Priority-Queue, Neighbors(v) for every *v* in *V*

Output: *CDS-Node-List* // contains the list of nodes part of the CDS.

Initialization:

Covered-Nodes-List = {*s*}; *CDS-Node-List* = Φ; *Priority-Queue* = {*s*}

```
Begin Construction of CDS
   while ( |Covered-Nodes-List| < |V| and Priority-Queue ≠ Φ) do
      CDS-Select-node s = Dequeue(Priority-Queue)
                        // where s ∈ Covered-Nodes-List and s ∉ CDS-Nodes-List
                        // CDS-Select-node s is selected according to the criteria
      CDS-Node-List = CDS-Node-List U {s}
      for all u ∈ Neighbors(s) and u ∉ Covered-Nodes-List
         Covered-Nodes-List = Covered-Nodes-List U {u}
         Priority-Queue = Priority-Queue U {u}
      end for
      Rearrange the Priority-Queue according to the criteria for ordering the nodes
   end while
   if (|Covered-Nodes-List| < |V| and Priority-Queue = Φ) then
      return NULL // the network is disconnected; there is no CDS covering all the nodes
   end if
  return CDS-Node-List
End Construction of CDS
```

ALGORITHM TO VALIDATE THE EXISTENCE OF A CDS

To reduce the control overhead, we intend to use a CDS as long as it exists and opt for a new CDS only if the currently known CDS ceases to exist. To determine whether a currently known CDS exists at a particular time instant, we construct a *CDS-Edge-List* comprising of edges that exist between any two nodes (according to the unit-disk graph model) in the *CDS-Node-List* known at that time instant. The two conditions that we test for are: (i) The CDS-induced graph comprising of the *CDS-Node-List* and the *CDS-Edge-List* should be connected and (ii) For every non-CDS node, there should be at least one CDS node as neighbor node. The pseudo code for the CDS validation algorithm is presented below. Condition (i) is validated by running the classical Breadth First Search (BFS) algorithm [19] on the CDS-induced graph. Condition (ii) is validated only if condition (i) holds true. The algorithm returns true only if both the conditions hold true; otherwise, it returns false.

Pseudo Code for the CDS Validation Algorithm

Input: *CDS-Node-List* // Set of vertices part of the CDS
Auxiliary Variables and Functions:
CDS-Edge-List – Set of edges, $\subseteq E$, between the vertices that are part of *CDS-Node-List*
connectedCDS – Boolean variable that stores information whether the CDS-induced sub graph of *G* (comprising of the *CDS-Node-List* and *CDS-Edge-List*) is connected
Output: *true* or *false*
// *true*, if the nodes in *CDS-Node-List* form a connected sub graph of *G* and every vertex $v \notin$ *CDS-Node-List* is at least a neighbor of a vertex $u \in$ *CDS-Node-List*
// *false*, if the nodes in *CDS-Node-List* do not form a connected sub graph of *G* and/or at least one vertex $v \notin$ *CDS-Node-List* with no neighbor in *CDS-Node-List*
Initialization: *CDS-Edge-List* = Φ
Begin CDS-Validation
for every pair of vertices u, $v \in$ *CDS-Node-List* **do**
if there exists an edge $(u, v) \in E$ at time instant t **then**
CDS-Edge-List = *CDS-Edge-List* U $\{(u, v)\}$
end if
end for
connectedCDS = Breadth-First-Search(*CDS-Node-List*, *CDS-Edge-List*)
if *connectedCDS* = true **then**
for every vertex $v \notin$ *CDS-Node-List* **do**
if there exists ***no*** edge $(u, v) \in E$ where $u \in$ *CDS-Node-List* at time instant t **then**
return *false*
end if
end for
return *true*
end if
return *false* // if *connectedCDS* = false
End CDS-Validation

Examples to Illustrate the Working of the ID-CDS and the Max-CDS Algorithms

We demonstrate the construction of the ID-CDS and MaxD-CDS through examples illustrated in Figures 2 and 3 respectively. As indicated in the legend (Figure 1) for these two figures wherein each circle indicates a node in the network graph, we represent: (i) a CDS node with a thick black-bordered circle that is gray-shaded inside; (ii) a covered node (a non-CDS node that is a neighbor of at least one CDS node) with a thick gray-bordered circle that has black-dots inside; (iii) a non-covered node (a node that is neither a CDS node nor a covered node) with a black thin circle with no shades or dots inside.

In Figure 2 (illustrating the construction of the ID-CDS), the integer values inside each circle represents the node ID; in Figure 3 (illustrating the construction of the MaxD-CDS), the integer values outside of each circle represents the number of uncovered neighbors for the corresponding node.

Both Figures 2 and 3 comprise of 16 nodes. The ID-CDS is constructed in 7 iterations and consists of 7 nodes and 8 edges; the MaxD-CDS is constructed in 5 iterations and also consists of 5 nodes and 5 edges.

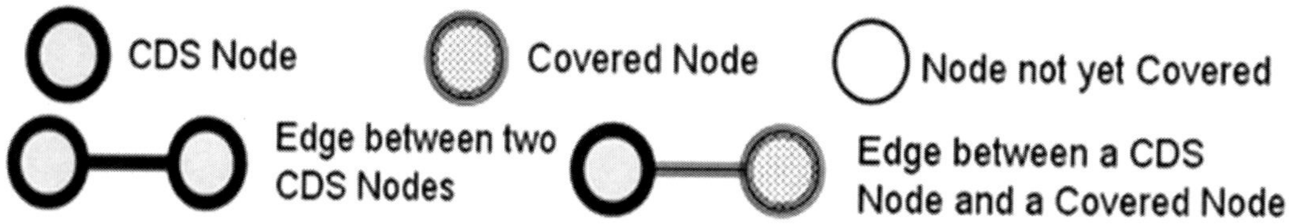

Figure 1. Legend for Figures 2 and 3.

Example to Illustrate the Working of the Minimum Velocity-Based CDS (MinV-CDS) Algorithm

We demonstrate the construction of the MinV-CDS through an example of a 24-node network illustrated in Figure 4 wherein each circle indicates a node. We represent: (i) a CDS node with a bold circle; (ii) a covered node (a non-CDS node that is a neighbor of at least one CDS node) with a shaded circle; (iii) a non-covered node (a node that is neither a CDS node nor a covered node) with a black thin circle that is neither shaded nor made bold. The integer values outside each circle represent the node ID; the integer values inside of each circle represent the number of uncovered neighbors for the corresponding node; the real-number inside the circle represents the node velocity (in m/s).

As observed in Figure 4, the MinV-CDS is constructed in 13 iterations and consists of 14 nodes and 16 edges.

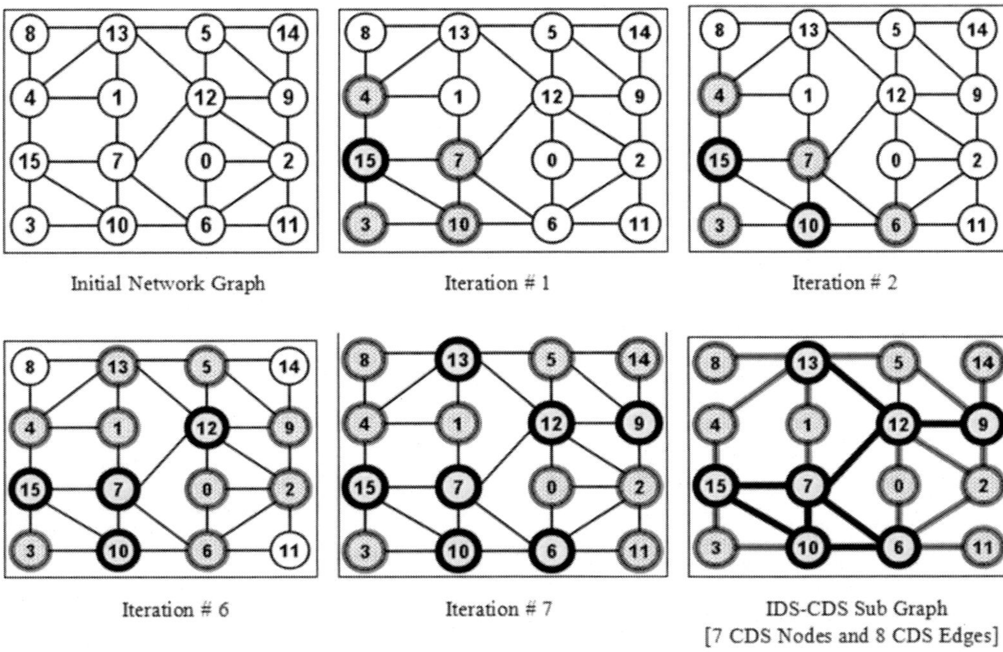

Figure 2. Example to Illustrate the Construction of an ID-based CDS (ID-CDS).

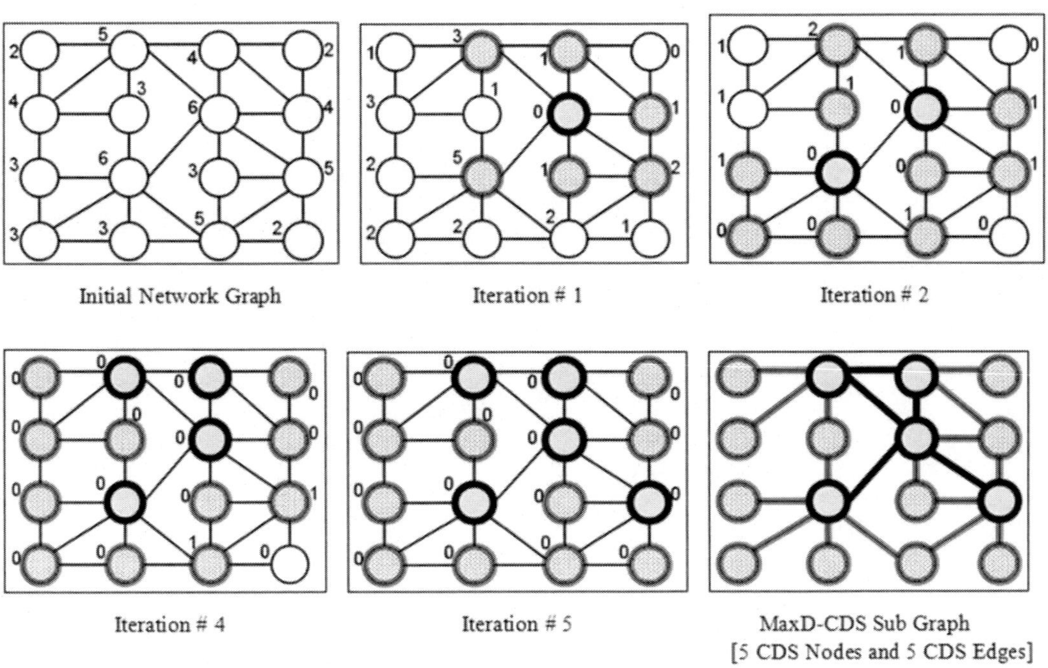

Figure 3. Example to Illustrate the Construction of a Maximum Density-based CDS (MaxD-CDS).

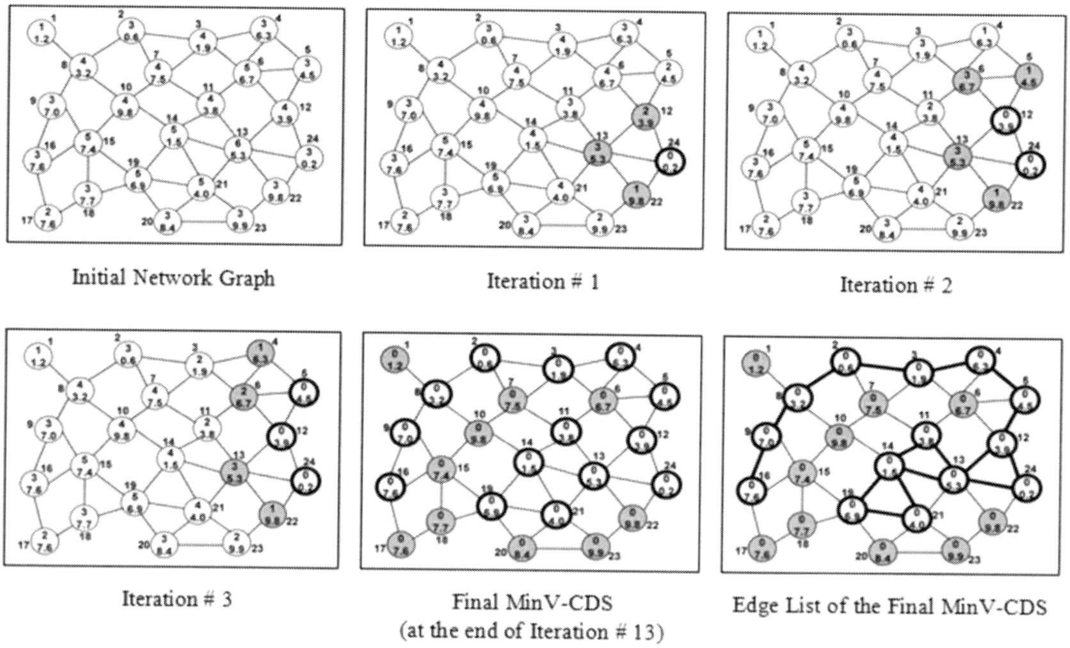

Figure 4. Example to Illustrate the Construction of the Minimum Velocity-based CDS (MinV-CDS).

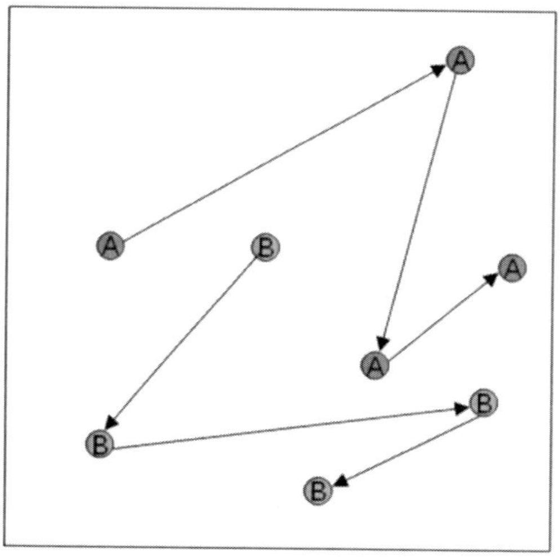

Figure 5. Movement under Random Waypoint Model.

DESCRIPTION OF THE MOBILITY MODELS

In this section, we provide a brief overview of the Random Waypoint mobility model commonly used in MANET simulation studies and the widely used City Section and Manhattan mobility models for VANET simulation studies. All the three mobility models [14] assume the network is confined within fixed boundary conditions. The Random Waypoint mobility model assumes that the nodes can move anywhere within a network region. The City Section and the Manhattan mobility models assume the network to be divided into grids: square blocks of identical block length. The network is thus basically composed of a number of horizontal and vertical streets. Each street has two lanes, one for each direction (north and south direction for vertical streets, east and west direction for horizontal streets). A node is allowed to move only along the grids of horizontal and vertical streets.

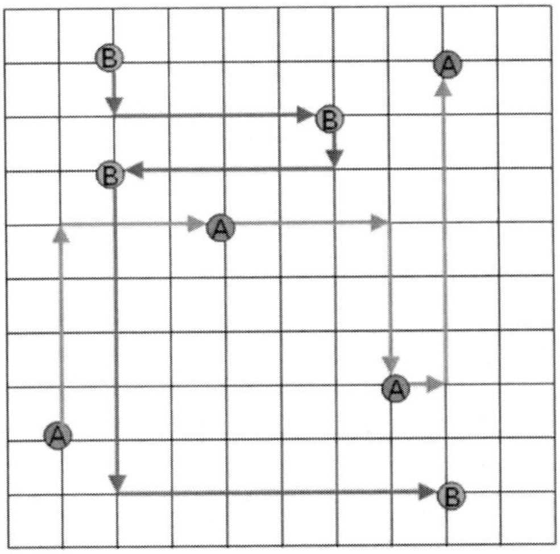

Figure 6. Movement under City Section Model.

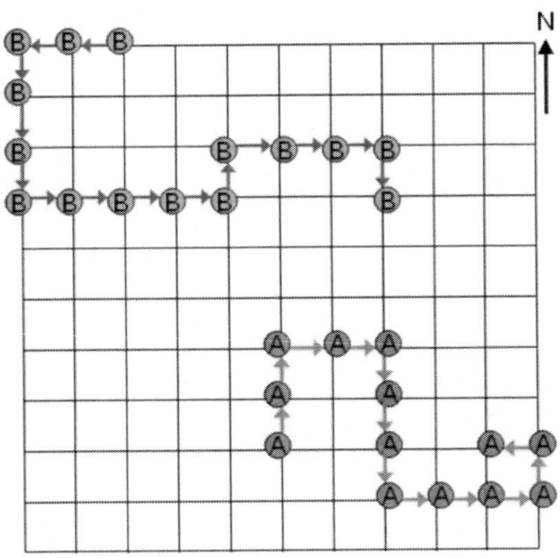

Figure 7. Movement under Manhattan Model.

Random Waypoint Mobility Model

Initially, the nodes are assumed to be placed at random locations in the network. The movement of each node is independent of the other nodes in the network. The mobility of a particular node is described as follows: The node chooses a random target location to move. The velocity with which the node moves to this chosen location is uniformly randomly selected from the interval [$v_{min},\ldots,v_{max}$]. The node moves in a straight line (in a particular direction) to the chosen location with the chosen velocity. After reaching the target location, the node may stop there for a certain time called the pause time. The node then continues to choose another target location and moves to that location with a new velocity chosen again from the interval [$v_{min},\ldots,v_{max}$]. The selection of each target location and a velocity to move to that location is independent of the current node location and the velocity with which the node reached that location. In Figure 5, we observe that nodes *A* and *B* move independent of each other, in random directions with randomly chosen velocities.

City Section Mobility Model

Initially, the nodes are assumed to be randomly placed in the street intersections. Each street (i.e., one side of a square block) is assumed to have a particular speed limit. Based on this speed limit and the block length, one can determine the time it would take move in the street. Each node placed at a particular street intersection chooses a random target street intersection to move. The node then moves to the chosen street intersection on a path that will incur the least amount of travel time. If two or more paths incur the least amount of travel time, the tie is broken arbitrarily. After reaching the targeted street intersection, the node may stay there for a pause time and then again choose a random target street intersection to move. The node then moves towards the new chosen street intersection on the path that will incur the least amount of travel time. This procedure is repeated independently by each node. In Figure 6, the movement of two nodes *A* and *B* according to the City Section mobility model has been illustrated.

Manhattan Mobility Model

Initially, the nodes are assumed to be randomly placed in the street intersections. The movement of a node is decided one street at a time. To start with, each node has equal chance (i.e., probability) of choosing any of the streets leading from its initial location. In Figure 7, to start with, node *A* has 25% chance to move in each of the four possible directions (east, west, north or south), where as node *B* can move only either to the west, east or south with a 1/3 chance for each direction. After a node begins to move in the chosen direction and reaches the next street intersection, the subsequent street in which the node will move is chosen probabilistically. If a node can continue to move in the same direction or can also change directions, then the node has 50% chance of continuing in the same direction, 25% chance of turning to the east/north and 25% chance of turning to the west/south, depending on the direction of the previous movement. If a node has only two options, then the node has an equal (50%) chance of exploring either of the two options. For example, in Figure 7, once node *A* reaches the rightmost boundary of the network, the node can either move to the north or to the south, each with a probability of 0.5 and the node chooses the north direction. After moving to the street intersection in the north, node *A* can either continue to move northwards or turn left and move eastwards, each with a probability of 0.5. If a node has only one option to move (this occurs when the node reaches any of the four corners of the network), then the node has no other choice except to explore that option. For example, in Figure 7, we observe node *B* that was traveling westward, reaches the street intersection, which is the corner of the network. The only option for node *B* is then to turn to the left and proceed southwards.

SIMULATIONS

The network dimensions are 1000m x 1000m. The Random Waypoint (RWP) model works by assuming an open network field without any grid constraints. For the City Section and Manhattan mobility models, the network is divided into grids: square blocks of length (side) 100m. The network for the two VANET mobility models is thus basically composed of a number of horizontal and vertical streets. Each street has two lanes, one for each direction (north and south direction for vertical streets, east and west direction for horizontal streets). A node is allowed to move only along the grids of horizontal and vertical streets. Simulations are conducted for grid block lengths (BL) of 50m, 100m and 200m. The wireless transmission range of a node is 250m. The network density is varied by performing the simulations with 50 (low-moderate) and 100 (moderate-high) nodes. The maximum node velocity values used for each of the three mobility models are 5 m/s (about 10 miles per hour), 25 m/s (about 50 miles per hour) and 50 m/s (about 100 miles per hour), representing levels of low, moderate and high node mobility respectively. The pause time is 0 seconds; so, all the nodes are constantly in motion.

A centralized view of the network topology is obtained by generating mobility trace files for 1000 seconds under each of the three mobility models. The network topology is sampled for every 0.25 seconds to generate the graphs. Two nodes *a* and *b* are assumed to have a bi-directional link at time *t*, if the Euclidean distance between them at time *t* (derived using the locations of the nodes from the mobility trace file) is less than or equal to the wireless transmission range of the nodes. Each data point in the performance figures shown in this section is an average computed over 5 mobility trace files and 20 randomly selected *s-d* pairs from each of the mobility trace files. The starting time of each *s-d* session is uniformly distributed between 1 to 20 seconds.

Overall, the simulations are conducted for six different combinations of network density and node mobility:

(1) *Low-moderate density and low node mobility*: represented by network of 50 nodes and v_{max} = 5 m/s per node, corresponding to an average neighborhood size of 10 nodes and average node velocity of about 2.5 m/s
(2) *Moderate-high density and low node mobility*: represented by network of 100 nodes and v_{max} = 5 m/s per node, corresponding to an average neighborhood size of 20 nodes and average node velocity of about 2.5 m/s
(3) *Low-moderate density and moderate node mobility*: represented by network of 50 nodes and v_{max} = 25 m/s per node, corresponding to an average neighborhood size of 10 nodes and average node velocity of about 12.5 m/s
(4) *Moderate-high density and moderate node mobility*: represented by network of 100 nodes and v_{max} = 25 m/s per node, corresponding to an average neighborhood size of 20 nodes and average node velocity of about 12.5 m/s

(5) *Low-moderate density and high node mobility*: represented by network of 50 nodes and v_{max} = 50 m/s per node, corresponding to an average neighborhood size of 10 nodes and average node velocity of about 25 m/s

(6) *Moderate-high density and high node mobility*: represented by network of 100 nodes and v_{max} = 50 m/s per node, corresponding to an average neighborhood size of 20 nodes and average node velocity of about 25 m/s

Randomization of the Node IDs for the ID-CDS Algorithm

In the simulations, to be fair to all nodes in the network, the node IDs are randomized before every reconfiguration of the ID-CDS. In other words, before the ID-CDS algorithm is reinitiated after the failure of the currently known ID-CDS, the node IDs are randomly redistributed and the ID-CDS algorithm is run based on the network graph formed based on the new node IDs. In each such reconfiguration, the appropriate mapping between the new randomized node IDs and the original node IDs (that will never change throughout the simulation) is maintained. While the original node IDs are used to determine the location and mobility of the nodes (from the mobility profile) at any time instant; the randomized node IDs are used to decide the inclusion of nodes from the Covered-Nodes-List to the CDS-Node-List as part of the ID-CDS algorithm. Note that the neighbors of a node that is recently added to the CDS-Node-List are considered covered based on their original node IDs; however they are listed in the Covered-Nodes-List based on their randomized node IDs.

Overall Simulation Methodology

The overall simulation methodology is as follows: For each mobility model, snapshots (static graphs) of the network topology are constructed for every 0.25 seconds, starting from time 0 to the simulation time of 1000 seconds. If a CDS is not known at a particular time instant, the appropriate CDS construction algorithm is run on the network snapshot. The CDS determined at a particular time instant is used in the subsequent time instants until the CDS ceases to exist. For a CDS to be considered to exist at a particular time instant, two conditions have to hold good: (i) All the CDS nodes have to stay connected – i.e., reachable from one another directly or through multi-hop paths; and (ii) Every non-CDS node should have at least one CDS node as its neighbor. If a CDS ceases to exist at a particular time instant, the appropriate CDS construction algorithm is again run and the new CDS is continued to be used as explained above. This procedure is continued for the duration of the simulation time.

Performance Metrics

The following two performance metrics are measured under the three mobility models:

- *Effective CDS Lifetime*: The duration of time each instance of a CDS actually exists is measured and the average of the CDS lifetimes observed across the entire simulation time period (for all the mobility profiles representing a particular combination of network density and node mobility) is computed. These average values of the actually observed CDS lifetimes are referred to as the Absolute CDS Lifetime. However, since the connectivity of the different CDSs are less than 1.0 for most of the scenarios evaluated, a better representative metric called the Effective CDS Lifetime is introduced – defined as the product of the Absolute CDS Lifetime and the CDS Connectivity – to effectively capture the stability of a CDS taking into consideration the chances of determining the CDS. For example, if a CDS has an average absolute lifetime of 10 seconds; but its connectivity is only 0.8 – it is more prudent to use the effective lifetime of 10*0.8 = 8 seconds as a more realistic measure of the stability (lifetime) of the CDS. The effective CDS lifetime incurred under the three mobility models under diverse conditions of network density and node mobility is illustrated in Figures 8, 10, 12, 14, 16 and 18.

- *CDS Node Size*: This is a time-averaged value for the number of nodes that are part of the CDS used for every time instant over the entire simulation. For example, if there exists a sequence of three CDS of size 30 nodes, 40 nodes and 20 nodes in a network for 6, 10 and 4 seconds respectively, then the average CDS Node Size for a total of 20 seconds is (30*6 + 40*10 + 20*4)/(6 + 10 + 4) = 33.0 and not simply the average of 30, 40 and 20 nodes = 30. The CDS Node Size incurred under the three mobility models under diverse conditions of network density and node mobility is illustrated in Figures 9, 11, 13, 15, 17 and 19.

Effective MaxD-CDS Lifetime

The MaxD-CDS incurs the largest lifetime under the Random Waypoint model for 5 of the 6 simulation conditions; for the condition of low-moderate density and moderate node mobility, the MaxD-CDS incurs the largest lifetime under the City Section model operated with a block length of 50m. The ratio of the difference between the maximum and minimum values of the effective MaxD-CDS lifetime incurred under the different simulation conditions ranges from 1.4 to 2.2. Between the two VANET mobility models, the MaxD-CDS is observed to incur a larger lifetime under the Manhattan mobility model for all the 6 simulation conditions. The effective MaxD-CDS lifetime incurred under the Manhattan model could be as large as 60% more than that incurred under the City Section model. For a given simulation condition, it is observed that the difference in the effective MaxD-CDS lifetime incurred with the two VANET mobility models decreases with increase in the block length (from 50m to 200m). It is also observed that for a given block length and node mobility, for most of the simulation conditions, the absolute values for the effective MaxD-CDS lifetime decreases with increase in network density; on the other hand, the relative difference in the effective MaxD-CDS lifetime incurred between the Manhattan model and the City Section model increases with increase in network density. For both the VANET mobility models, it is observed that the effective MaxD-CDS lifetime decreases with increase in the block length from 50m to 200m. This could be attributed to the nature of the MaxD-CDS algorithm to include only as minimal nodes as possible in the CDS; with a larger block length, even though the number of nodes constituting the MaxD-CDS reduces, the physical distance between the edges that are part of the CDS edges increases. As a result, a MaxD-CDS is more vulnerable to failure when operated in a VANET grid of larger block length.

MaxD-CDS Node Size

The MaxD-CDS incurs the lowest value for the node size under the Random Waypoint model for 5 of the 6 simulation conditions. For the condition of low-moderate density and low node mobility, the MaxD-CDS incurs a lower node size under the City Section model (block length of 50m). Thus, it is possible to simultaneously maximize the MaxD-CDS lifetime as well as minimize the node size when operated under the Random Waypoint model; there is no significant tradeoff.

The ratio of the maximum MaxD-CDS node size (incurred mostly with the Manhattan model) and the minimum MaxD-CDS node size (incurred mostly with the Random Waypoint model) typically ranges from 1.2 to 1.5. Between the two VANET mobility models, the MaxD-CDS is observed to sustain a lower node size for the City Section model. This indicates a CDS lifetime-node size tradeoff between the two VANET mobility models. In Section 4.4, it is observed that under a given simulation condition, the MaxD-CDS incurs a larger effective CDS lifetime under the Manhattan model; but, this is accompanied by a larger CDS node size. The relative difference in the MaxD-CDS node size between the Manhattan and City Section models could be as large as 25%, and the relative difference decreases with increase in the grid block length from 50m to 200m.

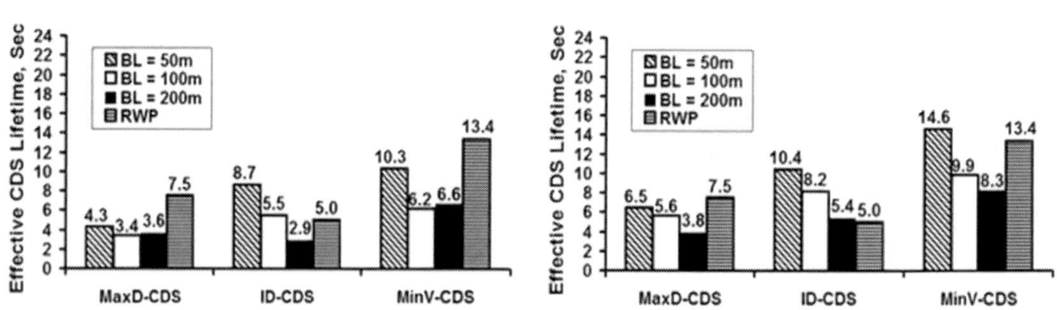

City Section vs. Random Waypoint Manhattan vs. Random Waypoint

Figure 8. Effective CDS Lifetime [50 nodes, v_{max} = 5 m/s].

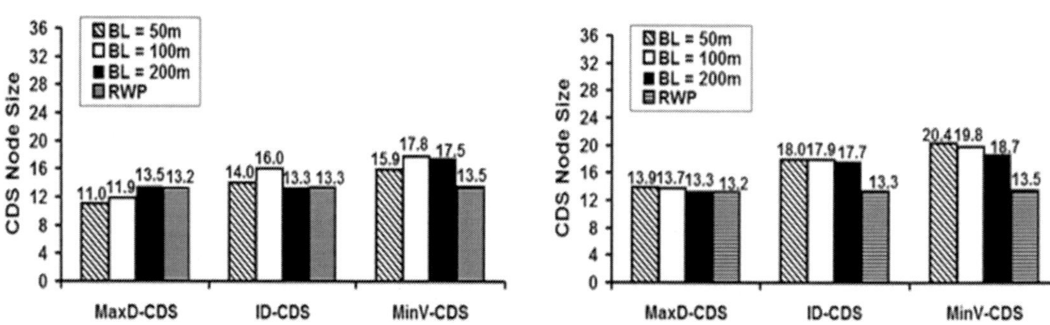

City Section vs. Random Waypoint Manhattan vs. Random Waypoint

Figure 9. CDS Node Size [50 nodes, v_{max} = 5 m/s].

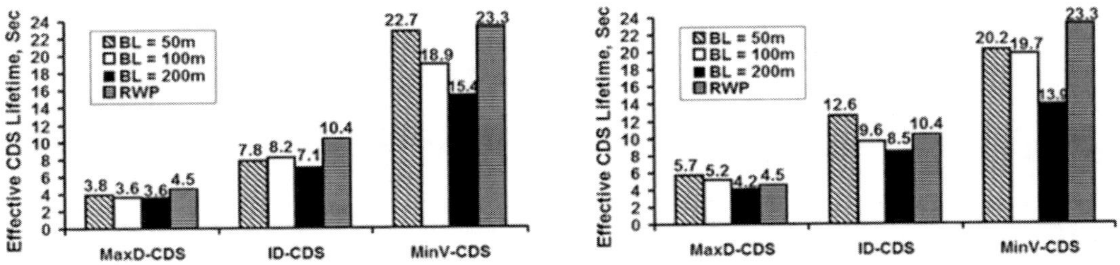

City Section vs. Random Waypoint Manhattan vs. Random Waypoint

Figure 10. Effective CDS Lifetime [100 nodes, v_{max} = 5 m/s].

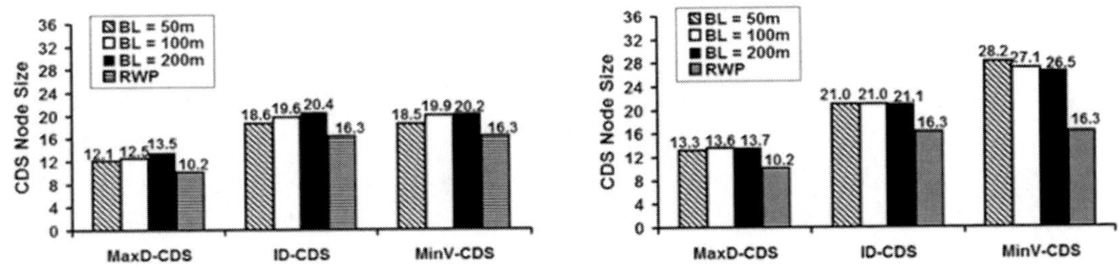

City Section vs. Random Waypoint Manhattan vs. Random Waypoint

Figure 11. CDS Node Size [100 nodes, v_{max} = 5 m/s].

For the Random Waypoint model, as the network density is doubled from 50 to 100 nodes for a given mobility level, the MaxD-CDS node size decreases by about 10-25%. This decrease, rather than an increase that is typically expected, could be attributed to the nature of the MaxD-CDS algorithm to include only those nodes as part of the CDS so that as many non-CDS nodes could be covered as possible. The negative impact of this greedy approach is observed in the effective CDS lifetime that decreases with increase in network density, due to the need to cover an increased number of non-CDS nodes with a reduced number of CDS nodes at high network density. Under the Manhattan mobility model, there is no appreciable change in the MaxD-CDS node size as the network density is doubled. For the City Section mobility model, for a given block length and node mobility, as the network density is doubled from 50 to 100 nodes, the MaxD-CDS node size increases minimally, only at most by 10%.

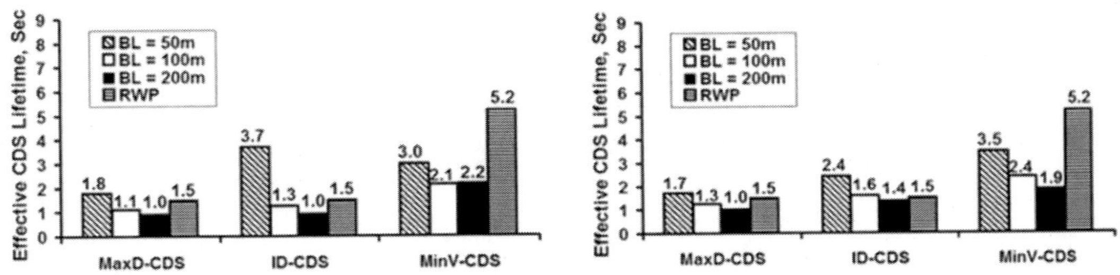

City Section vs. Random Waypoint Manhattan vs. Random Waypoint

Figure 12. Effective CDS Lifetime [50 nodes, v_{max} = 25 m/s].

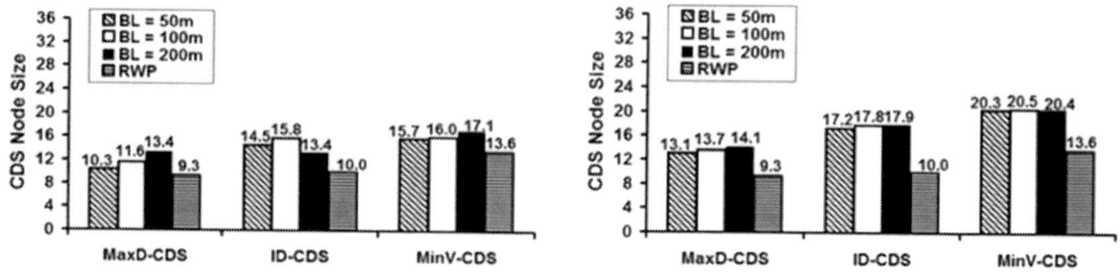

City Section vs. Random Waypoint Manhattan vs. Random Waypoint

Figure 13. CDS Node Size [50 nodes, v_{max} = 25 m/s].

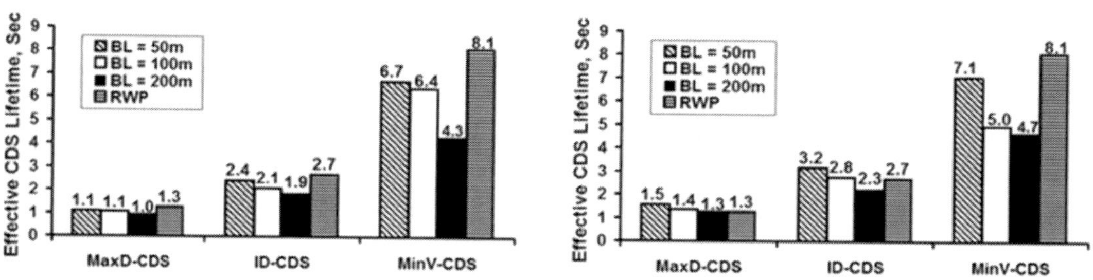

City Section vs. Random Waypoint Manhattan vs. Random Waypoint

Figure 14. Effective CDS Lifetime [100 nodes, v_{max} = 25 m/s].

Effective ID-CDS Lifetime

The ID-CDS incurs a larger effective lifetime under the two VANET mobility models compared to the Random Waypoint model under all the 6 simulation conditions. This is a trend different from what was observed in Section 4.4 for the MaxD-CDS which incurred the largest effective lifetime under the Random Waypoint model. The effective ID-CDS lifetime was the largest under the Manhattan model (with a block length of 50m) for 4 of the 6 mobility conditions. For conditions corresponding to low-moderate network density coupled with moderate and high node mobility conditions, the ID-CDS incurred the largest effective lifetime under the City Section model (for block lengths of 50m and 200m in moderate and high node mobility conditions respectively). For any given block length, the difference in the effective ID-CDS lifetime under the two VANET mobility models ranges from 15 to 90%, with the typical difference ranging from 20 to 40%. For any level of node mobility and block length, the ratio of the difference between the maximum effective CDS lifetime ranges from 2 to 3 in networks of low-moderate density and ranges from 1.4 to 1.8 in networks of moderate-high density. Under networks of low-moderate density, the effective ID-CDS lifetime incurred with the Random Waypoint model could be significantly lower (by about 50-60%) compared to the maximum effective ID-CDS lifetime incurred (with either of the two VANET mobility models). However under networks of moderate-high density, the effective ID-CDS lifetime incurred with the Random Waypoint model is only marginally lower (by about 5-20%) compared to the maximum effective ID-CDS lifetime incurred with the

VANET mobility models. Overall, it is also observed that for the two VANET models, the effective ID-CDS lifetime decreases with increase in the grid block length from 50m to 200m.

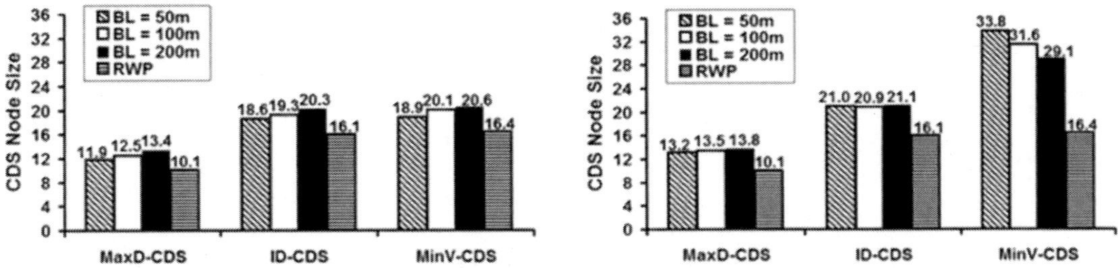

City Section vs. Random Waypoint Manhattan vs. Random Waypoint

Figure 15. CDS Node Size [100 nodes, v_{max} = 25 m/s].

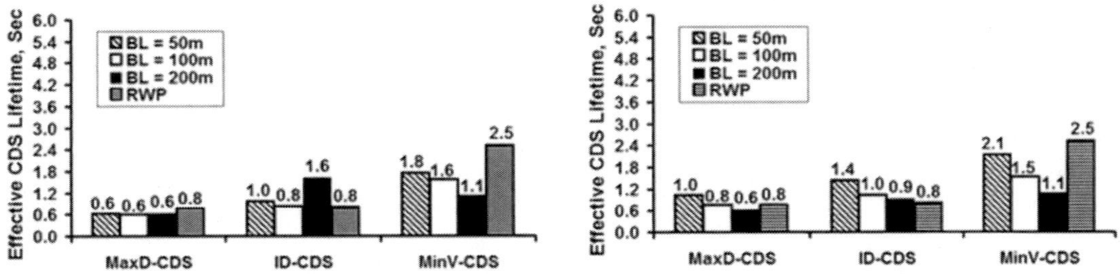

City Section vs. Random Waypoint Manhattan vs. Random Waypoint

Figure 16. Effective CDS Lifetime [50 nodes, v_{max} = 50 m/s].

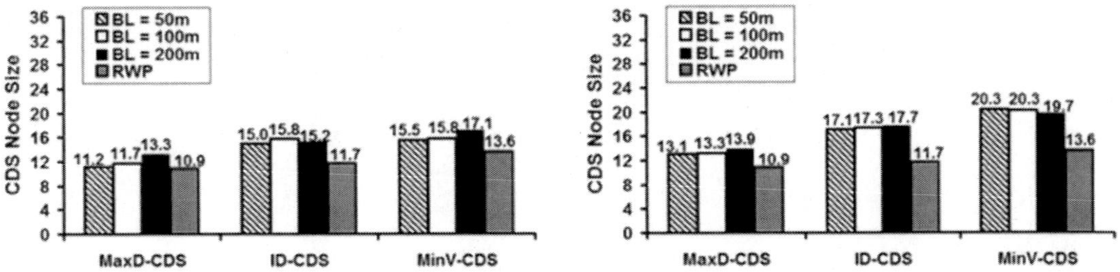

City Section vs. Random Waypoint Manhattan vs. Random Waypoint

Figure 17. CDS Node Size [50 nodes, v_{max} = 50 m/s].

ID-CDS Node Size

The ID-CDS exhibits a significant lifetime-node size tradeoff. The ID-CDS node size is the lowest under the Random Waypoint model and is the largest under the Manhattan model that also yielded the largest effective lifetime. Thus, it is not possible to simultaneously maximize the effective ID-CDS lifetime by incurring a lower node size under any mobility model. The ratio of the maximum ID-CDS node size to that of the minimum node size ranges from 1.2 to 1.8; the difference increases with increase in the network density and/or node mobility. Between the two VANET mobility models, the ID-CDS node size is larger when run the Manhattan mobility model compared to the City Section model. For a given block length and level of node mobility, the difference in the ID-CDS node size between the two mobility models is larger (by about 20-40%) when operated in networks of low-moderate density. In networks of moderate-high density, the difference in the ID-CDS node size incurred under the two VANET mobility models is only at most 15%. Another interesting observation is that the grid block length does not significantly impact the ID-CDS node size under both the VANET mobility models.

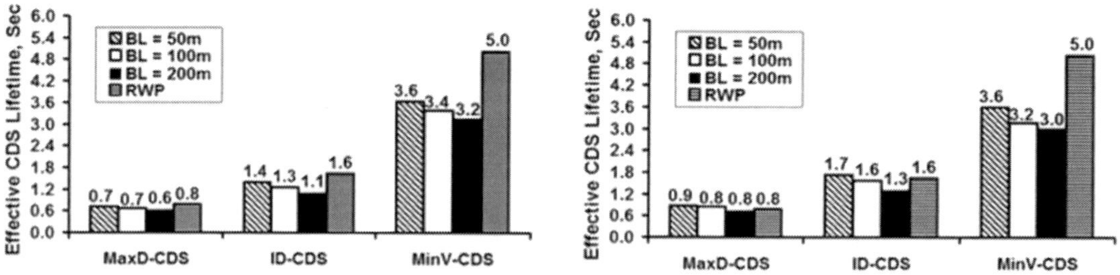

City Section vs. Random Waypoint Manhattan vs. Random Waypoint

Figure 18. Effective CDS Lifetime [100 nodes, v_{max} = 50 m/s].

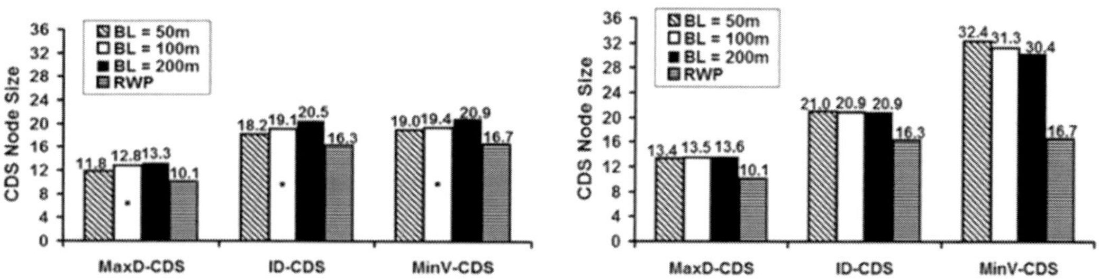

City Section vs. Random Waypoint Manhattan vs. Random Waypoint

Figure 19. CDS Node Size [100 nodes, v_{max} = 50 m/s].

Effective MinV-CDS Lifetime

The minimum velocity-based CDS (MinV-CDS) incurs the largest effective lifetime under the Random Waypoint model for 5 of the 6 simulation conditions. For the simulation condition of low-moderate network density and low node mobility, the effective MinV-CDS lifetime is slightly larger (by about 9%) under the Manhattan model (block length of 50m) compared to the Random Waypoint model. The ratio of the maximum effective MinV-CDS lifetime (incurred typically under the Random Waypoint model) and the minimum effective MinV-CDS lifetime (incurred typically under the City Section model for low-moderate density scenarios and under the Manhattan model for moderate-high density scenarios) is about 1.6 to 2.8; the difference in the effective MinV-CDS lifetime between the Random Waypoint model and that of the two VANET mobility models decreases with increase in the network density (for a fixed node mobility) and increases with increase in node mobility (for a fixed network density). Between the two VANET mobility models, it is observed that the effective MinV-CDS lifetime incurred under the Manhattan model is greater (by about 20%) than that incurred under the City Section model in low-moderate network density and low-moderate node mobility scenarios. With increase in the network density and/or node mobility, the effective MinV-CDS lifetime incurred under the City Section model is larger (at most by about 25%) compared to that incurred under the Manhattan model. The grid block length significantly influences the effective MinV-CDS lifetime under both the VANET mobility models. The effective MinV-CDS lifetime incurred under a grid block length of 50m could be as large as twice the grid block lengths of 100m and 200m. This could be attributed to the presence of physically longer edges in the MinV-CDS determined under larger values of the grid block lengths.

MinV-CDS Node Size

The MinV-CDS node size is the lowest under the Random Waypoint model for all the simulation conditions. Thus, one could obtain a larger MinV-CDS lifetime and a lower MinV-CDS node size when operated under the Random Waypoint model. The difference in the MinV-CDS node size incurred with the Random Waypoint model and the two VANET mobility models increases predominantly with increase in the network density. The difference could range from 25% to 100%, with the difference increasing with increase in the grid block length. For a given network density, there is no significant impact of the node mobility levels on the MinV-CDS node size. Between the two VANET mobility models, it is observed that the MinV-CDS node size is larger when run under the Manhattan mobility model for all the 6 simulation conditions, with the difference increasing with increase in network density and/or node mobility. For a given condition of network density and node mobility, the difference in the MinV-CDS node size decreases with increase in the grid block length from 50m to 200m. Even though the effective MinV-CDS lifetime is not always the greater under the Manhattan model, it is interesting to observe the MinV-CDS node size to be always larger than that incurred with the City Section model. The MinV-CDS node size incurred under the Manhattan model could be relatively (compared to the City Section model) as large as 30% and 80% respectively under the low-moderate and moderate-high network density scenarios. Thus, between the two VANET mobility models, it is possible to simultaneously optimize both the MinV-CDS lifetime and the node size when operated under the City Section model vis-à-vis the Manhattan model.

CONCLUSION

The following significant conclusions can be drawn from this chapter: (1) The MinV-CDS incurs the largest effective lifetime under all the three mobility models; and at the same time incurs the largest node size. Even though this indicates a CDS lifetime-node size tradeoff, it is interesting to observe that the effective MinV-CDS lifetime can be as large as 4 times the MaxD-CDS lifetime with just double the CDS node size. Similarly, the effective

MinV-CDS lifetime could be double that of the ID-CDS lifetime with just at most a 33% increase in the CDS node size. (2) The MaxD-CDS and MinV-CDS incur the largest effective lifetime under the Random Waypoint model and also can sustain the lowest node size under this mobility model vis-à-vis the two VANET mobility models. On the other hand, the ID-CDS incurs the largest effective lifetime under the VANET mobility models (predominantly with the Manhattan model) and the lowest node size with the Random Waypoint model. Thus, there is a CDS lifetime-node size tradeoff with respect to using an appropriate mobility model for the ID-CDS. (3) With regards to the two VANET mobility models, the MaxD-CDS and ID-CDS yielded the largest effective lifetime under the Manhattan model for most of the simulation conditions; whereas the MinV-CDS yielded the largest effective lifetime under the City Section model for a majority of the simulation conditions. On the other hand, all the three connected dominating sets sustained a larger CDS node size under the Manhattan mobility model compared to the City Section model. This illustrates a CDS lifetime – node size tradeoff for the MaxD-CDS and ID-CDS with respect to the choice of usage between the two VANET mobility models. (4) With regards to the impact of the grid block length on the stability of the connected dominating sets, one can conclude that the lower grid block lengths yielded more stable connected dominating sets compared to larger grid block lengths. Also, there is no appreciable increase in the CDS node size when operated at lower grid block lengths for all the three CDS algorithms under both the VANET mobility models.

REFERENCES

[1] Broch, J., Maltz, D. A., D. B. Johnson, Hu, Y. C., Jetcheva, J. A., 1998. Performance Comparison of Multi-hop Wireless Ad hoc Network Routing Protocols. *Proceedings of the 4th Annual International Conference on Mobile Computing and Networking*. 85-97.

[2]] Johansson. P., Larson, T., Hedman, N., Mielczarek, B., DegerMark, M., 1999. Scenario-based Performance Analysis of Routing Protocols for Mobile Ad hoc Networks. *Proceedings of the 5th Annual ACM/IEEE International Conference on Mobile Computing and Networking*. 195-206.

[3] Siva Ram Murthy, C., Manoj, B. S., (2004). *Ad Hoc Wireless Networks: Architectures and Protocols*, 1st ed., Prentice Hall.

[4]] Sinha, P., Sivakumar, R., Bhargavan, V., 2001. Enhancing Ad hoc Routing with Dynamic Virtual Infrastructures. *Proceedings of the 20th Annual Joint Conference of the IEEE Computer and Communications Societies*. 3, 1763 -1772.

[5] Wang, F., Min, M., Li, Y., Du, D., 2005. On the Construction of Stable Virtual Backbones in Mobile Ad hoc Networks. *Proceedings of the IEEE International Performance Computing and Communications Conference*. 1-19.

[6]] Sakai, K., Sun, M-T., Ku, W-S., 2008. Maintaining CDS in Mobile Ad hoc Networks," Wireless Algorithms Systems and Applications. *Lecture Notes in Computer Science*. 5258, 141-153.

[7]] Sheu, P-R., Tsai, H-Y., Lee, Y-P., Cheng, J. Y., 2009. On Calculating Stable Connected Dominating Sets Based on Link Stability for Mobile Ad hoc Networks. *Tamkang Journal of Science and Engineering*. 12, *4*, 417-428.

[8]] Bao, L., Garcia-Luna-Aceves, J. J., 2010. Stable Energy-aware Topology Management in Ad hoc Networks. *Ad hoc Networks*, 8, *3*, 313-327.

[9] Meghanathan, N., 2012. A Node Stability Index-based Connected Dominating Set Algorithm for Mobile Ad hoc Networks. *Proceedings of the 3rd International Conference on Wireless & Mobile Networks*. 84, 253-262.

[10] Meghanathan, N., 2006. An Algorithm to Determine the Sequence of Stable Connected Dominating Sets in Mobile Ad hoc Networks. *Proceedings of the 2nd Advanced International Conference on Telecommunications*. 1-6.

[11] Velummylum, N., Meghanathan, N., 2010. On the Utilization of ID-based Connected Dominating Sets for Mobile Ad hoc Networks. *International Journal of Advanced Research in Computer Science*. 1, *3*, 36-43.

[12] Meghanathan, N., 2010. Use of Minimum Node Velocity Based Stable Connected Dominating Sets for Mobile Ad hoc Networks. *International Journal of Computer Applications: Special Issue on Recent Advancements in Mobile Ad hoc Networks*. 2, 89-96.

[13] Bettstetter, C., Hartenstein, H., Perez-Costa, X., 2004. Stochastic Properties of the Random-Way Point Mobility Model. *Wireless Networks*. 10, *5*, 555-567.

[14] Camp, T., Boleng, J., Davies, V., 2002. A Survey of Mobility Models for Ad Hoc Network Research. *Wireless Communication and Mobile Computing*. 2, *5*, 483-502.

[15] Bai, F., Sadagopan, N., Helmy, A., 2003. IMPORTANT: A Framework to Systematically Analyze the Impact of Mobility on Performance of Routing Protocols for Ad hoc Networks. *Proceedings of the IEEE International Conference on Computer Communications*, 825-835.

[16] Kuhn, F., Moscibroda, T., Wattenhofer, R., 2004. Unit Disk Graph Approximation. *Proceedings of the Workshop on the Foundations of Mobile Computing*. 17-23.

[17] Hofmann-Wellenhof, B., Lichtenegger, H., Collins, J., (2004). *Global Positioning System: Theory and Practice*, 5th ed., Springer.

[18] Keiss, W., Fuessler, H., Widmer, J., 2004. Hierarchical Location Service for Mobile Ad hoc Networks. *ACM SIGMOBILE Mobile Computing and Communications Review*. 8, *4*, 47-58.

[19] Cormen, T. H., Leiserson, C. E., Rivest, R. L., Stein, C., (2009). *Introduction to Algorithms*, 3rd ed., MIT Press.

In: Recent Advances in Ad Hoc Networks Research
Editor: Natarajan Meghanathan
ISBN: 978-1-63321-337-1

Chapter 2

A PERFORMANCE COMPARISON OF ZONE-DISJOINT AND NODE-DISJOINT MULTI-PATH ROUTING WITH SINGLE-PATH ROUTING FOR MOBILE AD HOC NETWORKS

Natarajan Meghanathan*
Jackson State University, Jackson MS, US

ABSTRACT

The high-level contribution of this paper is a simulation-based analysis to evaluate the tradeoffs between zone-disjoint routing, node-disjoint routing and single-path routing for mobile ad hoc networks. Two paths are said to be zone-disjoint if the intermediate nodes of the two paths are not neighbors of each other; where as two paths are said to be node-disjoint if the intermediate nodes on one path do not appear as intermediate nodes on the other path. The zone-disjoint path routing algorithm proposed in this paper can be used to arrive at benchmarks for the time between successive zone-disjoint multi-path discoveries, the number of zone-disjoint paths per multi-path set and the hop count per zone-disjoint multi-path set. We compare the performance of the zone-disjoint multi-path routing algorithm with that of the single-path minimum-hop routing algorithm as well as with the node-disjoint multi-path routing algorithm proposed in our earlier work. Simulation results indicate that the number of zone-disjoint paths per multi-path set can be at most 2, which is far lower than the number of node-disjoint paths available per multi-path set. Also, the time between zone-disjoint multi-path discoveries would be far lower than the time between node-disjoint multi-path route discoveries and can be at most 10% more than the time between single minimum-hop path route discoveries. However, there is no appreciable difference in the average hop counts per zone-disjoint multi-path set and node-disjoint multi-path set and they can be only at most 12% more than the average minimum hop count determined using single-path routing.

---

* Mailbox 18839, Jackson State University, Jackson, MS 39217, USA. Email: natarajan.meghanathan@jsums.edu.

Keywords: Multi-path Routing, Zone-Disjoint, Node-Disjoint, Route Discoveries, Hop Count

INTRODUCTION

A Mobile Ad hoc Network (MANET) is a dynamic distributed system of wireless nodes that move independent of each other and have limited battery charge. The wireless medium is shared among the nodes and the channel is of limited bandwidth. MANET nodes often operate in limited transmission range to conserve battery charge as well as to reduce interference that may result due to long-range transmissions. As a result, routes in MANETs are often multi-hop in nature and a node assists its peers in route discovery and data propagation. MANET routing protocols are predominantly of two different types: reactive and proactive. Reactive or on-demand routing protocols use a network-wide flooding of Route Request (RREQ) messages to build and maintain routes, but only when needed. Proactive routing protocols tend to maintain routes between all pairs of nodes all the time and hence in the presence of a dynamically changing topology, incur considerable route maintenance overhead compared to on-demand protocols [2]. Hence, most of the recent research in MANETs is on reactive on-demand routing and we restrict ourselves to this routing technique in this paper.

On-demand routing protocols incur higher route discovery latency and also incur frequent route discoveries in the presence of a dynamically changing topology, typical of MANETs. Recent research has started to focus on multi-path routing for reduced route discovery overhead, fault tolerance and load balancing. Three different multi-path routing strategies have been proposed in the MANET literature: link-disjoint routing, node-disjoint routing and zone-disjoint routing. For a given source *s* and destination *d*, the set of link-disjoint *s-d* routes comprises of paths that have no link present in more than one constituent *s-d* path. A set of node-disjoint *s-d* routes comprises of paths that have no node (other than the source and destination) present in more than one constituent *s-d* path. A set of zone-disjoint *s-d* routes comprises of paths such that an intermediate node in one path is not a neighbor node of an intermediate node in another path. Multi-path on-demand routing protocols tend to compute multiple paths between a source-destination (*s-d*) pair, in a single route discovery attempt. A new network-wide route discovery operation is initiated only when all the *s-d* paths fail. Throughout the paper, we use the terms 'path' and 'route' interchangeably. They mean the same.

Multi-path routing can provide fault tolerance, load balancing and higher aggregate bandwidth. However, in order to achieve maximum level of fault tolerance and effectively balance the load as well as maximize the aggregate bandwidth across the multiple *s-d* paths, it is important to discover paths that are as independent as possible. Metrics such as correlation factor and coupling factor are used to calculate the relative degree of independence among the multiple paths [10]. The coupling factor, measured only for node-disjoint paths, indicates the number of links connecting two node-disjoint paths. The correlation factor, measured for all the three types of multi-paths, is the average number of nodes that are blocked from receiving data on one of the paths when a node in the other path is transmitting. Network topology and channel characteristics (measured with the correlation and coupling factors) have been observed to severely limit the gain from multi-path routing [11].

The three multi-path routing strategies can be ranked as follows, in the increasing order of independence: link-disjoint routing, node-disjoint routing and zone-disjoint routing. It may not be always possible to simultaneously send data across two link-disjoint paths or two node-disjoint paths as the transmission of data in a link that is part of one path may require a node that is part of another path to remain idle (controlled by the channel access mechanism). It has been observed earlier [18] that larger the correlation factor between two node-disjoint paths, the larger will be the average end-to-end delay for both the paths and also the larger will be the difference in the end-to-end delay along the two paths. If two link-disjoint or node-disjoint routes are physically close enough to interfere with each other during data communication, the nodes in these multi-path routes may constantly contend for accessing the shared channel and the multi-path routing protocol may end up performing worse than any single-path routing protocol [14]. In [17], the authors argue that benefits (improvement in throughput and reduction in end-to-end delay) obtained with multi-path routing become insignificant with respect to single-path routing if we take into consideration the interference between the multiple paths and the cost of discovering these paths. Thus, multi-path routing may not be a sound strategy if the constituent multiple paths suffer interference among themselves. This motivates the need to consider zone-disjoint path routing as a potentially effective multi-path routing strategy because the intermediate nodes of the zone-disjoint paths are not located in the neighborhood of each other and zone-disjoint paths have a coupling factor of zero.

Zone-disjoint routing with directional antennas has been observed to yield a significant improvement in network throughput and reduction in end-to-end delay compared to zone-disjoint routing using omni-directional antennas [14]. Zone-disjoint routing has a non-zero correlation factor in an omni-directional network system. With omni-directional antennas, a source node will not be able to simultaneously transmit data to more than one of its neighbors and a destination node will not be able to simultaneously receive data from more than one of its neighbors. Hence, zone-disjoint paths exhibit a correlation factor of 2 in an omni-directional antenna system. Nevertheless, this value is far less than the correlation factors observed for link-disjoint and node-disjoint paths [13]. The correlation factor of zone-disjoint paths in a directional antenna system is zero as each node could set its transmission to only the target node. The zone-disjoint paths in a directional antenna system are thus 100% independent as one can simultaneously send data on all of these paths.

The tradeoff between the three multi-path routing strategies is that for a given network topology, network density and node mobility, the number of link-disjoint paths may be more than the number of node-disjoint paths, which may be more than the number of zone-disjoint paths. In an earlier work [8], we have observed that the number of link-disjoint paths can be as large as 40% more than the number of node-disjoint paths and the time between two successive link-disjoint multi-path route discoveries can be at most 30% more than the time between two successive node-disjoint multi-path route discoveries. However, no such results are available comparing the number of node-disjoint paths vis-à-vis the number of zone-disjoint paths as well as the time between two successive node-disjoint multi-path route discoveries vis-à-vis the time between two successive zone-disjoint multi-path route discoveries. This forms the motivation for our research in this paper.

The rest of the paper is organized as follows: Section II briefly reviews the zone-disjoint routing protocols proposed in the literature. Section III proposes the algorithm used in this paper to determine the sequence of zone-disjoint routes over the duration of a source-destination (*s-d*) session. Section IV describes the simulation environment, illustrates the simulation results comparing zone-disjoint routing, node-disjoint routing and single-path routing and interprets the results. Section V concludes the paper.

Review of Zone-Disjoint Multi-Path Manet Routing Protocols

In this section, we review zone-disjoint multi-path routing protocols that are based on the concepts of Active Neighbors, Zone-radius and Clusters. In addition, we also discuss some miscellaneous zone-disjoint multi-path routing protocols.

Zone-Disjoint Multi-Path Routing Protocols Based on Active Neighbors

The number of active neighbors for a node indicates the number of neighbor nodes that have received and forwarded the Route Request (RREQ) message during a route discovery process. The multi-path routing protocols that are based on the notion of active neighbors are the zone-disjoint extensions of the well-known single-path routing protocols such as the Dynamic Source Routing (DSR) [7] protocol and the Ad hoc On-demand Distance Vector (AODV) [12] routing protocol. We describe below two zone-disjoint extensions for the DSR protocol based on the notion of Active Neighbors and similar zone-disjoint extensions have been also proposed for AODV (e.g., ZD-AOMDV [6]).

The Zone-Disjoint Multi-path extension of the Dynamic Source Routing (ZD-MPDSR) protocol [5] proposed for an omni-directional system works as follows: Whenever a source node has no route to send data to a destination node, the source node initiates broadcast of the Route-Request (RREQ) messages. The RREQ message has an *ActiveNeighborCount* field and it is updated by each intermediate node before broadcasting the message in the neighborhood. When an intermediate node receives the RREQ message, it broadcasts a 1-hop RREQ-query message in its neighborhood to determine the number of neighbors who have also seen the RREQ message. The number of RREQ-query-replies received from the nodes in the neighborhood is the value of the *ActiveNeighborCount* field updated by a node in the RREQ message. The destination node receives several RREQ messages and selects the node-disjoint paths with lower *ActiveNeighborCount* values and sends the Route-Reply (RREP) messages to the source along these paths. Even though the selection of the zone-disjoint paths with lower number of active neighbors will lead to reduction in the end-to-end delay per data packet, the route acquisition phase will incur a significantly longer delay as RREQ-query messages are broadcast at every hop (in addition to the regular RREQ message) and the intermediate nodes have to wait to receive the RREQ-query-reply messages from their neighbors. This will significantly increase the control overhead in the network.

In order to reduce the route acquisition delay associated with ZD-MPDSR, a Cluster-based Zone Multi-path Dynamic Source Routing (CZM-DSR) protocol was proposed in [16].

Here, an intermediate node upon receiving a RREQ message records the number of times it has seen the message in a locally maintained *ActiveNeighborCount* variable in memory and broadcasts the message further if it has been seen for the first time. The destination node sends back a Route-Reply (RREP) message to the source node for every RREQ received. The path traced by the RREQ message is included in the RREP message. When an intermediate node receives the RREP message, it includes its *ActiveNeighborCount* value in the message and forwards the message to the next hop node on the path towards the source. The source receives RREP messages through several paths and chooses the path whose maximum value for the *ActiveNeighborCount* is the minimum. However, CZM-DSR will still incur a larger control message overhead and possibly a RREP-storm as the destination node would send a RREP message for every RREQ message received.

Multi-Path Distance Vector Zone Routing Protocol

Multi-path Distance Vector Zone Routing Protocol (MDVZRP) for MANETs has been proposed in [4]. When a new node (say node *i*) joins a network, it broadcasts a Hello beacon message to its immediate neighbors. The neighbor nodes on receiving the Hello message update their routing table with a new entry for the sender of the message, node *i*, and in turn send their entire routing table (full dump) to their new neighbor, node *i*. In addition, the one-hop neighbor nodes broadcast the Hello message to their own neighbors (i.e., to the 2-hop neighbors of node *i*). This process of broadcasting the Hello message is repeated by every node if the node falls within the zone radius centered at node *i*. MDVZRP uses the notion of zone radius (measured in terms of the number of hops) to restrict the scope of the broadcast of the Hello message. Every *k*-hop neighbor node ($1 \leq k \leq$ zone radius) that receives the Hello message updates its routing table by adding an entry for the originating node of the Hello message and the neighbor node from which the Hello message was received the first time is included as the next hop node. Meanwhile, using the routing tables received from all of its neighbor nodes, the new node determines a set of node disjoint paths to every node in the entire network. If a distant node, say node *j*, falls outside the zone radius of a node, say node *i*, to which *j* wants to send data packets, then node *j* initiates a RREQ-based broadcast route search. When an intermediate node receives the RREQ message and it has a valid route (i.e., the next hop node information) for the targeted destination node of the RREQ message, the intermediate node sends back a RREP to the originating source node of the RREQ message. Such intermediate nodes are located at the periphery of the proactive routing zone centered at the targeted destination node. The RREQ message is thus not propagated all the way to the destination node. The source node, upon receiving RREPs from several of the peripheral nodes, learns the set of node-disjoint routes to the destination and starts sending the data packets through these routes.

Cluster-Based Multi-Path Routing Protocol

A Cluster-Based Multi-Path Routing (CBMPR) protocol has been recently proposed in [19]. Nodes are organized into clusters – the radius of each cluster is two to three hops. Each cluster is controlled by a clusterhead that is responsible for gathering the link state information from all its member nodes, constructing the cluster topology and advertising the cluster topology information back to the member nodes. Intra-cluster communication is managed through link-state routing, while inter-cluster communication is through gateway nodes that are present in both the clusters. When a source node in one cluster has to determine multiple disjoint paths to a destination node in another cluster, it sends a RREQ message to its clusterhead, which further broadcasts the message to the clusterheads of its adjacent clusters. The RREQ message propagation is continued all the way to the cluster in which the destination node is located. The destination node receives RREQ messages across several paths whose constituent nodes are the clusterheads. The destination node selects the clusterhead-disjoint paths (i.e., disjoint-paths in which a clusterhead does not appear more than once) and sends back the RREP messages to the source through these paths. The throughput obtained with CBMPR has been observed to increase proportionally with respect to the number of clusterhead-disjoint paths used, illustrative of the independence between these paths.

Miscellaneous Zone-Disjoint Multi-Path Routing Protocols

While determining a maximally zone-disjoint multi-path between a source-destination (*s*-*d*) pair, it is imperative to consider all the active routes (between every *s-d* pair) in the system rather than only considering the zone-disjoint paths between the particular source *s* and destination *d*. In [13], the authors have proposed a trial and error algorithm to determine two maximally zone-disjoint shortest paths between an *s-d* pair. The algorithm is based on determining an initial set of node-disjoint paths between the *s-d* pair and then iteratively discarding the *s-d* path that has the largest value for the hop count * correlation factor with all of the other active routes in the system.

A 3-directional zone-disjoint multi-path routing protocol (3DMRP) has been proposed in [15]. 3DMRP discovers up to three zone-disjoint paths (one primary path and two secondary paths) based on a greedy forwarding technique at a reduced control overhead without using directional antennas. The two secondary paths, if exist, are discovered by avoiding the RREP overhearing zone created during the acquisition of the primary path.

Algorithm to Determine the Set of Zone-Disjoint Paths

We now propose the algorithm used to determine the sequence of zone-disjoint paths in our simulation studies. Let *G* (*V*, *E*) be the graph representing a snapshot of the network topology collected at the time instant in which we require a set of zone-disjoint routes from a source node *s* to a destination node *d*. Note that *V* is the set of vertices (nodes) and *E* is the set of edges (links) in the network. We say there is a link between two nodes if the distance between the two nodes is less than or equal to the transmission range of the nodes. We assume all nodes are homogeneous, use omni-directional antennas and have identical transmission range.

We illustrate here (along with the pseudo code) the algorithm to determine the set of zone-disjoint *s-d* routes, P_Z, on a graph *G* collected at a particular time instant. We use the

Dijkstra $O(n^2)$ algorithm [3] to determine the minimum hop *s-d* path in a graph of *n* nodes. If there exist at least one *s-d* path in *G*, we include the minimum hop *s-d* path *p* in P_Z. We then remove all the intermediate nodes (nodes other than the source *s* and destination *d*) that were part of the minimum hop *s-d* path *p* and also all their neighbor nodes from the original graph *G* to obtain the modified graph *G*' (*V*', *E*'). We determine the minimum hop *s-d* path in the modified graph *G*', add it to the set P_Z and remove the intermediate nodes that were part of this *s-d* path and all their neighbor nodes to obtain a new updated graph *G*'(*V*', *E*'). We then repeat this procedure until there exists no more *s-d* paths in the network. The set P_Z is now said to contain the set of zone-disjoint *s-d* paths in the original network graph *G*. Note that when we remove a node *v* from a network graph, we remove all the links associated with the node (i.e., links belonging to the adjacency list *Adj-list*(*v*)). The algorithm to determine the set of node-disjoint *s-d* routes, P_N, on a network graph is very similar to the zone-disjoint multi-path routing algorithm described here. The only difference is that we only remove the intermediate nodes that were part of the minimum hop *s-d* path from a network graph. The procedure is repeated until no more *s-d* paths exist in the network. More information about the algorithm to determine the set of node-disjoint paths can be found in [8].

Algorithm to Determine the Set of Zone-Disjoint *s-d* Paths in a Network Graph

Input: Graph *G* (*V*, *E*), Source *s* and Destination *d*
Output: Set of Zone-Disjoint Paths P_Z
Auxiliary Variables: Graph *G*' (*V*', *E*')
Initialization: $G'(V', E') \leftarrow G(V, E)$, $P_Z \leftarrow \varphi$
Begin
While ($\exists$ at least one *s-d* path in *G*')
  $p \leftarrow$ Minimum hop *s-d* path in *G*'
  $P_Z \leftarrow P_Z \cup \{p\}$
  $$\forall_{\substack{vertex, u \in p, u \neq s,d \\ edge, e \in Adj-list(u)}} \quad G'(V', E') \leftarrow G'(V'-\{u\}, E'-\{e\})$$
  $$\forall_{\substack{vertex, u \in p, u \neq s,d \\ v \in Neighbor(u), v \neq s,d \\ edge, e' \in Adj-list(v)}} \quad G'(V', E') \leftarrow G'(V'-\{v\}, E'-\{e'\})$$
end While
return P_Z
End

The zone-disjoint and node-disjoint multi-path routing algorithms used in this research could be implemented in a distributed fashion in ad hoc networks by flooding the RREQ message, letting the destination node to select and inform about the zone-disjoint and node-disjoint routes to the source through the RREP messages. The source could send the data packets to the destination using these routes in the increasing order of hop count (i.e., use the least hop count route until it exists and then use the next highest hop count path as long as it exists and so on) or distribute the data packets simultaneously through several paths with paths that have minimum hop count being used more.

SIMULATION ENVIRONMENT AND RESULTS

We ran our simulations in both square and rectangular network topologies of dimensions 1000m x 1000m and 2000m x 500m respectively. Both these network topologies have the same area. The average neighborhood size is determined as follows: $N^* \pi R^2/A$, where N is the number of nodes in the network, R is the transmission range of a node and A is the network area. The transmission range per node used in all of our simulations is 250 m. The simulations on both the square and rectangular network topologies were conducted for different values of the average node densities representing the neighborhood size: 10 neighbors per node (50 nodes, low density), 20 neighbors per node (100 nodes, moderate density) and 30 neighbors per node (150 nodes, high density). By running the simulations in both square and rectangular network topologies, we intend to study the impact of the variation in node distribution for a fixed value of average node density. Square topologies will have more uniform node distribution compared to rectangular topologies.

We use the Random Waypoint mobility model [1], one of the most widely used models for simulating mobility in MANETs. According to this model, each node starts moving from an arbitrary location to a randomly selected destination with a randomly chosen speed in the range $[v_{min} .. v_{max}]$. Once the destination is reached, the node stays there for a pause time and then continues to move to another randomly selected destination with a different speed. We use $v_{min} = 0$ and pause time of a node is also set to 0. The values of v_{max} used are 10, 30 and 50 m/s representing low mobility, moderate mobility and high mobility levels respectively.

We obtain a centralized view of the network topology by generating mobility trace files for 1000 seconds under each of the above simulation conditions. We sample the network topology for every 0.25 seconds. Note that, two nodes *a* and *b* are assumed to have a bi-directional link at time *t,* if the Euclidean distance between them at time *t* (derived using the locations of the nodes from the mobility trace file) is less than or equal to the wireless transmission range of the nodes. Each data point in Figures 1 – 6 is an average computed over 10 mobility trace files and 15 *s-d* pairs from each of the mobility trace files. The starting time for each *s-d* session is uniformly distributed between 1 to 20 seconds.

Determining the Sequence of Multi-Path and Single-Path Routes

We determine the sequence of zone-disjoint routes over the entire simulation time period as follows: When an *s-d* path is required at a given sampling time instant and there is none known, run the zone-disjoint multi-path algorithm to determine the set of zone-disjoint routes for a given *s-d* pair. We assume *s-d* routes in a zone-disjoint path set are used in the succeeding sampling time instants in the increasing order of the hop count. In other words, the *s-d* route with the next highest hop count is used as long as it exists and so on. We thus persist with the determined zone-disjoint multi-path set of *s-d* routes as long as at least one path in the set exists. We repeat the above procedure till the end of the simulation time period.

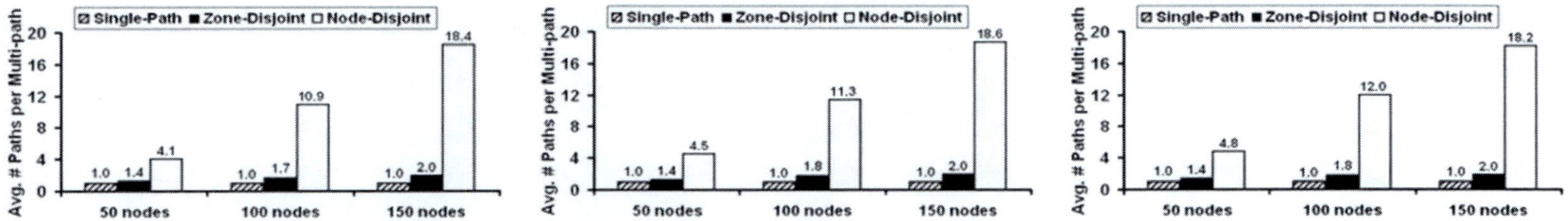

v_{max} = 10 m/s v_{max} = 30 m/s v_{max} = 50 m/s

Fig. 1. Average Number of Paths per Multi-path [Network: 1000m x 1000m].

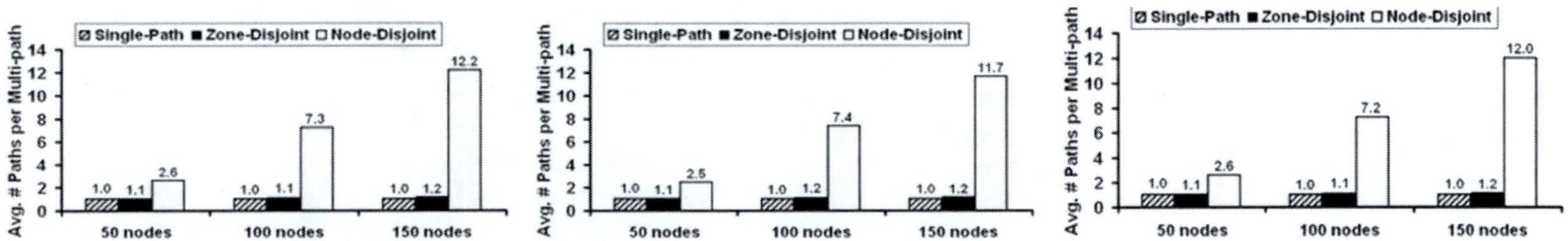

v_{max} = 10 m/s v_{max} = 30 m/s v_{max} = 50 m/s

Figure 2. Average Number of Paths per Multi-path [Network: 2000m x 500m].

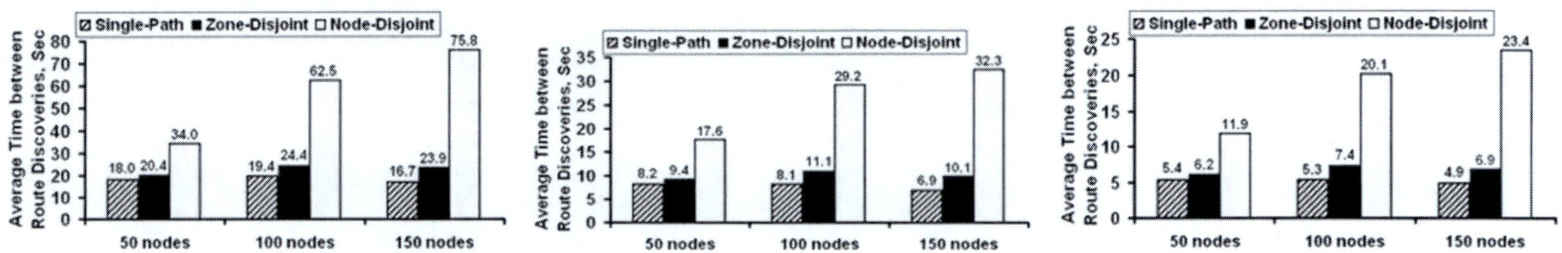

v_{max} = 10 m/s v_{max} = 30 m/s v_{max} = 50 m/s

Figure 3. Average Time between Multi-path Route Discoveries [Network: 1000m x 1000m].

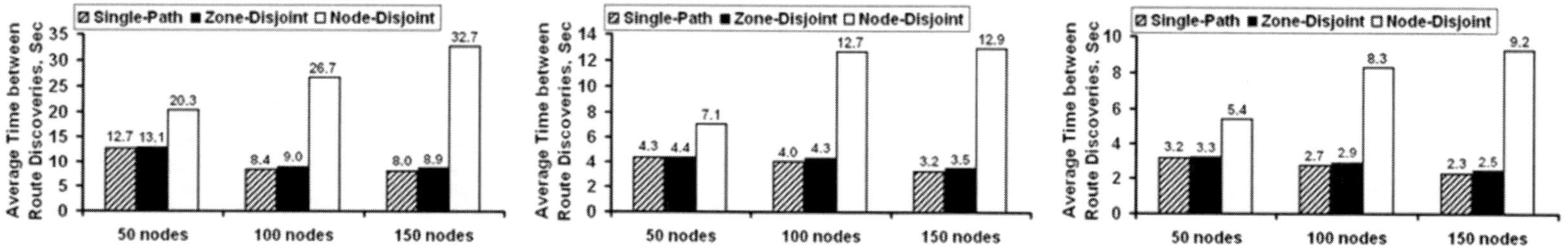

v_{max} = 10 m/sv_{max} = 30 m/sv_{max} = 50 m/s

Figure 4. Average Time between Multi-path Route Discoveries [Network: 2000m x 500m].

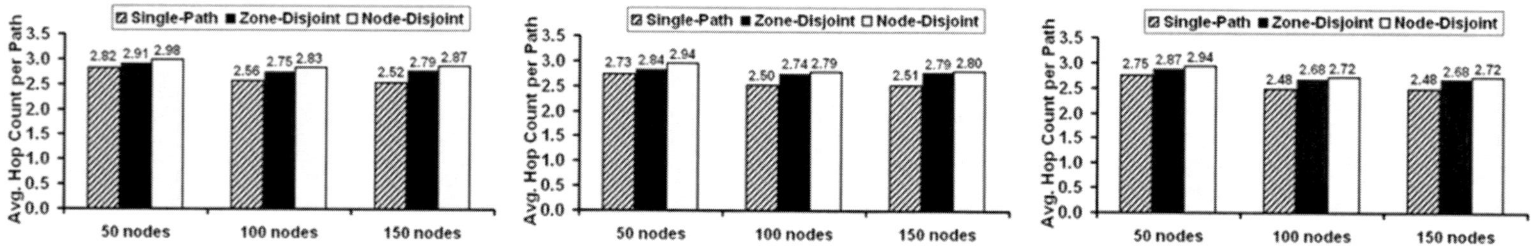

v_{max} = 10 m/sv_{max} = 30 m/s v_{max} = 50 m/s

Figure 5. Average Hop Count per Multi-path [Network: 1000m x 1000m].

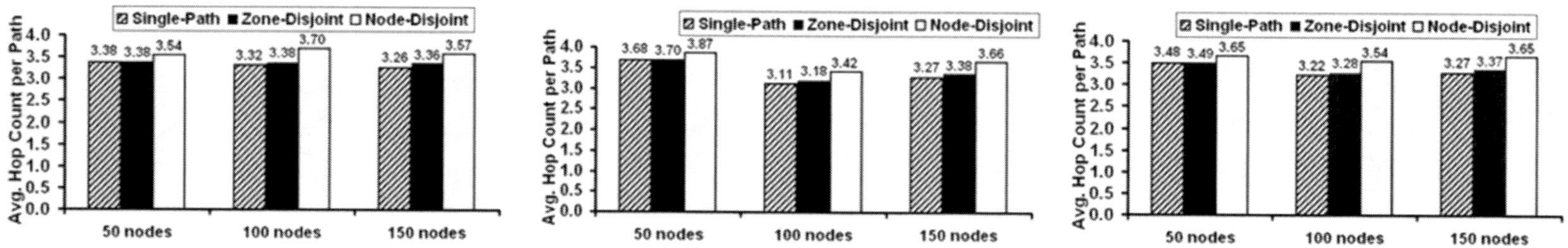

v_{max} = 10 m/s v_{max} = 30 m/s v_{max} = 50 m/s

Figure 6. Average Hop Count per Multi-path [Network: 2000m x 500m].

To determine the sequence of node-disjoint routes over the entire simulation time period, we follow a similar procedure except that we use the node-disjoint multi-path algorithm [8] to determine the set of node-disjoint *s-d* routes at a given sampling time instant, use these routes in the increasing order of the hop count as long as at least one path in the set exists, and repeat this procedure till the end of the simulation time period. We also determine the sequence of minimum-hop single-path *s-d* routes by running the Dijkstra algorithm [3] on the network graph generated at the simulation time instant when an *s-d* route is used until it exists and the procedure is repeated over the duration of the simulation session. The sequence of minimum-hop single-path *s-d* routes is used as a benchmark to evaluate the relative increase in the time between multi-path route discoveries vis-à-vis single-path discoveries and the corresponding increase in the average hop count for multi-path zone-disjoint and node-disjoint routes.

Performance Metrics

We measure the following performance metrics:

- *Average Number of Paths per Multi-Path Set*: This is the number of disjoint paths (zone-disjoint or node-disjoint, depending on the algorithm) determined during a multi-path route discovery, averaged over all *s-d* sessions. In the case of single-path routing, the number of paths determined per route discovery is 1.
- *Average Time between Successive Multi-Path/Single-Path Route Discoveries*: This is the time between two successive broadcast multi-path (or single-path) discoveries, averaged over all the *s-d* sessions over the simulation time. As we opt for a route discovery only when all the paths in a multi-path set fails, this metric is a measure of the lifetime of the set of multi-paths and a larger value is preferred for a routing algorithm or protocol.
- *Average Hop Count per Multi-Path/Single-Path*: The average hop count for a given routing strategy is the time-averaged hop count of the individual paths that are used in a sequence over the entire simulation time period. For example, if the sequence of minimum hop paths used comprise of a 2-hop path for 2 seconds, then a 3-hop path for 3 seconds and then again a 2-hop path for 5 seconds, the time-averaged hop count of the single-path routing strategy comprising the sequence of minimum hop paths over a 10-second simulation time period is (2*2+3*3+2*5)/10 = 2.3 seconds. Similarly, if the sequence of zone-disjoint paths determined comprise of a 2-hop path for 8 seconds, a 3-hop path for 3 seconds and a 4-hop path for 4 seconds, the time-averaged hop count of the zone-disjoint multi-path routing strategy over the 15-second simulation time period is (2*8+3*3+4*4)/15 = 2.7.

Average Number of Paths per Multi-Path Set

The number of paths per multi-path set for zone-disjoint routing has been observed to be significantly smaller than that observed for node-disjoint routing. With zone-disjoint routing, when the intermediate nodes of the minimum hop path and also their neighbor nodes are removed from the network graph, the probability of an alternate path between the source and destination decreases significantly. For a given network topology, node density and multi-path routing algorithm, the number of paths per multi-path set remains almost the same at all the three levels of node mobility. We also observe that for a given node density, level of node mobility and multi-path routing algorithm, the number of paths per multi-path set in square networks is more than that obtained for rectangular networks. This can be attributed to the uneven distribution (distribution of more nodes in one direction compared to the other direction) in rectangular networks compared to square networks. In square networks, for a given node velocity, as we increase the average node density from 10 neighbors per node (50 node network) to 30 neighbors per node (150 node network), the average number of paths per multi-path set for zone-disjoint routing increases from 1.38 to 1.97 (43% increase); but the average number of paths per multi-path set for node-disjoint routing increases from 4.44 to 18.41 (315% increase). In rectangular networks, for a given node velocity, as we increase the node density from 10 to 30 neighbors per node, the average number of paths per multi-path set for zone-disjoint routing increases from 1.07 to 1.18 (10% increase); while the average number of paths per multi-path set for node-disjoint routing increases from 2.57 to 11.96 (365% increase). It is important to note that on average, there can be at most two zone-disjoint paths and only one zone-disjoint path (i.e., nothing more than a single-path) when we operate in square and rectangular networks with node density as large as 30 neighbors per node.

Average Time between Successive Multi-Path and Single-Path Route Discoveries

In square network topologies, for a given level of node mobility, the time between successive node-disjoint multi-path route discoveries is 1.82 (node density of 10 neighbors per node) to 3.26 (node density of 30 neighbors per node) times more than the time between successive zone-disjoint multi-path route discoveries. In rectangular network topologies, for a given level of node mobility, the time between successive node-disjoint multi-path route discoveries is 1.59 (at 10 neighbors per node) to 3.67 (at 30 neighbors per node) times more than the time between successive zone-disjoint multi-path route discoveries. On the other hand, for a given level of node mobility, in square network topologies, the time between successive zone-disjoint multi-path route discoveries is 1.14 (at 10 neighbors per node) to 1.42 (at 30 neighbors per node) times more than the time between successive single-path route discoveries. In rectangular network topologies, the time between successive route discoveries for single-path routing and zone-disjoint routing is almost the same with the latter being at most 10% more than the former. Thus, we cannot significantly reduce the route discovery control overhead with zone-disjoint multi-path routing.

Even though we observe a direct correlation between the number of paths per multi-path set and the time between successive multi-path route discoveries, for both zone-disjoint and node-disjoint routing, the increase in the number of paths per multi-path set with increase in node density does not yield a corresponding proportional increase in the time between successive multi-path route discoveries. For example, in square network topologies, even though the number of zone-disjoint paths per multi-path set increases from 1.38 to 1.97 with increase in node density from 10 to 30 neighbors per node, the time between successive zone-disjoint multi-path route discoveries can be at most 20% larger. Similarly, for node-disjoint path routing, as we increase node density from 10 neighbors per node to 30 neighbors per node, even though the absolute value for the number of paths per multi-path set increases from 4.4 to 18.4, the time between successive multi-path route discoveries increases only by at most 120%.

For rectangular network topologies, the increase in the time between successive multi-path route discoveries with increase in node density from 10 to 30 neighbors per node is relatively low compared to that incurred with square network topologies. This can be also attributed to the relatively unstable nature of the minimum-hop routes in rectangular network topologies compared to square network topologies. The minimum-hop routes in rectangular network topologies have a larger hop count (explained more in Section 4.5) compared to those incurred with square network topologies. Each of the links in a minimum hop path has almost the same probability of failure in both square and rectangular network topologies [9]. As a result, since there are more hops, the probability of failure of a minimum hop path is more in rectangular network topologies compared to square network topologies.

The impact of the topology shape on the stability of the routes is also vindicated by the relatively rapid decrease in the lifetime per multi-path set in rectangular network topologies with increase in the level of node mobility compared to that incurred in square network topologies. For a given node density, as we increase the maximum node velocity from 10 m/s to 50 m/s, the time between successive multi-path route discoveries reduces at most by a factor of 3.3 in square network topologies and at most by a factor 0f 4.0 in rectangular network topologies.

Average Time between Successive Multi-Path and Single-Path Route Discoveries

In square network topologies, for a given level of node mobility, the time between successive node-disjoint multi-path route discoveries is 1.82 (node density of 10 neighbors per node) to 3.26 (node density of 30 neighbors per node) times more than the time between successive zone-disjoint multi-path route discoveries. In rectangular network topologies, for a given level of node mobility, the time between successive node-disjoint multi-path route discoveries is 1.59 (at 10 neighbors per node) to 3.67 (at 30 neighbors per node) times more than the time between successive zone-disjoint multi-path route discoveries. On the other hand, for a given level of node mobility, in square network topologies, the time between successive zone-disjoint multi-path route discoveries is 1.14 (at 10 neighbors per node) to 1.42 (at 30 neighbors per node) times more than the time between successive single-path route discoveries. In rectangular network topologies, the time between successive route discoveries for single-path routing and zone-disjoint routing is almost the same with the latter being at most 10% more than the former. Thus, we cannot significantly reduce the route discovery control overhead with zone-disjoint multi-path routing.

Even though we observe a direct correlation between the number of paths per multi-path set and the time between successive multi-path route discoveries, for both zone-disjoint and node-disjoint routing, the increase in the number of paths per multi-path set with increase in node density does not yield a corresponding proportional increase in the time between successive multi-path route discoveries. For example, in square network topologies, even though the number of zone-disjoint paths per multi-path set increases from 1.38 to 1.97 with increase in node density from 10 to 30 neighbors per node, the time between successive zone-disjoint multi-path route discoveries can be at most 20% larger. Similarly, for node-disjoint path routing, as we increase node density from 10 neighbors per node to 30 neighbors per node, even though the absolute value for the number of paths per multi-path set increases from 4.4 to 18.4, the time between successive multi-path route discoveries increases only by at most 120%.

For rectangular network topologies, the increase in the time between successive multi-path route discoveries with increase in node density from 10 to 30 neighbors per node is relatively low compared to that incurred with square network topologies. This can be also attributed to the relatively unstable nature of the minimum-hop routes in rectangular network topologies compared to square network topologies. The minimum-hop routes in rectangular network topologies have a larger hop count (explained more in Section 4.5) compared to those incurred with square network topologies. Each of the links in a minimum hop path has almost the same probability of failure in both square and rectangular network topologies [9]. As a result, since there are more hops, the probability of failure of a minimum hop path is more in rectangular network topologies compared to square network topologies.

The impact of the topology shape on the stability of the routes is also vindicated by the relatively rapid decrease in the lifetime per multi-path set in rectangular network topologies with increase in the level of node mobility compared to that incurred in square network topologies. For a given node density, as we increase the maximum node velocity from 10 m/s to 50 m/s, the time between successive multi-path route discoveries reduces at most by a factor of 3.3 in square network topologies and at most by a factor 0f 4.0 in rectangular network topologies.

Average Hop Count per Multi-Path and Single-Path

For any level of node mobility and node density, the average hop count per zone-disjoint multi-path set and node-disjoint multi-path set can be respectively at most 10% and 12% (for square network topologies) and 3% and 8% (for rectangular network topologies) more than that of the minimum hop count obtained via single-path routing. Thus, there is relatively insignificant difference in the hop count incurred by the zone-disjoint or node-disjoint and the single-path routing strategies.

In terms of the absolute numbers, for a given level of node mobility, routing strategy and network topology, the average hop count incurred with the multi-path routes as well as the single-path routes decreases with increase in node density. The decrease is more predominant (by a factor of at most 10%) with the single-path routing strategy compared to the two multi-path routing strategies (only by a factor of at most 5%). This can be attributed to the fact that the constituent routes of the zone-disjoint multi-paths and node-disjoint multi-paths may not be minimum hop routes. Also, both the number of paths per multi-path set and the time between successive multi-path route discoveries increase with increase in node density. The above observation is especially more relevant for node-disjoint multi-path routing.

We also observe that for a given level of node mobility and node density, the average hop count per routing strategy in a rectangular network topology can be 40% - 50% more than that incurred in a square network topology. This can be attributed to the fact that in the rectangular network topologies the nodes are more predominantly distributed in one-dimension (actually in the longer of the two dimensions) and this contributes to the relatively larger hop count compared to the square network topologies where nodes are more uniformly distributed [9]. The relatively larger hop count contributes to the unstable nature of the minimum hop routes in rectangular network topologies compared to those discovered in square network topologies.

CONCLUSION AND FUTURE WORK

Based on the simulation results obtained in this paper, one could conclude that, on the average, the number of zone-disjoint paths can be as large as 2 and the time between successive zone-disjoint multi-path discoveries can be at most 42% (for square topologies) and 10% (for rectangular topologies) more than that incurred with single-path routing. On the other hand, the time between successive node-disjoint multi-path route discoveries can be as large as 225%-267% more than that incurred with zone-disjoint routing. The corresponding increase in the average hop count per node-disjoint multi-path set is only 12% more than that of the minimum hop single-paths. Also, the worst-case difference in the average hop count per zone-disjoint multi-path set and node-disjoint multi-path set is within 5% and this is relatively insignificant compared to the significant reduction in the route discovery overhead that can be potentially brought about through node-disjoint routing. As future work, we would develop distributed routing protocols based on our zone-disjoint and node-disjoint routing algorithms and compare the two routing protocols with respect to metrics such as throughput and end-to-end delay. We will study the benefits and drawbacks associated in simultaneously routing through at most two zone-disjoint paths vis-à-vis routing through multiple node-disjoint paths.

REFERENCES

[1] Meghanathan, N., Farago, A., 2008. On the Stability of Paths, Steiner Trees and Connected Dominating Sets in Mobile Ad Hoc Networks. *Ad hoc Networks*. 6, 5, 744-769.

[2] Bettstetter, C., Hartenstein, H., Perez-Costa, X., 2004. Stochastic Properties of the Random-Way Point Mobility Model. *Wireless Networks*. 10, 5, 555-567.

[3] Ariyakhajorn, J., Wannawilai, P., Sathitwiriyawong, C., 2006. A Comparative Study on Random Waypoint and Gauss-Markov Mobility Models in the Performance Evaluation of MANET. *Proceedings of the International Symposium on Communications and Information Technologies*. 894-899.

[4] Liang, B., Haas, Z., 1999. Predictive Distance-based Mobility Management for PCS Networks. *Proceedings of the IEEE International Conference on Computer Communications*. 3, 1377-1384.

[5] Cormen, T. H., Leiserson, C. E., Rivest, R. L., Stein, C., (2001). *Introduction to Algorithms*, 2nd ed., MIT Press.

[6] Perkins, C. E., Royer, E. M., 1999. Ad-hoc On-demand Distance Vector Routing. *Proceedings of the 2nd IEEE Workshop on Mobile Computing Systems and Applications*. 90-100.

[7] Xie, G., Xu, M., Lam, K-Y., Wu, Q., 2005. The Impact of Mobility Modeling in Mobile IP Multicast Research. *Lecture Notes in Computer Science*. 3619, 295-304.

[8] Camp, T., Boleng, J., Davies, V., 2002. A Survey of Mobility Models for Ad Hoc Network Research. *Wireless Communication and Mobile Computing*, 2, *5*, 483-502.

[9] Rahman, M. A., Al Muktadir, A. H., 2007. The Impact of Data Send Rate, Node Velocity and Transmission Range on QoS Parameters of OLSR and DYMO MANET Routing Protocols. *Proceedings of the 10th International Conference on Computer and Information Technology*. 1-6.

[10] Jacquet, P., Muhlethaler, P., Clausen, T., Laouiti, A., Qayyum, A., Viennot, L., 2001. Optimized Link State Routing Protocol for Ad hoc Networks. *Proceedings of the IEEE International Multi Topic Conference*. 62-68.

[11] Chakeres, I., Perkins, C., 2009. "draft-ietf-manet-dymo-17.txt," Mobile Ad hoc Networks Working Group, Internet-Draft for Dynamic MANET On-demand (DYMO) Routing.

[12] Prabhakaran, P., Sankar, R., 2006. Impact of Realistic Mobility Models on Wireless Networks Performance. *Proceedings of the IEEE International Conference on Wireless and Mobile Computing, Networking and Communications*. 329-334.

[13] Agrawal, C. P., Tiwari, M. K., Vyas, O. P., 2008. Evaluation of AODV Protocol for Varying Mobility Models of MANET for Ubiquitous Computing. *Proceedings of the 3rd International Conference on Convergence and Hybrid Information Technology*. 1, 769-774.

[14] Lin, Q., Chan, K-M., Tan, K-S., Yeo, B-S., 2006. Partition-Aware TCP for Mobile Ad hoc Networks. *Proceedings of the IEEE International Conference on Communications*. 8, 3777-3782.

[15] Farago, A., Syrotiuk, V. R., 2003. MERIT: A Scalable Approach for Protocol Assessment. *Mobile Networks and Applications*. 8, *5*, 567-577.

[16] Abolhasan, M., Wysocki, T., Dutkiewicz, E., 2004. A Review of Routing Protocols for Mobile Ad hoc Networks. *Ad hoc Networks*. 2, *1*, 1-22.

[17] Meghanathan, N., 2009. Multicast Extensions to the Location-Prediction Based Routing Protocol for Mobile Ad hoc Networks. *Proceedings of the International Conference on Wireless Algorithms, Systems and Applications, Lecture Notes of Computer Science Series* 5682, 190-199.

[18] Meghanathan, N., 2008. Location Prediction Based Routing Protocol for Mobile Ad hoc Networks. *Proceedings of the IEEE Global Communications (GLOBECOM) Conference*.

[19] Meghanathan, N., 2009. A Density and Mobility Aware Energy-Efficient Broadcast Strategy to Minimize the Number of Route Discoveries in Mobile Ad hoc Networks. *Proceedings of the 2009 International Conference on Wireless Networks*.

In: Recent Advances in Ad Hoc Networks Research
Editor: Natarajan Meghanathan
ISBN: 978-1-63321-337-1

Chapter 3

ALTRUISTIC NETWORKS: WHERE EVERY NODE MATTERS

Pau Arce*[*], *Santiago González and Juan Carlos Guerri
Universitat Politècnica de València (UPV), Valencia, Spain

ABSTRACT

Traditionally, wireless ad hoc networks have been used for emergency situations due to the feasibility of fast deployment and connectivity. However, multimedia services are much demanded nowadays and bandwidth and delay requirements of these kinds of services are very restrictive. Offering real-time video services in wireless ad hoc networks is not an easy task because of the difficulty of guaranteeing certain quality in a shared medium. In this kind of network, nodes should be ready to route and forward data packets coming from other nodes. The cooperation of every node is essential for the proper operation of the network because there are many factors that may cause video quality degradation, from radio interferences to node mobility, which causes link breakages until a new route is calculated, producing annoying video interruptions to the receiver. The variability in network capacity and link quality, together with the dynamic network topology, has clearly influenced emerging wireless mesh networks, which tend to maintain a static backbone in order to provide sufficient Quality of Service. Moreover, since wireless propagation nature allows any node to overhear any neighbor transmission, the way opportunistic and cooperative routing protocols take advantage of the broadcast nature of wireless medium can be adopted for new routing proposals. In this sense, this chapter proposes and describes a new cross-layer mechanism for recovering lost packets by means of caching overheard packets in neighbor nodes and retransmitting them to their destination. Additionally, a video-aware cache is implemented in order to recover full frames and prioritize more significant frames. On the other hand, energy consumption is critical in mobile nodes because they may rely on battery power, and the whole network connectivity may be affected if some of the routing nodes run out of battery eventually. Thus, energy consumption is also taken into account in the recovering algorithm design to ensure longer network connectivity life. Finally, results show the improvement in reception, increasing the throughput as well as video quality, and reduce

---

[*] Multimedia Communications Group, Universitat Politècnica de València, València. Email: paarvi@iteam.upv.es.

large video interruptions considerably. Moreover, by being aware of nodes energy consumption, the proposed algorithm is able to maintain network lifetime longer.

Keywords: Routing Protocols, OLSR, Quality of Service, Video Streaming, Quality of Experience, Wireless Ad Hoc Networks, ARQ

INTRODUCTION

Mobile wireless ad hoc networks (MANETs) are characterized by versatility, feasibility and ease of deployment without infrastructure. This kind of network consists of a series of nodes that cooperate in order to create and maintain packet routes. In large networks, communications might have to cross some intermediate nodes in order to reach their destination. These intermediate nodes act as routers so that packets can travel from one node to another through multi-hop routes. Consequently, every node should be able to forward packets addressed to other nodes. In fact, every node forming part of the network which can be a potential source or destination of data transmissions, has also to be able to route and forward packets from other communications. As far as fairness is concerned, this may be seen as initial condition to be part of an ad hoc network. This way, every node cooperates towards the proper operation of the network, with the aim of providing connectivity among nodes. However, besides the basic connectivity service offered, the number of real-time video services and multimedia applications is growing nowadays, and delay and bandwidth requirements of these kinds of services are very restrictive.

This sort of network represents a hostile environment for this kind of real-time data transmission to the extent that obtaining a good quality of viewer experience is challenging and still under study. Besides the research point of view, providing high-quality multimedia services is decisive for the practical usability and feasibility of wireless ad hoc networks so that service providers can broaden the range of services offered. So far, mobile wireless ad hoc networks have been used to provide network connection among users who could not have connectivity otherwise. However, quality expectations and requirements have been increased notably, fostered by the advent of real-time multimedia applications over mobile devices. Due to the considerable processing and bandwidth constraints underlying these types of devices, coupled with their ability to move freely, it becomes a difficult task to achieve an acceptable Quality of Service (QoS) throughout the entire video transmission.

In MANETs, routing protocols are in charge of establishing routes towards destination. Because of the multi-hop nature of this kind of network, when the number of hops increases in a route, the throughput is negatively affected. This is due to the fact that the packet loss probability and the interferences caused by the intra-flow contention are increased in every additional link [1]. Moreover, mobility of nodes makes it difficult to create and maintain these routes. In case a node moves out of coverage of its neighbors, part of the communication path has to be calculated again. During this rerouting time, following packets cannot be delivered and most of them are dropped, causing packet losses and non-negligible delays.

It is well known that MANETs can be set up at very low cost compared with networks based on access points that need wired infrastructure support. However, due to the difficulty of maintaining minimal QoS conditions, actual ad hoc networks tend to be designed with a static wireless backbone, which provides them with the minimal structure to assure connectivity and stability to a certain extent, like in emerging wireless mesh networks (WMNs) [2]. This could become a trade-off between cost effort and the transmission quality offered [3]. The hierarchical structure of WMNs can help in stabilizing routes despite the mobility of some terminals. A typical wireless mesh scenario is depicted in Figure 1.

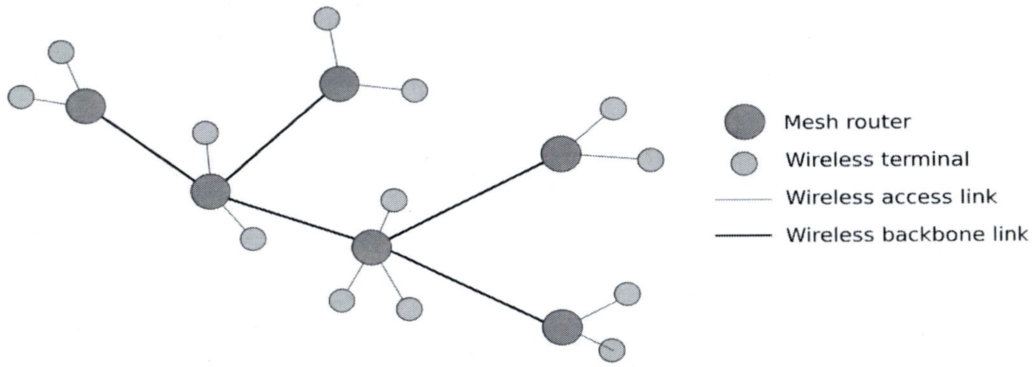

Figure 1. Typical Ad hoc Mesh Network with a Wireless Backbone.

In case the destination node is moving around in such environment, packet losses are likely to be concentrated on the last hop, when such node moves out of the forwarding neighbor range. When this occurs, next packets cannot be sent and could be discarded as long as the new route is not established. In case these packets arrive correctly at the node preceding the destination, it should be worth an effort to make those packets finally arrive at destination without having to be discarded or sent again through a new route, consuming time and resources. Since any neighbor of the destination node may have overheard those undelivered packets, it could send them again, although it does not take part of the original packet path. This can be achieved due to a particularity inherent to the wireless channel nature. Despite the fact of being one of the main reasons of interferences and contention, which affect the transmission quality negatively, the shared medium can be exploited to reinforce routes and build more robust packet paths, such in opportunistic [4] and cooperative routing protocols [5].

Even in mesh networks, where a backbone provides more topological stability, it is not assured high Quality of Experience (QoE). In such scenario, mobility of terminal nodes still causes link breakages until a new route is calculated. In the meanwhile, lost packets cause annoying video interruptions to the receiver. With this in mind, the main objective of this proposal is to provide throughput gains in wireless communications and improve the QoS of video transmissions, providing the user with a higher QoE. To this end, this chapter proposes a cross-layer technique that uses information drawn from link, routing and application layers in order to increase the overall packet delivery ratio and, in case of video transmissions, reduce packet delay so as to avoid playback interruptions. Furthermore, in order to maintain compatibility with existent wireless devices and network standards, no modifications to link layer are performed and only slight changes in the routing protocol are needed.

Additionally, and aiming at improving video transmissions particularly, this cross-layer proposal allows using video aware cache, which would provide altruistic nodes with the ability to recover full frames and prioritize more significant frames. Furthermore, energy consumption is a key factor for the proper operation of an ad hoc network, since the majority of nodes are mobile and battery-dependent devices. Therefore, despite the significant progress in battery capacity and duration, power resources in mobile devices are limited and, consequently, it is worth taking energy consumption into account. In this regard, nodes using the proposed mechanism may choose the better neighbor to retransmit lost packets according to their residual energy so that the overall lifetime of the network is increased. With this proposal, both throughput and video quality are improved and, in addition, large video interruptions are considerably reduced, as results show. Energy consumption is also taken into consideration in order to increase the network lifetime.

This chapter is organized as follows. Next section exposes some related work. Then, the main challenges for video streaming in mobile ad hoc networks are briefly described. The proposal is explained in the next section and the performance and results are shown in the assessment section. Finally, conclusions are discussed.

Related Work

Usually, MANETs present a mesh topology where every node may have one or more neighbors and any of them may act as a router. This network arrangement allows multipath routing protocols to choose among several possible routes if the current one results broken [6] [7]. Furthermore, Automatic Repeat Request (ARQ) mechanisms can be implemented to retransmit lost packets from the source through one of the alternative routes, increasing the overall throughput and even providing the possibility of changing to a new route seamlessly without video interruption [8]. In multi-hop networks, transmission paths are usually established taking into account the number of hops, but there are also other alternatives and measures such as path loss, available bandwidth, packet delay or link quality [9] [10]. In some cases, these routing protocols can even control video quality parameters in a cross-layer manner in order to adapt the transmission rate to the current network conditions and path bandwidth [11].

One of the drawbacks of the ARQ mechanism is that it negatively affects real-time video streaming when packets are retransmitted frequently, because additional traffic overload is generated throughout the network and, moreover, higher end-to-end delay is introduced for each retransmitted packet, which can become deprecated and discarded, leading to video playback interruptions. Some related works propose the utilization of special intermediate nodes along the path that act as video assistants [12]. These video assistants are in charge of buffering video packets and retransmit them when destination node sends an ARQ. By using an intermediate node instead of the source node, the requested packet is sent back to the destination in shorter time than the source could do. For this purpose, routes are built dynamically and the shortest path is selected in which a suitable video assistant is located. This mechanism reduces the delay of those packets that have to be retransmitted in comparison with end-to-end ARQ methods, at the cost of introducing some complexity when routes are created. As aforementioned, the shared nature of the wireless medium allows nodes to hear packets sent by neighbors to other nodes. Taking advantage of this feature, retransmitter nodes in the ARQ scheme should not be limited to nodes belonging to the transmission path. Reference [13] proposes a method that uses neighboring terminals of the nodes along the route, not only the nodes that are currently part of the route, to forward packets cooperatively. Therefore, lost packets acquire more chances to be retransmitted, improving the effectiveness of retransmission, although more complexity is introduced in order to coordinate possible retransmitters. Also, reference [14] proposes a cooperative relaying algorithm for interference reduction, where idle nodes can be used as potential video relays. Video rate and transmission power are controlled and distributed in order to maximize the overall video quality. Generally, however, cooperative routing may cause additional energy consumption since more nodes than in deterministic routing are participating in the transmission path. Taking this into account, reference [15] proposes a cooperative routing mechanism that uses variable transmission power in order to balance achievable throughput and battery life.

In general, many proposals involving energy-aware mechanisms are based on a cross-layer scheme, which combine information collected from different protocol layers and operate on a particular function within the protocol stack. Particularly, interaction between data link layer and network layer may contribute to provide routing protocols with some sort of energy awareness in order to deal with battery life limitations inherent to mobile devices. Some of these approaches make use of additional metrics in order to select better routes. In this sense, reference [16] proposes an algorithm that reduces network congestion by means of establishing routes using the nodes with maximum residual energy. Another approach proposes to build different routing entries according to the node power levels on demand, and select the minimum power level route for data delivery [17]. In [18] and [19], both the balance of the route and power conservation are considered, leading to cross-layer routing protocols that perform load balancing across multiple paths and extend network lifetime. Energy consumption is therefore an important point to consider because energy-aware algorithms could improve the overall network performance in the sense that some route breakages and packet losses might be prevented. Commonly, actual implementations of wireless mesh networks [20] rely on an ad hoc backbone with stable topology, and consequently, link losses are usually low within these backbone nodes. This can be the case of real practical scenarios, such as in smart cities or campus universities. This fact causes that most of packet losses likely occur on the last hop due to possible movements of the destination node or some of its contiguous neighbors. Therefore, limiting retransmission mechanisms to the last hop surroundings is certainly reasonable, because interference caused to other nodes is minimized and the overall energy consumption and packet delay is consequently reduced, which is desirable in real-time video transmissions. In a similar wireless scenario, reference [21] proposes a buffering scheme during handoff between access points in order to avoid packet losses. In this case, signal strength is measured in these access points to foresee when client nodes are moving.

Challenges for Video Streaming Services over MANETs

Shared Channel Limitations

The shared nature of the wireless channel in ad hoc networks may cause packet collisions within the carrier-sensing distance of the transmission node. Such situations can be avoided with proper mechanisms to access the wireless medium. The medium access control algorithm used in IEEE 802.11 (i.e., CSMA/CA) presents several basic mechanisms in order to avoid packet collisions, such as random back-off time or the RTS/CTS handshake mechanism. This kind of collision avoidance medium access entails some limitations in wireless ad hoc networks and, particularly, one of these limitations is the achievable transmission capacity. Specifically, the RTS/CTS mechanism does avoid collisions that would decrease throughput due to retries, but on the other hand, this additional process adds a significant amount of protocol overhead that also results in a decrease in network throughput. All in all, the maximum bandwidth is reduced due to the fact that nodes cannot simultaneously access the shared medium. That is, when a node is transmitting a packet, neighbor nodes within its interference range must not transmit. As a result, an overall degradation in data rate is produced.

These results are not unexpected at all, but they have to be taken into account when analyzing wireless networks and especially when assessing services that consume an important amount of bandwidth, such as video streaming services. Medium contention and transmission interferences do worsen the average network throughput when several data sources are competing for the medium access, but this contention exists even when only a single transmission is carried out through the network (or it is locally isolated in the network).

In multi-hop ad hoc networks, when a transmission is established, the nodes must cooperate to forward the packets through the network, which means that the available throughput on each host is limited not only by the access channel, but also by the forwarding load. As hop count increases, the maximum throughput of one flow decreases substantially and falls down because of the overhead of MAC layer and the mutual interference between packets of the same flow. This effect is called intra-flow contention [22] and represents the contention between packets of the same flow being forwarded at different hops along a multi-hop path, causing the actual bandwidth consumption.

Although node interference and intra-flow contention are constraining factors that affect the maximum throughput achieved in transmissions, there are still other issues that may cause additional packet losses and may also difficult good quality transmissions in such distributed networks, such as, for instance, mobility of nodes.

Ad hoc networks have the ability of self-organization and self-configuration but the topology of these networks is usually highly dynamic. Due to mobility and the multi-hop nature of ad hoc networks, any node can move out of the coverage area for a short time, losing the packet route to destination and even causing route breakages to other communications. Therefore, the node ability to move freely can become a problem because of these induced link breakages and the necessity to discover new routes towards destination for data transmission. These facts cause packet losses and delay while new routes are being configured, with the consequent loss of quality at the receiver.

Video Streaming over MANETS

Video streaming services, which are increasingly demanded nowadays, are bandwidth consuming and have high restrictive delay and loss constraints. Deploying such real-time services turns out difficult on wireless ad hoc networks due to the aforementioned issues. While video streaming requires a steady flow of information and delivery of packets by a deadline, wireless radio networks have difficulties to provide such a service reliably. Hence, the problem is challenging due to contention from other network nodes, as well as intermittent interference from external radio sources. Besides this, it is likely that any node might move away and therefore, the network topology may be altered causing link breakages and packet loss. Because of their nature, video streaming services are very sensitive to packet loss and delay. Figure 2 illustrates this video quality loss (PSNR degradation) when throughput is degraded because of node mobility, radio interferences or intra-flow contention.

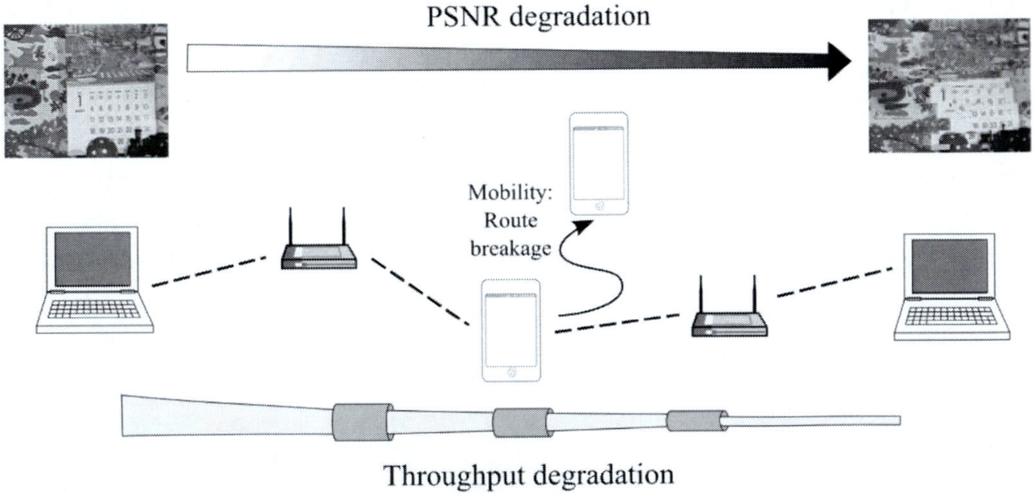

Figure 2. Video Quality Degradation in Multi-hop Wireless Networks.

Nowadays, most of video encoders are capable of reaching a quite low data rate and ensuring a rather good video quality. This is due to the use of a hierarchical coding, which causes many frames to be time dependent on others within the same video flow (e.g., MPEG-4, H.264, VP8). However, just because of this type of video encoding, the loss of a few packets can provoke the loss of one or several dependent video frames. Even a slight delay on some packets could result in deprecated frames, and therefore it would be better to skip them rather than play them back late. It is true that this time dependency is reduced to slice domain or even block domain within a frame in cutting-edge encoders, but the inter-frame dependency will be eventually unavoidable if a high compression rate is aimed to be achieved. This is why many video decoders have been developed with error concealment mechanisms in case of transmission failures.

Network simulators are useful tools that allow building huge network topologies and testing new protocols and algorithms that could not be assessed otherwise. However, it would also be interesting to check some results whenever possible over real networks and devices. In order to illustrate more clearly what happens when a node moves out of the coverage of the routing neighbor and how it affects the video quality, a real video transmission has been assessed, which not only is useful for a better understanding of the actual performance of wireless transmissions but also to measure the video quality received in a hostile environment. For scalability reasons, however, only a small-scale scenario has been assessed. Thus, real devices have been configured and arranged forming an ad hoc network.

The testbed has been built with laptops and smartphones. Source and destination nodes are laptops with Linux and 802.11b/g wireless cards. For multi-hop transmission, Android smartphones are used as intermediate nodes, which are in charge of routing video packets. These devices have been intentionally arranged so that the source node must always use any of the intermediate nodes to forward packets to the destination node. Therefore, transmission route is always forced to have two hops. During the experiment, the destination node moves at approximately 1 m/s, following the itinerary depicted in Figure 3.

Note that node 1 and node 2 do not see one another due to the thick walls. Hence, the experiment is carried out as follows. First, the destination is receiving the video transmission from source through node 1, which acts as a router (1). Then, destination moves away from the coverage of node 1, causing a route breakage and the consequent packet losses (2). Right away, destination node enters within the coverage of node 2. Video packets are then transmitted from source to destination through node 2. This route change does not occur immediately, because the routing protocol must first realize that the link has fallen and then recalculate the best route (3). The routing protocol used is an implementation of OLSR [23], which uses HELLO and Topology Control (TC) messages to perform routing operations. The main parameters used to configure the testbed regarding wireless card and routing protocol are described in Table 1.

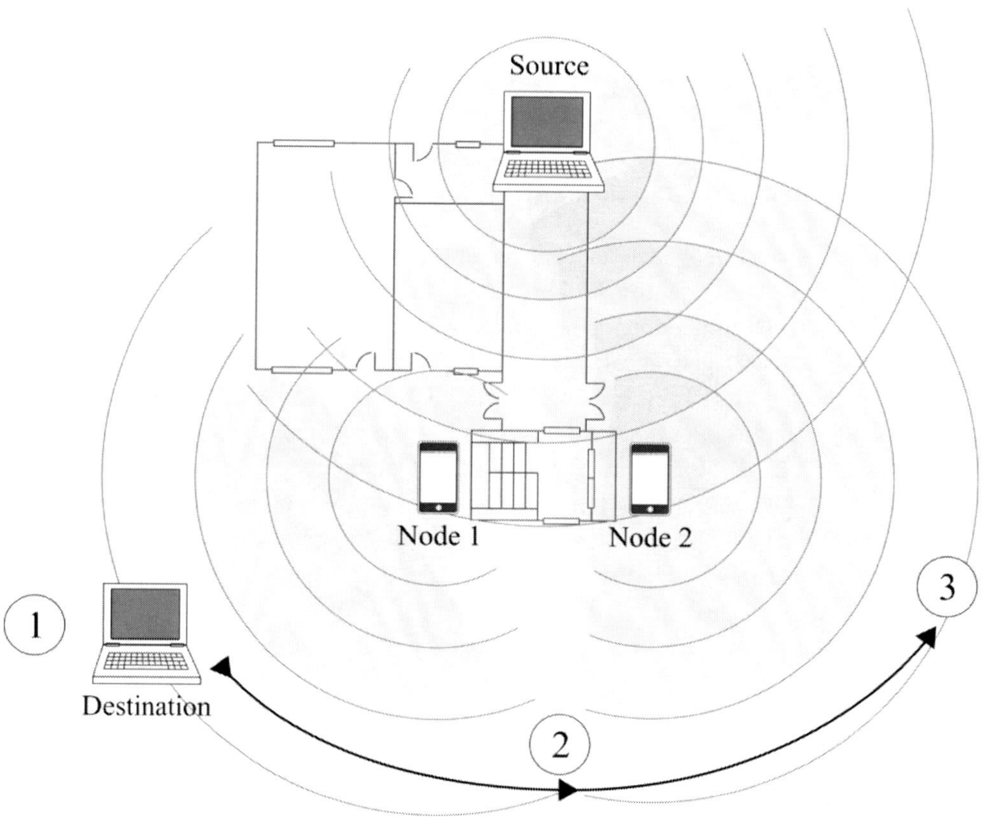

Figure 3. Network Setup for Testbed.

Table 1. Testbed Wireless Configuration Parameters

Parameter	Value
Wireless Standard	802.11g
Data Rate	54 Mbps
Transmission Power	0 dBm
RTS/CTS, Fragmentation	Off
Power Management	Off
Routing Protocol	OLSR
OLSR HELLO Interval	2 seconds
OLSR TC Interval	5 seconds

Once the network is set up, real video traffic is sent through the network. Source node transmits a video of 70 s of duration, the size of which is 352x288 pixels, with a frame rate of 30 fps (the video is a loop of *mobile.yuv* [24], available on the Internet and commonly used for video assessment) encoded at 500 kbps on average using H.264 with a GoP size of 30 frames, without B-frames (bidirectional). Then, it has been packetized to add RTP headers into packets of an MTU of 1400 bytes. So far, video is suitable to be streamed through the network.

During the experiment, the Received Signal Strength Indicator (RSSI) has been measured at destination node to depict the signal quality received from node 1 and node 2. Figure 4 shows the RSSI variation caused by destination movement along the scenario layout, highlighting the three stages.

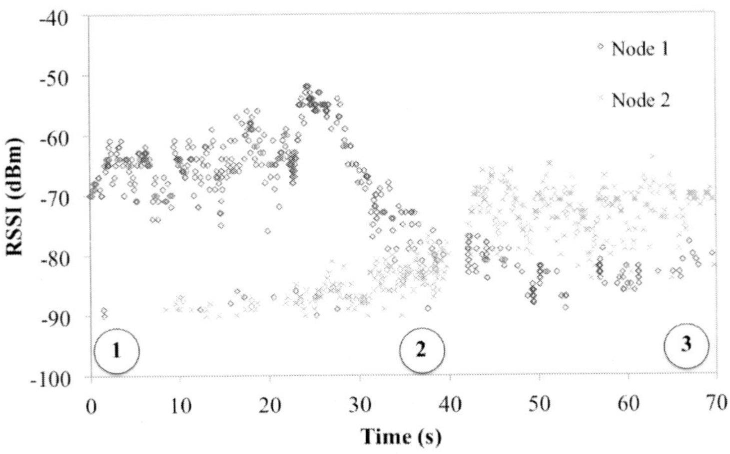

Figure 4. RSSI from Node 1 and Node 2 Measured at Destination.

As long as destination remains within the coverage of node 1, RSSI values are high enough to guarantee the proper reception of video transmission. As destination moves out of range, depicted as stage 2, the signal received from node 1 decreases but signal strength from node 2 is progressively increasing. When destination node arrives at stage 3, RSSI values from node 2 indicate that destination falls within the coverage of node 2, and a new route can be established now. Finally, results regarding instant PSNR and packet delay are depicted in Figure 5.

Average PSNR of the encoded video used as reference is 28.31 dB. However, average PSNR of the received video drops to 22.39 dB. This is due to the video playback interruption generated when OLSR is trying to discover the new route. Even in a rather simple scenario like this, the rerouting time is remarkable. OLSR takes about 20 seconds to realize that a link has fallen and recalculate the new route. It is true that this interval could be slightly shorter if OLSR is configured to keep routing tables updated faster (e.g., by reducing OLSR HELLO and TC intervals), but at the expense of increasing control traffic overhead. Regarding instant packet delay, it can be seen a noticeable increase when destination is arriving at stage 2. This fact coincides with the decrease in the signal strength received from node 1. A thorough analysis of packet delay and RSSI could be performed in order to anticipate link failures, as can be seen in other studies in the literature [25].

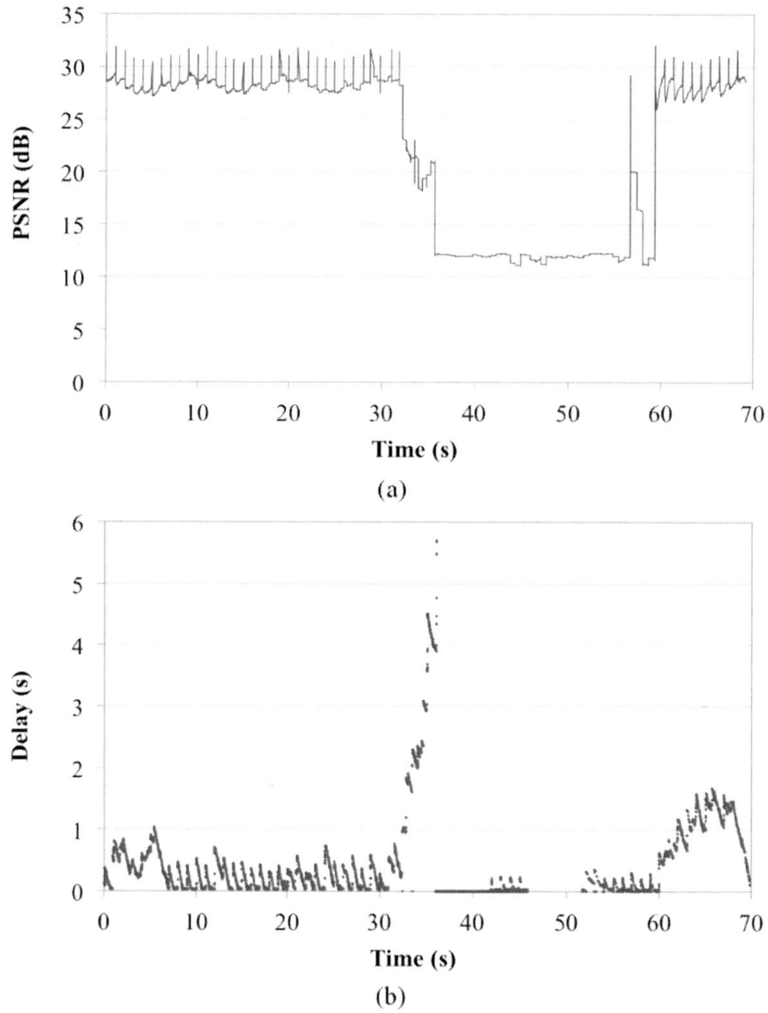

Figure 5. Average PSNR (a) and Packet Delay (b) in the Real Testbed Layout.

Recovering Algorithm in Altruistic Networks

In general, in ad hoc networks nodes must cooperate and work for the common good. Every node should be able to become a router and to forward packets from flows originated from or destined to other nodes. Particularly, in wireless mesh networks, packet routes rely on backbone nodes because they hardly suffer modifications and provide long-term stability to the wireless links. Logically, nodes that are likely to move around are devices that make use of the wireless backbone to communicate. These mobile nodes are usually the transmission source, the destination or any of their nearest neighbors. This mobility could affect the current packet route partially so recovering mechanisms should be implemented at network edges, where the mobility is more plausible, especially at the destination surroundings. Hence, the proposed mechanism tries to recover lost packets by means of caching overheard packets in the surrounding of the destination node and retransmit them to destination.

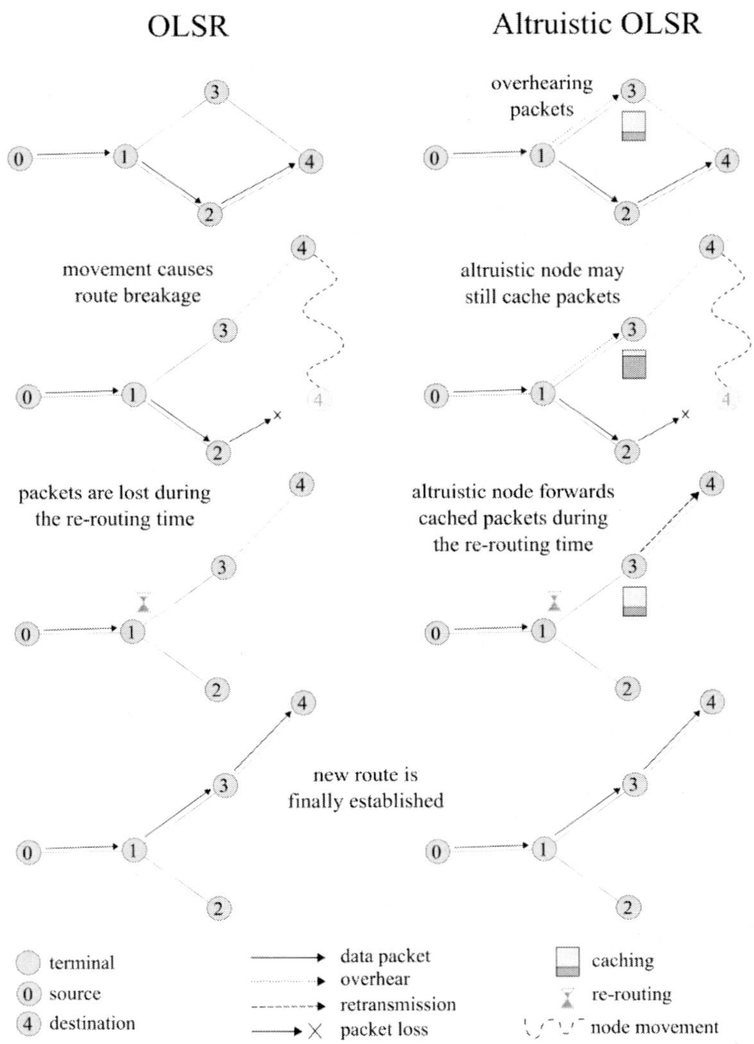

Figure 6. Behavior before a Route Breakage in OLSR (left) and Altruistic OLSR (right).

On traditional routing, e.g., OLSR, when a route is broken due to the movement of nodes, packets are likely to be discarded on the queue of any intermediate node during the rerouting time, causing a negative effect on the throughput. Figure 6 depicts this situation in a reduced scenario with 5 nodes to assess the effect of node mobility. Node 4 is the destination and has two neighbors (node 2 and node 3).

The packet route calculated by the routing protocol (OLSR in this case) is 0->1->2->4. Suppose now that node 4 moves and gets out of the transmission range of node 2. The transmission route results broken and then, by means of the routing protocol signaling, a new route towards node 4 is established through the node 3. Therefore, the new route will be 0->1->3->4 (Figure 6 left).

As a feature common to wireless ad hoc networks, all nodes within the radio range of a sender terminal can take advantage of the shared medium and overhear packets even if they are not the genuine receivers. In common data-link layer protocols, the overheard packets are discarded if the destination address is not the terminal's address. In the approach proposed, the neighbors of the destination node (i.e., node 3) may cache packets that they overhear in promiscuous mode and are addressed to their neighbors (Figure 6 right). In this example, node 3 can keep sending previously overheard packets that it retains in the cache, until the new route is completely established.

The ideal case is given when every packet that was not received at destination has been overheard by a neighbor node and in addition, this neighbor node is able to retransmit it to destination. In practice, when the routing algorithm detects a link failure, source node queues outgoing packets (i.e., stops transmitting) and waits until a new route has been found. Packets that remain in the outgoing queue during a long time might be discarded.

In this approach, not every node forming the path has to buffer packets for retransmission, in contrast to other cooperative caching techniques, which use every possible node near the transmission route as a retransmitter candidate [26]. Usually, most of ad hoc mobile nodes are resource-limited devices so it would be worth limiting the amount of nodes that should perform packet caching and retransmission. In this scheme, a node caches most recently received packets only if they are addressed to a neighbor. If destination is no longer in the neighborhood (one-hop nodes), the cache is emptied for this node and no more packets addressed to it are cached.

In order to avoid an excessive memory usage, this cache has a maximum size for each neighbor and packets are cached only for a short time. In addition, every cache entry stores both the packet and the arrival time so that packets that are older than a certain validity time (VT) are discarded, avoiding deprecated packets to be retransmitted.

For a better understanding, Figure 7 draws the main events that are taking place in this scenario. During the initial steady state, video transmission is being received correctly. When the destination node starts to move, there comes a time when packets cannot reach the destination and finally, the routing protocol notices that there has been a route breakage. Then, when the destination node comes into coverage again, transmission can be resumed after this rerouting time. Note that destination can benefit from cached packets of altruistic neighbor nodes if they are still in range.

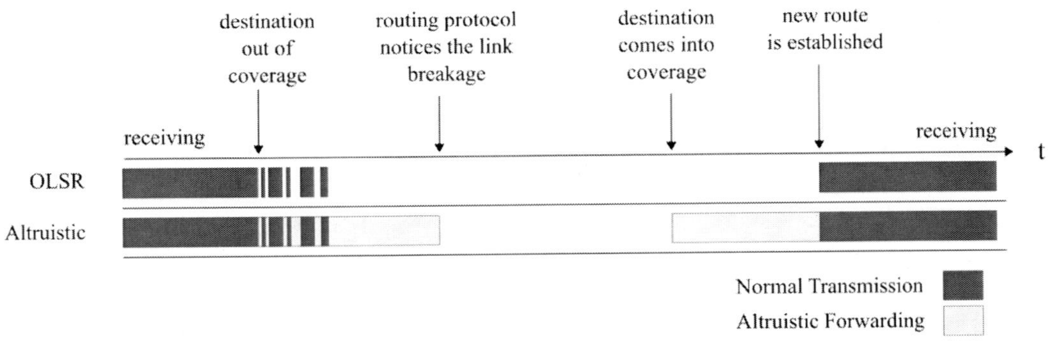

Figure 7. Timeline Comparing the Rerouting Behavior between OLSR and Altruistic OLSR.

Candidate Selection

When relaying on extra nodes to retransmit lost packets, candidate selection becomes an important process to ensure the best performance. Reference [12] chooses the candidate before the route has been established, assuring a good position for the retransmitter throughout the path. Instead, opportunistic routing protocols [27] track all possible routes for each packet (or batch of packets [28]) and mark the priority of each route.

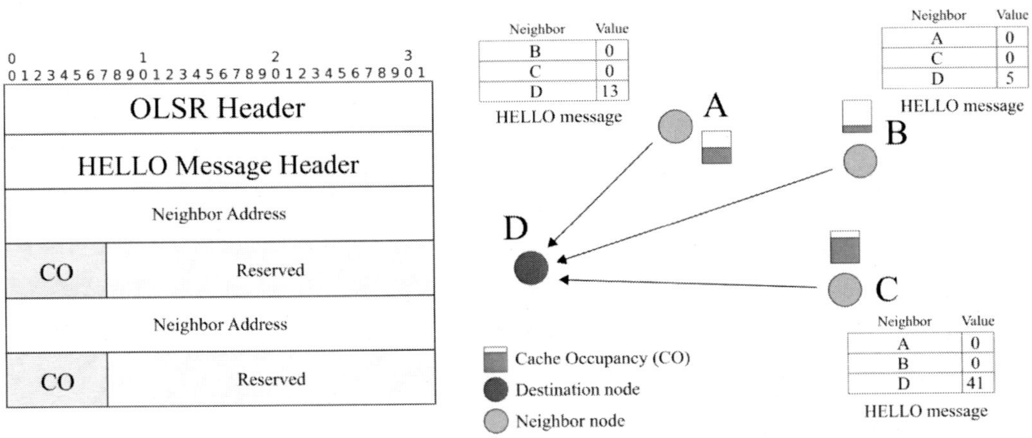

Figure 8. Modification to HELLO Packets for the Candidate Selection Mechanism.

Actually, among the nodes that have cached packets for retransmission, there will be some of them holding more packets and fresher ones, which make those nodes be more effective retransmitters. Therefore, the way the retransmitter node is selected has to be considered carefully. In the scheme presented in this proposal, the candidate selection process is carried out by the destination node so that no coordination function is needed among all possible retransmitters, reducing complexity and overhead. In order to select the best retransmitter candidate, destination node chooses one of its neighbors attending to a measurement value. This value, which can be estimated according to several methods, will help the destination node choose the most suitable neighbor to retransmit lost packets. Each node periodically informs its neighbors about this measurement value by means of a new field in OLSR HELLO message. As occurs in other proactive routing protocols, OLSR periodically broadcasts HELLO messages in order to discover and update neighboring information, which is very convenient for the aim of this proposal. When HELLO messages are generated to inform about neighbors' connectivity, each neighbor entry will also contain a value representing the goodness of the cache content for this neighbor. It is worth noting that the frequency of this update is closely related to the frequency configured for HELLO messages. As the interval of HELLO messages are configured shorter, cache information is updated more frequently, but the overhead is also higher. When destination node receives HELLO messages from its neighbors, it is able to compare and finally decide which one has the most valuable set of packets to be retransmitted. This decision is made from the values that neighbors have sent inside the modified HELLO messages and it will be explained in detail later. When cache is empty for all of its neighbors, no additional fields are inserted into the traditional HELLO packet format, not increasing message size and overhead. Otherwise, it is indicated using the reserved field of the HELLO message header. Figure 8 depicts an example, where node D is the destination, and nodes A, B and C inform periodically about their suitability to be retransmitters. In this example, node C will be chosen because it has a higher value.

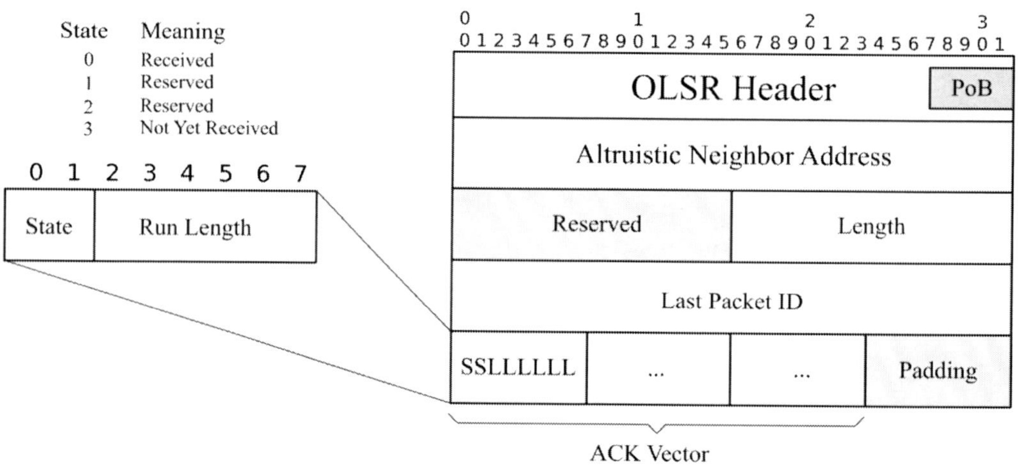

Figure 9. AR Message Format.

The aforementioned measurement value can be calculated in several ways, including but not limited to: 1) geoposition, where nearest neighbors would achieve greater values; 2) Expected Transmission Count (ETX), i.e., nodes with greater delivery probability would be more suitable; 3) Cache Occupancy (CO), that is, attending to the total amount of packets cached for a specific destination; or 4) residual energy, where nodes that have higher remaining battery would be selected. Other methods could also be used as long as they provide a measurement value to be set in HELLO messages, or even a combination of them. For instance, by knowing the position of the neighboring nodes and the cache occupancy in each of them, destination node could choose a candidate more accurately taking into account also the direction in case it is moving. Diverse local positioning methods could be used for this purpose [29]. Initially, in order to evaluate the proposed algorithm, CO has been used as the measurement value, so that caches that contain more packets are given higher values. Packets older than a certain validity time are discarded and therefore are not taken into account. Hence, as long as destination chooses a retransmitter neighbor that maximizes CO value, the amount of useful video packets for destination will also be maximized. Reserved bytes could be further used to send additional information about each neighbor node (ETX, geoposition, remaining battery, etc.), which could be employed jointly to select the best retransmitter.

Then, the proposed scheme acts as follows. When the destination node detects any packet loss (examining sequence numbers in video packet headers or more generally, in RTP headers), it generates and sends a report by means of a new kind of OLSR message: the Application Report (AR) message. This AR packet contains the identifier (sequence number) of the last correctly received packet (Last Packet ID) and an ACK Vector, which gives a run-length encoded history of previous data packets received at destination, as carried out in other standards such as Datagram Congestion Control Protocol (DCCP) [30]. Moreover, original OLSR packets contain a header field indicating how long after a reception of this packet, the information is still valid (Vtime). In AR packets this field is used to inform neighbors about the maximum time a retransmitted packet will still be valid for video playback, i.e., the play-out buffer (PoB) size. As explained before, destination node holds information about which neighbor has been estimated the most suitable for retransmitting lost packets (Altruistic Neighbor Address). All these parameters are encapsulated in a new AR message according to Figure 9. The ACK Vector itself consists of two fields: State, which informs about reception or loss; and Run Length, which specifies how many consecutive packets have the given State.

Nevertheless, during a long link failure it may well be the case that no packets were received and therefore, packet loss cannot be detected from sequence numbers. For this reason, the destination node (and only this node) periodically informs about the last received packets through AR messages. This is also carried out in order to update neighbors' cache regularly so that both deprecated as well as correctly received packets could be deleted.

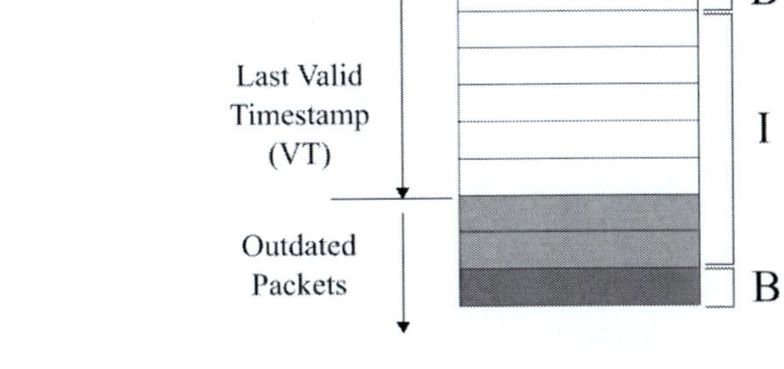

Figure 10. Discarding policy for Cached Video Packets.

Cache

Network nodes are configured with a certain maximum cache size and timeout in order to limit the total amount of packets stored and avoid retaining stale packets, respectively. When a node receives an AR message from one of its neighbors, it checks every packet in the cache addressed to this node and compares the packet arrival time stamp with the validity timestamp set in the AR message. Deprecated packets are immediately deleted. The rest of packets are checked against the ACK Vector, and those that are not set as received by destination are then retransmitted. Packets remaining in the cache are deleted after a preconfigured validity time. Optimal timeout period for caching packets closely depends on the size and state of the play-out buffer at destination node. If this buffer eventually underruns, QoE will be seriously degraded. Hence, by means of AR messages, destination node can inform other nodes about which is the maximum PoB time allowed for the current video transmission. Neighbors can now configure the cache validity time more accurately according to this. This way not only is the amount of packets the altruistic node caches optimized but also the amount of video packets that are retransmitted, with the concomitant bandwidth and energy saving.

Video Awareness

As explained, this proposal could be appropriate for managing time-constraint transmissions because it takes into account temporal considerations and restrictions. Nevertheless, the relative importance of video frames (I, P or B) and the policy taken for which frames to cache and forward are other considerable parameters, at the expense of adding some complexity to the algorithm. It is worth noting that this could be done below frame level with video codecs that support slicing. This sort of video awareness is carried out in altruistic neighbors that are able to discern and inspect video packets, and classify them according to the kind of frame they belong to (i.e., packets from I-frames are more critical than those from P- or B-frames). Moreover, intra-frame packets can be prioritized so that other packets will be discarded instead if node cache fills up. From a practical point of view, although deep packet inspection could consume extra time and computation, it could be feasible to check only the Differentiated Services Code Point (DSCP) field from IP headers or a Header Extension in RTP. In this case, video source must use this field to mark packets belonging to higher priority frames before sending them. In any case, this enhancement could be feasible for static power-supplied nodes with higher processing capabilities (e.g., backbone nodes).

Another interesting consideration can also be taken into account. Outdated packets that belong to a frame from which some packets are not deprecated yet, are not discarded until all packets from that frame are completely obsolete (Figure 10). This way, the algorithm tries not to split I-frames especially, because they are usually formed by a considerable number of packets.

This scheme is not only valid for making decisions according to the type of frame, but also, it is useful when using other sort of video coding that could be arranged into layers, such as Scalable Video Coding (SVC) [31]. By using this coding scheme, video packets from base layer can be prioritized over other improvement layers in order to reduce interruptions considerably.

Energy Awareness

Proper energy management could be essential for maintaining routes as steady as possible and foresee any upcoming link breakage in order to forestall packet losses. Due to the retransmission mechanism proposed, altruistic neighbors might have extra battery consumption while sending not-acknowledged packets. Hence, exchanging information about the battery levels of neighbors can help in the selection of the proper altruistic neighbor, taking into account that a longer network lifetime is also desired. In this sense, HELLO messages are modified again in order to include a new metric so that the remaining battery level of a node can be known by its neighbors. This energy parameter will help at destination in the decision of selecting which neighbor fits better as an altruistic forwarder. Hence, Figure 11 illustrates how HELLO message can be modified using the reserved field in the header to house the new Residual Battery parameter.

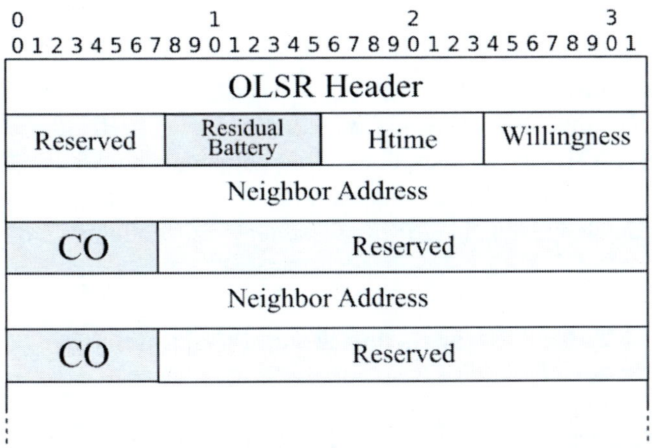

Figure 11. New HELLO Message Containing Information about Node Residual Battery.

Proposal Evaluation

In order to offer a general overview of some of the related work and solutions mentioned in previous sections, Table 2 compares them with the mechanism proposed in this chapter in order to show the main differences attending to some distinctive qualitative parameters. It is worth noting that, unlike other cooperative routing protocols, this proposal is not a routing algorithm itself but take advantage of OLSR information to implement an ARQ mechanism that also exploits the wireless shared medium and performs caching in order to retransmit lost packets when needed. Moreover, the presented cross-layer solution is video-aware, which allows discerning video traffic; and energy-aware, which both help improve QoE by reducing video interruptions when node mobility causes route breakages.

Sample Network

Firstly, the scenario depicted in Figure 6 is assessed regarding throughput, PSNR, packet delay and packet losses, using a video streaming source. All PSNR values cover both encoding distortion as well as channel-induced distortion. This first scenario consists of 5 nodes, where destination node moves causing a route change.

Table 2. Qualitative Comparison among Recovery Solutions

Mechanisms	ARQ	Video Awareness	Exploits shared medium	Caching	Adaptive	Multipath
Reference [8]	Yes	No	No	No	No	Yes
Reference [11]	Yes	Yes	No	No	Yes	No
Reference [12]	Yes	Yes	No	Yes	Yes	No
Reference [13]	No	No	Yes	No	No	Yes
Altruistic OLSR	Yes	Yes	Yes	Yes	No	No

This scenario has been simulated in NS-3 and the most relevant simulation parameters regarding wireless channel and transmission conditions, as well as video properties, are shown in Table 3. RTS/CTS mechanism does avoid collisions that would decrease throughput due to retries, but on the other hand, this additional process adds a significant amount of protocol overhead that also results in a decrease in network throughput, so it is not used in the simulations.

Table 3. Scenario and Simulation Parameters

Parameter	Value
Wireless Standard	802.11g
Data Rate	54Mbps
Transmission range	30m
RTS/CTS	Off
Video resolution	352x288
Video duration	70 seconds
Average video rate	500 kbps
Max. queue delay	1s
Cache validity time	2s
HELLO interval	1s

The following figures show the results comparing the scheme proposed with the standard OLSR. Figure 12 illustrates the instantaneous throughput received in the destination node. It can be observed that packet reception is interrupted during a gap of time in traditional OLSR, due to the movement of the receiving node. A considerable decrease is stated in the altruistic scheme, but even though some glitches or slight interruptions may appear, it manages to recover a number of packets that allow video to keep playing almost seamlessly. This effect can be corroborated in Figure 13, where PSNR is represented. There can be seen the effect of the interruption in the quality of the received video. Comparing with OLSR, the altruistic scheme manages to recover some additional video frames, thus improving the overall quality of video.

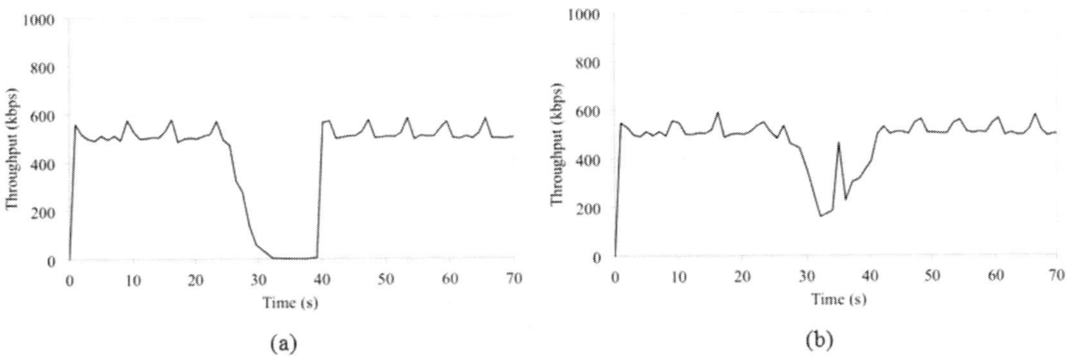

Figure 12. Throughput Comparison between OLSR (a) and Altruistic OLSR (b).

Besides PSNR, time instants of early AR packets are also depicted in the same figure, so it can be clearly shown the temporal relevance between the changes suffered in PSNR and the moment an AR packet is early transmitted. These are AR packets that are not sent periodically, but only when a packet loss is detected. By sending these packets instantaneously, destination node may recover some useful packets in time, being able to recover video frames that would be lost otherwise. After the rerouting process, altruistic neighbor become part of the actual route of packets and stops caching video packets (in case there would be more neighbors, they could become altruistic nodes).

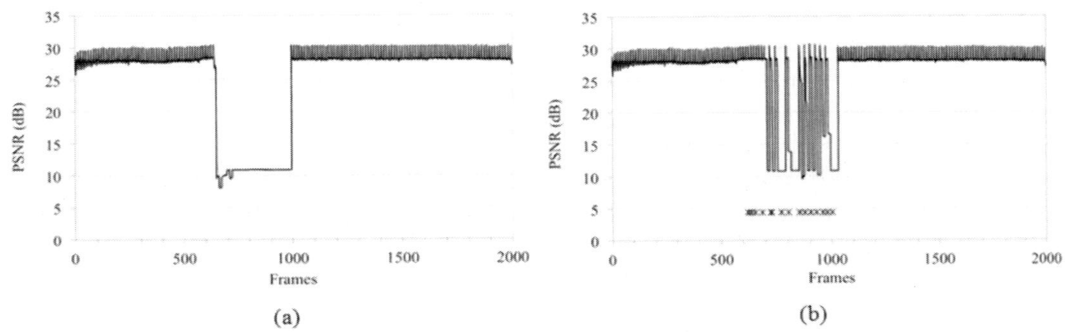

Figure 13. PSNR Comparison between OLSR (a) and Altruistic OLSR (b).

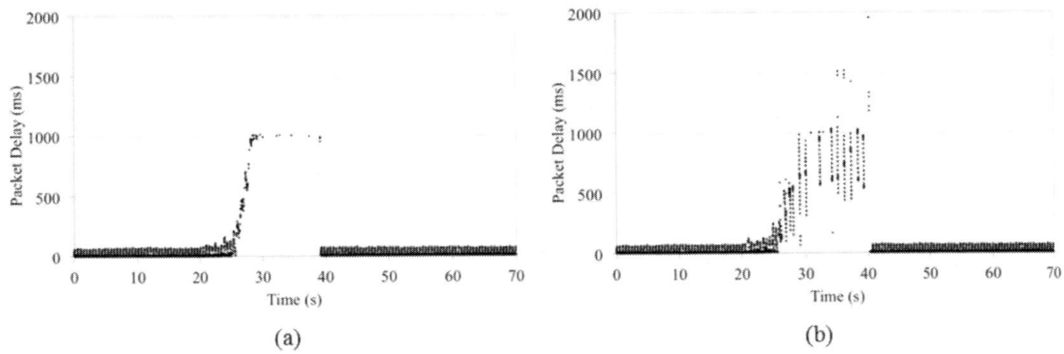

Figure 14. End-to-end Packet Delay Comparison between OLSR (a) and Altruistic OLSR (b).

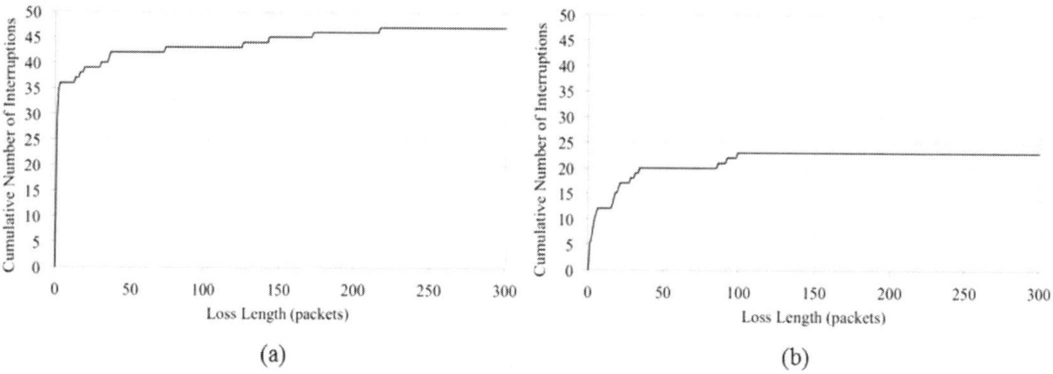

Figure 15. Cumulative Number of Interruptions Comparison between OLSR (a) and Altruistic OLSR (b).

Figure 14 illustrates end-to-end packet delay. As long as the maximum queue delay is set to 1 second, packets that stay longer than this delay in the queue are dropped. In this particular scenario, only one node is likely to suffer packet losses. Consequently, maximum packet delay reaches just over 1 second and below in OLSR. On the other hand, the altruistic recovering mechanism may present some packets with a higher delay due to retransmissions, even beyond 1 second, and there can also be distinguished some packet bursts retransmitted by the altruistic neighbor.

Figure 15 shows the cumulative number of interruptions or burst losses regarding their length in packets. It can be stated that there is a higher number of interruptions in traditional OLSR, especially burst losses that last few packets. In this case, altruistic retransmission recovers most of the small burst losses. Moreover, the maximum burst loss length is reduced considerably, as well as the number of bigger interruptions, compared with standard OLSR.

Finally, it is worth mentioning that even though the average PSNR along the whole simulation increases from 25.12 dB in OLSR to 26.38 dB in the altruistic scheme, the improvement is even more noticeable if only the frames within the zone of interest (from second 20 to second 44, i.e., approximately the rerouting time) would be taken into account (from 15.99 dB in OLSR to 21.01 dB in the altruistic scheme). PSNR reference value is 28.31 dB, which is the average PSNR obtained from comparing the original video sequence with the encoded one, not taking into account any transmission loss. It is also worth mentioning that the goal is to show the relative improvement that this proposal offers over traditional OLSR routing and the exact absolute values are not to be necessarily concerned, since they strongly depend on the current video enconding parameters and network conditions. The fact of prioritizing I-frames has also slightly helped improve PSNR, since more interdependent frames could be decoded. However, such particularized analysis cannot be carried out in random scenarios where destination node moves freely, resulting in one or several (or none) rerouting occasions and link breakages.

Energy Consumption

In general, wireless ad hoc networks are resource-demanding networks, especially because nodes that belong to a transmission route are consuming their own resources (e.g., processing time, memory and battery) although they are neither the source nor the destination of the communication. This tradeoff between connectivity and energy consumption has been analyzed in [32] and the feasibility and convenience of implementing ad hoc networks have been demonstrated, despite the fact that incentives to the users could be necessary to persuade them to share the capabilities of their devices with other users. In addition, if any of these router nodes has to become an altruistic node and it also has to cache packets to retransmit, this resource consumption increases inevitably.

Regarding this energy consumption, the fact of adding further mechanisms that use packet retransmission necessarily entails an increase in battery consumption. Taking into account that in ad hoc networks most of the nodes are mobile nodes or battery-dependent devices, new proposed techniques should not be very energy demanding in general. Therefore, energy consumption is analyzed in the situation that nodes become altruistic nodes and compared with the introduced improvement about energy-awareness.

Usually, wireless radio interfaces consume different amount of energy depending on the state they are working in, which can be transmission (TX), reception (RX), idle and busy. A node in TX or RX state is likely to consume more power than in busy or idle state. Nodes that are not taking part of the actual path are also receiving packets and dismissing them, which mean non-negligible consumption. Power consumption parameters used in the simulations are described in Table 4.

Table 4. Power Consumption Parameters for Wireless Network Cards Configuration

Parameter	Value
Transmission	2.6 W (transmitting at 17 dBm)
Reception	60 mW
Idle mode current	1.3 mW
Busy mode current	1.3 mW
Operating voltage	3 V

Figure 16 shows a similar scenario but there are now two additional nodes that can potentially become altruistic neighbors. In this scenario, both node 4 and node 5 have the same initial battery level. With the aim of assessing the algorithm, node 6 moves following the diagram during the simulation at 2 m/s, causing routes to be recalculated. Specifically, the packet path keeps changing among nodes 2, 4 and 3.

When destination node (node 6) is moving, packet route is lost during the transition from the coverage of one neighbor to another. When the transmission path is broken, both node 4 and node 5 are candidates to become altruistic neighbors and retransmit possible lost packets. However, as route suffers several changes along the simulation, this will cause video degradation and reduction in PSNR during the rerouting time. The video flow (with the same encoding parameters as in previous evaluation) is sent after 25 seconds from the beginning of the simulation and during 200 seconds. Figure 17 depicts the average PSNR and frame loss depending on the protocol used.

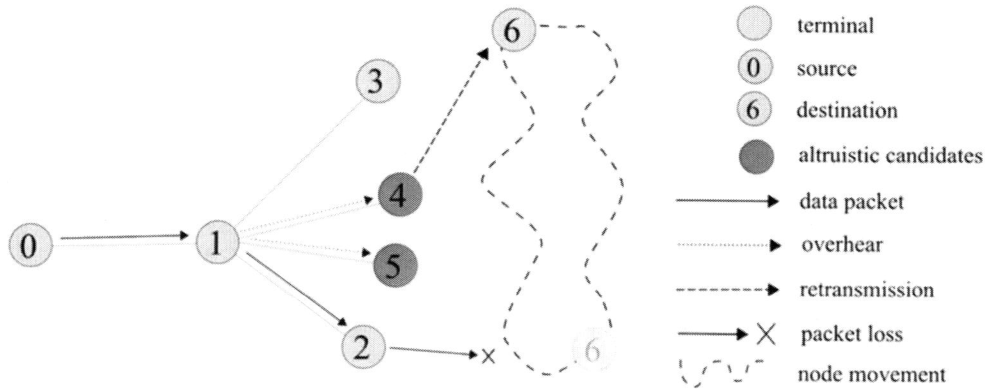

Figure 16. Scenario for Energy Assessment.

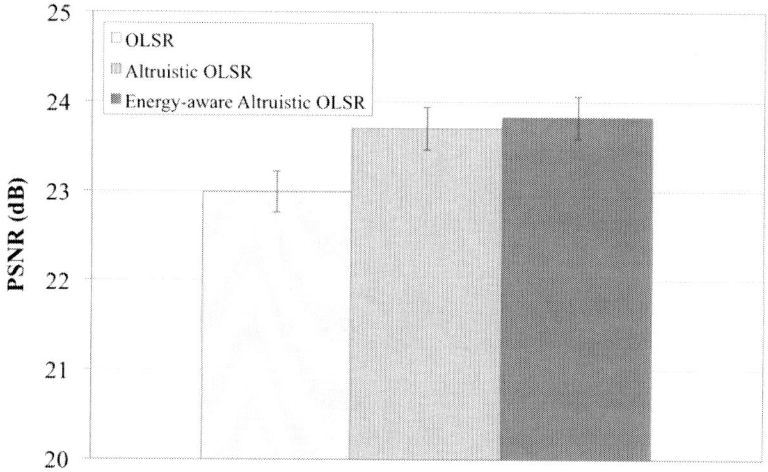

(a)

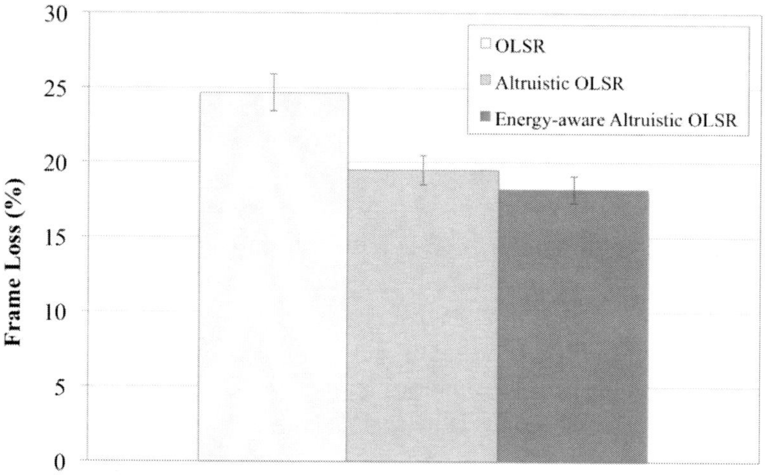

(b)

Figure 17. Average PSNR (a) and Average Frame Loss (b) for OLSR, Altruistic OLSR and Energy-aware Altruistic OLSR.

Average PSNR is increased from 22.99 dB in OLSR to 23.7 dB in Altruistic OLSR and 23.82 dB using the energy-aware enhancement. As long as PSNR is measured for the whole video sequence, these are average values, so the improvement is not as remarkable as though it was measured just during the rerouting time, as mentioned in previous results. Frame loss is reduced from 24.66% in OLSR to 19.48% and 18.18% in Altruistic OLSR without and with energy improvement, respectively.

As aforementioned, besides the improvement in video quality, additional enhancing mechanisms may cause an increase in power consumption, which can be critical in some situations since ad hoc networks usually consist of battery-dependent devices. In this sense, Figure 18 shows the energy consumption for the altruistic nodes in the scenario under analysis.

Particularly, it can be seen that when node 4 is performing routing operations, the energy consumption is higher, as can be seen in the steep slope at certain points. In OLSR, only node 4 is participating in the packet route and node 5 only has minimal consumption. In Altruistic OLSR, node 4 sometimes becomes an altruistic neighbor and retransmits cached packets to destination. The residual energy is affected and is depleted faster. However, node 5 has never been chosen as altruistic neighbor, probably because it would have cached the same amount of packets as node 4. It is worth noting that in the case that node 4 run out of battery, packet route would be broken. In this example, this happens after 177 seconds using Altruistic OLSR whereas in OLSR, node 4 is still running after 202 seconds. Nevertheless, using the energy-aware improvement for Altruistic OLSR, energy consumption is balanced among the altruistic candidates. Therefore, node 5 is sometimes selected to be the altruistic neighbor, as far as it has cached packets to retransmit. Hence, node 4 can save energy to perform routing operations, although it can become altruistic neighbor when no other altruistic candidates are present. Node 4's lifetime has been increased about 14%, practically like in OLSR, but with the advantage that PSNR and video quality is increased as well.

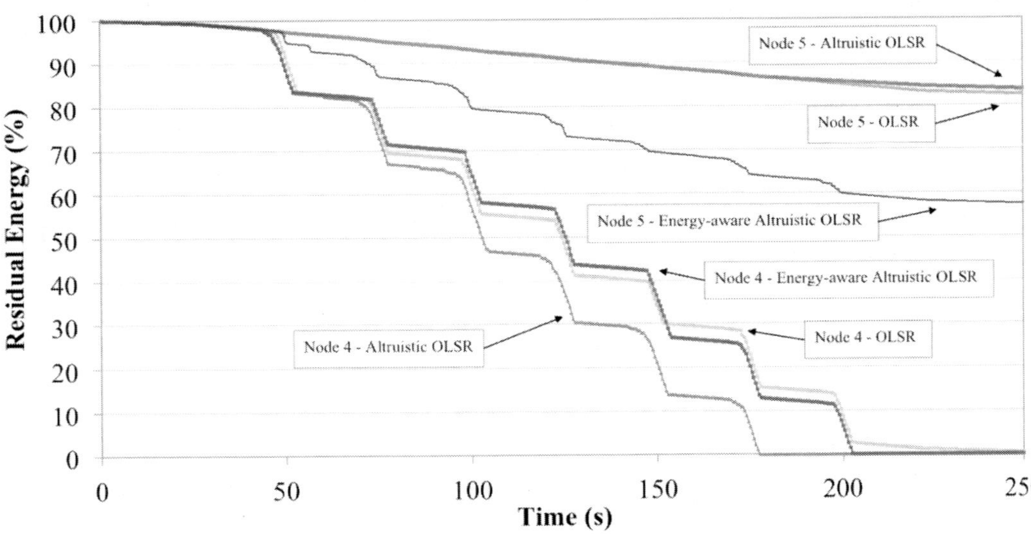

Figure 18. Power Consumption of Altruistic Candidates (Node 4 and Node 5).

Finally, it is worth mentioning that other ARQ mechanisms that use caching nodes near the source will ensure that video packets have been cached, but at the same time, retransmitting packets through a high number of hops would entail higher energy consumption, not only in the nodes that take part in the path but also in neighboring nodes, which are actually receiving these packets as well (RX state). Then, by using this altruistic scheme, only the surrounding area of destination node is affected by retransmissions. Moreover, the proposed energy-aware improvement can achieve higher network energy balance, which definitely enhances route stability.

CONCLUSION

Wireless ad hoc networks are altruistic networks by nature, that is, every node should be ready to serve as a router and forward packets from other communications in order to ensure connectivity and the proper network operation. However, node mobility hinders the creation and maintenance of steady routes in this kind of network. Hence, providing real-time services, such as video streaming, which is very sensitive to packet loss and delay, is still a topic under research because of the difficulty of guaranteeing a certain QoE. When any node moves out of range, routes have to be recalculated and, in the meanwhile, packets could be lost, with the consequent video interruptions and quality degradation.

In order to deal with video interruptions, a cross-layer technique is proposed, which uses information gathered from data-link, routing and application layers in order to increase the overall packet delivery ratio and reduce frame losses in video transmissions. This mechanism proposes that neighbors of the destination node can help in recovering lost packets by using cache and retransmission when a route breakage occurs.

Results show that the altruistic recovering solution reduces video playback interruptions considerably (about 50% on average) and frame losses (21%), and therefore improves the average PSNR from 1% to 5%, even achieving about 31% of improvement when considering only the rerouting period. Because of retransmitted packets, average packet delay is considerably increased (37%). However, due to the proximity of the retransmitter to the destination, packets are delivered faster than in source ARQ solutions.

Furthermore, by taking into account energy metrics, the algorithm has been enhanced in order to take into account the residual battery of the nodes. Hence, it can be possible to decide which retransmitters are optimal to guarantee a longer network lifetime, and consequently, preventing excessive usage and fast depletion of the altruistic nodes' battery. With this improvement, altruistic nodes can increase battery life about 14%. However, energy issues are rather complex because of the wide amount of variables that come into play regarding power consumption in mobile devices, so a thorough analysis would need further research.

Finally, it is worth noting that this kind of altruistic network is based on the concept that every node could perform caching and retransmitting functions when required and, moreover, there should not be other limitations, such as processing constraints or user restrictions.

REFERENCES

[1] Gupta, P., Kumar, P.-R., 2000. The Capacity of Wireless Networks. *IEEE Transactions on Information Theory*. 46, *2*, 388-404.

[2] Aguiar, E. S., Pinheiro, B. A., Figueirêdo, J. F. S., Cerqueira, E., Abelém, A. J. G., Gomes, R. L., (2011). Trends and Challenges for Quality of Service and Quality of Experience for Wireless Mesh Networks. *Wireless Mesh Networks*, 1st ed., InTech. 127-148.

[3] Guerri, J. C., Arce, P., Acelas, P., Castellanos, W. E., Fraile, F., (2012). Routing and Coding Enhancements to Improve QoS of Video Transmissions in Future Ad hoc Networks. *Multimedia Services and Streaming for Mobile Devices: Challenges and Innovations*, 1st ed., IGI Global. 244-261.

[4] Hsu, C.-J., Liu, H.-I., Seah, W. K. G., 2011. Opportunistic Routing: a Review and the Challenges Ahead. *Computer Networks*. 55, *15*, 3592-3603.

[5] Huang, X., Zhai, H., Fang. Y., 2008. Robust Cooperative Routing Protocol in Mobile Wireless Sensor Networks. *IEEE Transactions on Wireless Communications*. 7, *12*, 5278-5285.

[6] Marina, M. K., Das, S. R., 2006. Ad hoc On-demand Multipath Distance Vector Routing. *Wireless Communications and Mobile Computing*. 6, *7*, 969-988.

[7] Zhou, X., Lu, Y., Ma, H. G., 2006. Routing Improvement using Multiple Disjoint Paths for Ad hoc Networks. *Proceedings of the International Conference on Wireless and Optical Communications Networks*. 1-5.

[8] Fujisawa, H., Minami, H., Yamamoto, M., Izumi, Y., Fujita, Y., 2006. Route Selection using Retransmission Packets for Video Streaming on Ad hoc Networks. *Proceedings of the IEEE Conference on Radio and Wireless Symposium*. 607-610.

[9] Badis, H., Agha, K. A., 2004. QOLSR Multi-path Routing for Mobile Ad hoc Networks based on Multiple Metrics: Bandwidth and Delay. *Proceedings of the IEEE 59th Vehicular Technology Conference*. 2181-2184.

[10] Wu, Z., Wu, J., 2010. Cross-layer routing optimization for video transmission over wireless ad hoc networks. *Proceedings of the 6th International Conference on Wireless Communications Networks and Mobile Computing*. 1-6.

[11] Schier, M., Welzl, M., 2012. Optimizing Selective ARQ for H.264 Live Streaming: A Novel Method for Predicting Loss-Impact in Real Time. *IEEE Transactions on Multimedia*. 14, *2*, 415-430.

[12] Nikoupour, M., Nikoupour, A., Dehghan, M., 2008. A Cross-Layer Framework for Video Streaming over Wireless Ad hoc Networks. *Proceedings of the 3rd International Conference on Digital Information Management*. 340-345.

[13] Yamamoto, R., Miyoshi, T., 2008. Distributed Retransmission Method using Neighbor Terminals for Ad hoc Networks. *Proceedings of the 14th Asia-Pacific Conference on Communications*. 1-5.

[14] Guan, Z., Melodia, T., Yuan, D., 2013. Jointly Optimal Rate Control and Relay Selection for Cooperative Wireless Video Streaming. *IEEE Transactions on Networking*. 21, *4*, 1173-1186.

[15] Gravalos, I., Kokkinos, P., Varvarigos, E. A., 2013. Multi-Criteria Cooperative Energy-Aware Routing in Wireless Ad hoc Networks. *Proceedings of the 9th International Wireless Communications and Mobile Computing Conference*. 387-393.

[16] Vijayan, R., Mareeswari, V., Samyukta, V., 2013. Enhancing Energy Efficiency of Routing Protocol through Cross Layer Interactions in MANET. *International Journal of Engineering and Technology*. 5, *2*, 1147-1152.

[17] Haojun, H., Guangmin, H., Fucai, Y., 2010. A Routing Algorithm Based on Cross-Layer Power Control in Wireless Ad Hoc Networks. *Proceedings of the 5th International ICST Conference in Communications and Networking*. 1-6.

[18] Jian, C., Zhen, L., Juanwei, L., 2011. QoS Multipath Routing Protocol Based on Cross Layer Design for Ad hoc Networks. *Proceedings of the International Conference on Internet Computing & Information Services*. 261-264.

[19] Chen, S., Lu, X., 2010. A Novel Energy-Balanced Cross-layer Multi-Path Routing Algorithm for Wireless Ad hoc Networks. *Proceedings of the 2nd International Conference on Advanced Computer Control*. 5, 494-497.

[20] Abid, R. M., Benbrahim, T., Biaz, S., 2010. IEEE 802.11s Wireless Mesh Networks for Last-Mile Internet Access: An Open-Source Real-World Indoor Tstbed Implementation. *Wireless Sensor Networks*. 2, *10*, 725-738.

[21] Yen, Y.-S., Chang, R.-S., Wu, C.-Y., 2013. A Seamless Handoff Scheme for IEEE 802.11 Wireless Networks. *Wireless Communications and Mobile Computing*. 13, *2*, 157-169.

[22] Sanzgiri, K., Chakeres, I. D., Belding-Royer, E. M., 2004. Determining Intra-Flow Contention Along Multihop Paths in Wireless Networks. *Proceedings of the 1st International Conference on Broadband Networks*. 611-620.

[23] Clausen, T., Jacquet, P., 2003. Optimized Link State Routing Protocol (OLSR). IETF RFC 3626.

[24] Video Trace Library, (2013). http://trace.eas.asu.edu/yuv, last accessed on: May 2, 2014.

[25] Suarez, A., Macias, E., Espino, F., (2012). Multi-Platform Video Streaming Implementation on Mobile Terminals. *Multimedia Services and Streaming for Mobile Devices: Challenges and Innovations*. 1st ed., IGI Global. 288-314.

[26] Yin, L., Cao, G., 2006. Supporting Cooperative Caching in Ad hoc Networks. *IEEE Transactions on Mobile Computing*. 5, *1*, 77-89.

[27] Biswas, S., Morris, R., 2005. ExOR: Opportunistic Multi-Hop Routing for Wireless Networks. *Proceedings of the 2005 Conference on Applications, Technologies, Architectures, and Protocols for Computer Communications*. 133-144.

[28] Chachulski, S., Jennings, M., Katti, S., Katabi, D., 2007. Trading Structure for Randomness in Wireless Opportunistic Routing. *Proceedings of the 2007 Conference on Applications, Technologies, Architectures, and Protocols for Computer Communications*. 169-180.

[29] Karbasi, A., Oh, S., 2013. Robust Localization from Incomplete Local Information. *IEEE Transactions on Networking*. 21, *4*, 1131-1144.

[30] Kohler, E., Handley, M., Floyd, S., (2006). Datagram Congestion Control Protocol (DCCP). IETF RFC 4340.

[31] Schierl, T., Ganger, K., Hellge, C., Wiegand, T., Stockhammer, T., 2006. SVC-Based Multisource Streaming for Robust Video Transmission in Mobile Ad hoc Networks. *IEEE Wireless Communications*. 13, *5*, 96-103.

[32] Iera, A., Molinaro, A., Paratore, S. Y., Ruggeri, G., Zurzolo, A., 2011. Making a Mesh Router/Gateway from a Smartphone: Is that a Practical Solution? *Ad Hoc Networks*. 9, *8*, 1414-1429.

In: Recent Advances in Ad Hoc Networks Research
Editor: Natarajan Meghanathan

ISBN: 978-1-63321-337-1

Chapter 4

VEHICULAR AD HOC NETWORKING FOR TRANSPORTATION CYBER PHYSICAL SYSTEMS

***Danda B. Rawat**[*1]**, Sachin Shetty**[2]** and Bhed B. Bista**[3]*
[1]Georgia Southern University, GA, US
[2]Tennessee State University, TN, US
[3]Iwate Prefectural University, Japan

ABSTRACT

Vehicular networking is an emerging concept for intelligent transportation Cyber-Physical System (IT-CPS) for safety and infotainment applications where vehicles exchange information using vehicle-to-vehicle (V2V) through vehicular ad hoc network (VANET) and/or vehicle-to-roadside (V2R) communications. Unlike other wireless systemsm, VANET has unique characteristics such as network topology changes based on the behavior of drivers, speed of the vehicles, road structure, location (urban vs. rural), weather condition, etc. Furthermore, VANET users have virtually unlimited on-board power, computation, communication, and storage resources unlike other mobile communication systems. Vehicular network for IT-CPS offfers huge societal, economical and safety benefits. However, there are several challenges to be tackled to realize full potential of vehicular communications. This chapter presents different wireless communication technologies and their suitability in VANET for V2V and V2R communications. Challenges in deployment of the wireless communication in vehicular network for IT-CPS are also presented. With this chapter, readers can have a thorough understanding of wireless technologies and communications in VANETs for IT-CPS, the research trends and challenges in this area.

Keywords: Vehicular Networking, VANETs, Vehicular Cyber-Physical Systems, Information and Communication Technologies, ITS

---

* Department of Electrical Engineering, Georgia Southern University, Statesboro, Georgia, USA
Email: db.rawat@ieee.org.

INTRODUCTION

Vehicular communication for the development of Intelligent Transportation System (ITS) is an important rudiment that allows the forwarding of upcoming traffic information and entertainment messages to the drivers. Recently vehicular communication has attracted researchers from both academia and industries all over the world, notably, in the United States of America, Japan and European Union [2, 4, 5, 6]. Road traffic crashes are one of the largest problems being faced not only in the US but also all over the world. A report published by National Highway Traffic Safety Administration (NHTSA) in 2012 estimates that one person dies in a vehicle crash every 15 minutes in the US [19]. Moreover, the US Department of Transportation (US-DOT) estimates that traffic congestions and crashes cause a waste of billions of dollars in lost worker productivity and fuel costs every year. Studies [20, 21] have shown, that "about 60% roadway collisions could be avoided if the operator of the vehicle was provided warning at least one-half second prior to a collision." The number of death, injuries and the excessive cost of traffic collisions can be significantly lowered if the drivers are provided with upcoming traffic information in a timely manner [4, 9, 16, 19, 21]. Existing information dissemination mechanisms for vehicular network require a driver or a passenger to tune a radio or dial a certain number to get current traffic information. This process is slow and cannot guarantee timely dissemination of information. Devising an automatic wireless based mechanism for communicating traffic information in a timely manner can help drivers make informed travel decisions and avoid hazardous situations. Wireless systems can provide a better alternative for forwarding upcoming traffic information.

A vehicular network is a wireless mobile network where moving vehicles act as nodes in a network, and communicate with each other via Vehicle-to-Vehicle (V2V) communications through Vehicular Ad hoc Networks (VANETs), as well as, with roadside base stations via Vehicle-to-Roadside (V2R), along with possible Roadside-to-Roadside (R2R) communications. Vehicular communications can be used for providing timely information to drivers and to concerned authorities, thereby making the roads safer. For instance, when a road accident occurs, emergency responders could provide information about road closure and the estimated time of re-openings using vehicular communications. In a vehicular network, messages have to be routed from the information source to one or to several destinations as quickly as possible and efficiently [5, 10, 11, 21].

There are several challenges in realizing the full potential of vehicular communications for intelligent transportation systems. Ongoing research in this area is bridging the gap between theory and practice [2, 18, 21]. The US-DOT [18] plans to develop an architecture for vehicle infrastructure integration based largely on roadside equipment for collecting data from passing vehicles and for disseminating it to other interested vehicles or concerned authorities. Cellular telephone system has been studied at the University of Virginia for vehicular traffic monitoring in limited deployments [14]. Santa, et al. [15] have successfully tested cellular network based on Universal Mobile Telecommunications System (UMTS) for vehicular communications. Since the information exchange between participating vehicles happens through V2R and R2V with possible R2R communications, one can expect higher delay (few milliseconds to a few seconds). Because of the high delay/latency introduced by cellular systems, it is not suitable for forwarding emergency messages in vehicular networks.

In addition, cellular networks use licensed bands and users need to pay a usage fee. Unlicensed communication such as Wi-Fi (i.e., WLAN), Bluetooth, etc., would provide a better alternative for communication as users do not have to pay licensing fees. However, because of installation cost and limited availability of Wi-Fi networks, it is not an attractive choice [8,17, 21]. In this context, V2V based communications through VANETs, where devices and associated technologies use unlicensed bands, is a suitable option. It introduces negligible delay for emergency message communication.

This chapter presents the wireless communication framework for vehicular networks to forward upcoming traffic information including time critical emergency messages as quickly as possible so that drivers can take intelligent decision about any accidents, risks or delays. The idea is to use wireless devices which have the least connection setup time to form an ad hoc network of moving vehicles to exchange emergency messages among them. It is worth pointing out that non-critical messages such as information about gas station/price, roadside restaurants, etc. could also be forwarded using existing cellular wireless systems. Thus, the framework uses V2V communications for emergencies messages and V2R and R2V communications for other non-emergency or comfort-related messages.

VEHICULAR COMMUNICATIONS FRAMEWORK FOR IT-CPS

Cyber physical system for intelligent transportation and vehiclular applications will have ability to interact with, and expand the capabilities of, the physical world through computation, communication, and control as shown in Figure 1. Vehicles would exchange information about vehicle operating behavior, driving route, destination, vehicle speed, drivers' condition, etc. Then, using copmputing capability, vehicles would analize the data and select the parameters for the the best response which would result in safer and more efficient road travel. Vehicular communitation is one of the important components of IT-CPS.

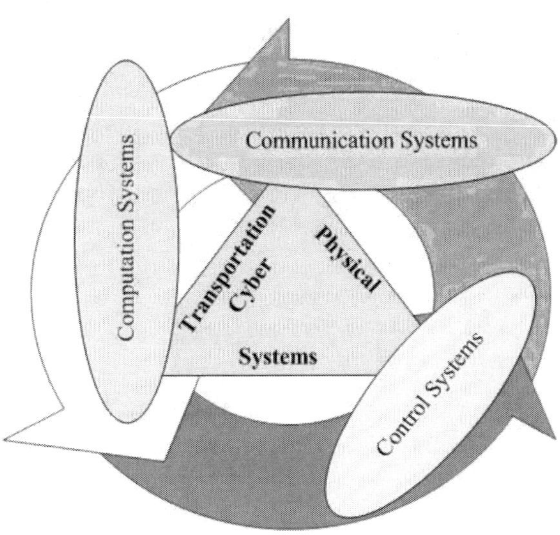

Figure 1. Wireless communication framework for vehicular networks.

Future vehicular communication systems are expected to use a variety of wireless technologies such as WiMAX, Wi-Fi, Bluetooth, Zigbee, WAVE, cellular, satellite, etc. and communications among vehicles could be acomplished using peer-to-peer networks or through the road side infrastructures as shown in Figure 2.

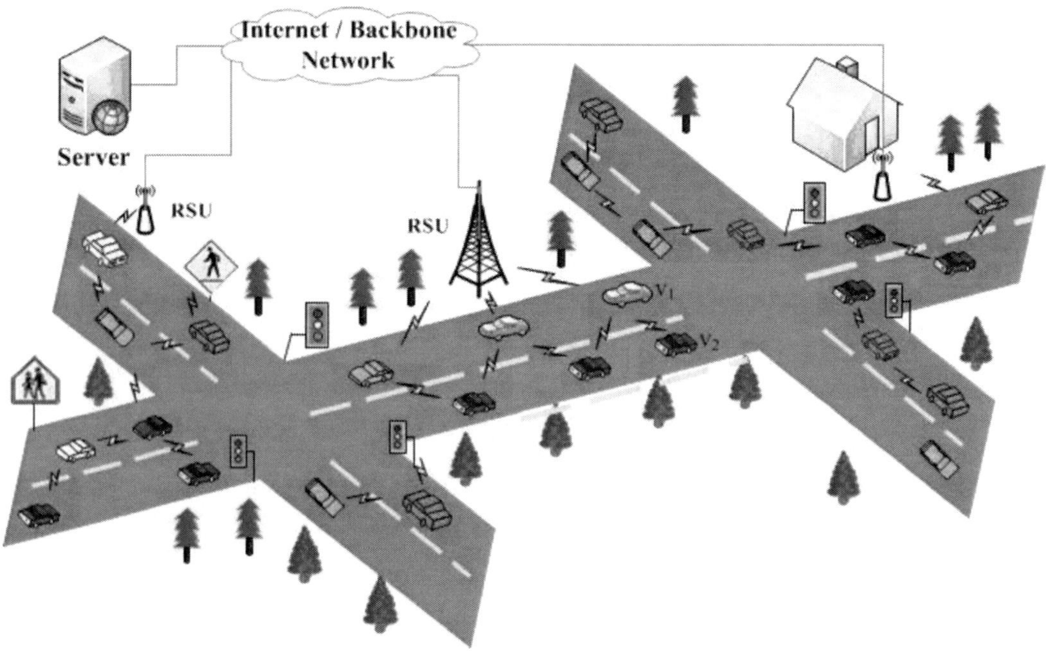

Figure 2. Wireless communication framework for vehicular networks.

Vehicular Network

Vehicular network is a network of vehicles to disseminate the traffic related information. In a vehicular network, vehicles are assumed to be capable of receiving, processing (if needed) transmitting and/or routing the messages in the networks. This is possible with the integration of different technologies such as Global Positioning System (GPS), on-board computers and sensors with intelligence. This gives an opportunity to create powerful vehicular communication system to support different applications. With such computing and communication equipment, numerous applications can be deployed in the vehicular networks.

Cellular networks, ad hoc networks, Wi-Fi and Wireless Personal Area Networks (PANs) [21, 22] are possible candidates for mobile vehicular communications. The selection of wireless technology depends on the application that the vehicular network is envisioned to support. There are several factors that influence highly mobile vehicular communications. VANET is considered as a special case of Mobile Ad hoc Network (MANET) with some peculiar features:

- Constantly changing topology of VANETs: vehicles moves with high speed ranging from 15 miles/hour to 75 miles/hour. As a result, network topology changes frequently. However the topology follows the road pattern and thus is not random like in MANETs.

- Human/driver behavior affects the topology of vehicular network: Drivers can join or take exit at any time when it is possible to do so. Furthermore, some drivers travel with higher speed than others. This makes change in network topology and number of vehicles within a communication range. Human or driver behaviors have huge impact in the VANET topology.
- Highly dynamic network density and frequent network fragmentation in VANET: High mobility of vehicles and human behaviors results in different vehicle density. In highly dense network, there would be vehicles within a communication range and network connection is not an issue. However, when vehicle density is low such as in rural highways, network connection among vehicles could easily be lost.
- Wireless access technology: There are different technologies for wireless communications. However all technologies are not designed for highly dynamic VANETs. Without any modification of protocols, architecture or framework, existing wireless technologies might not fulfill the demand of VANETs.
- High RF Interference: In urban environment, vehicle density can easily be high and because of it, there would be high interference from other neighbor vehicles and other wireless services that operate in the same band.
- Virtually no power constraints: Generally power is most important commodity in almost all wireless networks and is the main constrains in wireless resource allocation. However, it is not an important resource for VANET as it can be easily supplied through vehicles.
- Virtually no storage constraints: Vehicular users could have big storage units within the vehicles and thus it is not a major concern.
- Low latency requirement for safety applications: safety applications require message transmission in a timely manner.
- Security and privacy of drivers or owners of vehicles: Privacy of drivers is directly associated with the vehicle. When identity of vehicle is compromised, the privacy of the driver could be easily compromised resulting in related security concerns. Thus securing vehicular network is challenging.
- High bandwidth requirement for multimedia application in highly mobile environment: Multimedia applications are bandwidth hungry so these applications could easily suffered in low bandwidth vehicular communication networks.

Applications of Vehicular Network

The main goal of vehicular communications is to provide safety and comfort for passengers by forwarding upcoming traffic information in a timely manner. A special communication device will be mounted in each vehicle that is capable of receiving (and of processing if needed) along with forwarding to other vehicles through V2V and/or V2R communications. These wireless devices could also facilitate multimedia and Internet connectivity for passengers, provide lane merge assistance, receive information about road side facilities (such as roadside restaurants, gas stations and price, shopping and entertainment centers), and pay automatic parking fees or tolls. In mobile vehicular communications, sending timely traffic updates is important. For instance, vehicles should not forward information about road closures after the road has re-opened. In a broad sense, vehicular communication has two applications: safety and comfort.

Emergency and Safety Related Applications

Primary purpose of vehicular communication is to forward the upcoming traffic information in timely manner to the drivers so that they could make a wise decision to avoid accidents and/or delays (11). The emergency and safety related applications include collision alert, emergency vehicle approaching, deceleration alert, road conditions warnings, merge assistance, etc. In these applications, central emphasis is to timely disseminate the safety related messages to nearby vehicles. In other words, safety applications require messages to be propagated from the point of occurrence to the target vehicles with very low latency (less than a half-second).

Information and Entertainment (Infotainment) Applications

Infotainment applications (multimedia and comfort applications) aim to improve passenger comfort and traffic efficiency and include information about road side facilities (such as shopping malls, fast foods, hotels, parking spots, gas station/price, etc.), electronic payments, weather condition, and interactive multimedia communications. These applications may require high speed continuous connectivity and thus are bandwidth-hungry, but they are typically not delay-sensitive like safety-related applications. In these applications, connectivity with high bandwidth is main concerns. In these applications, latency is not very important like in safety applications.

Communication and Data Dissemination Models

Wireless communications in vehicular networks can be an infrastructure based V2R or an ad hoc based V2V that forms VANETs. In V2R based communications, road-side-unit (RSU) is used as a relay unit between vehicles to exchange information. Whereas in VANETs, vehicles directly exchange information with each other using single hop or multiple hops V2V communications without using any RSUs.

Information Dissemination Models

In vehicular networks, vehicles that participate in communications are considered to be equipped with computing and communicating devices. Using these devices, vehicles would be able to receive, transmit or route the information over the vehicular network using V2V or V2R communications.

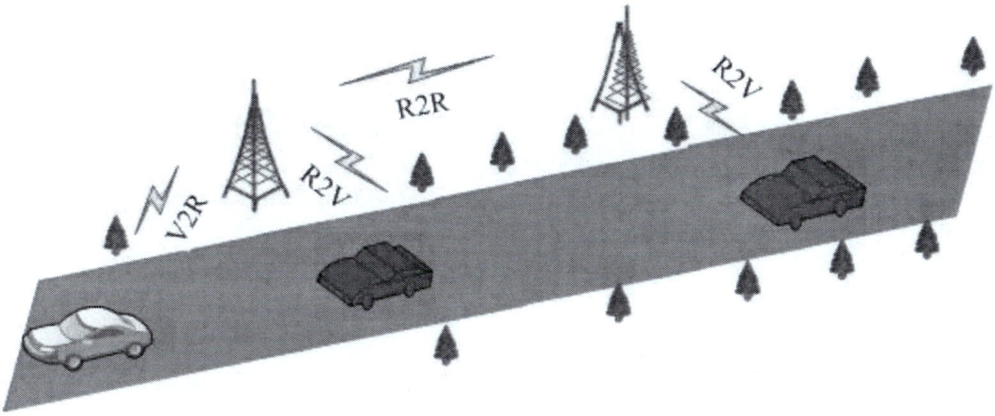

Figure 3. Vehicle-to-Roadside, Roadside-to-Roadside, and Roadside-to-Vehicle Communications.

Vehicle-to-Roadside (V2R) and Roadside-to-Vehicle (R2V) Model

In vehicular network, vehicles can exchange information using V2R and R2V communications as shown in Figure 3. In this model, one roadside unit can forward the information to others using R2R communications. This dissemination model could use existing wireless cellular infrastructures to forward messages. Alternatively, for vehicular networks, IEEE 802.11 wireless access points could be installed throughout the road to disseminate the traffic information. However, V2R and R2V based wireless communications in vehicular networks introduces the latency/delay [15] as message has to be transmitted from a source vehicle to a roadside unit and the roadside unit to a destination vehicle with possible intermediate R2R communications. It is important to note that the message delivery time should less than one half second [20]. When cellular infrastructures are used, vehicular network users have to pay usage fee as cellular bands are licensed to service providers that makes the vehicular communications more expensive. As a result they may not be able to remain online all the time to transmit information. As a result they need to establish a connection and be online when they have some information to transmit. Thus this method introduces high delay as vehicular users have to set up a call before transmitting the actual information. In the alternative approach, as IEEE 820.11 wireless/Wi-Fi networks use unlicensed Industry, Scientific and Medical (ISM) bands, usage cost could be almost none compared to cellular networks. However there are no such IEEE 820.11 wireless network infrastructures installed throughout the highways or roads to cover all areas for vehicular communications. In this regards, in addition to delay introduced by roadside communication, installation cost of IEEE 820.11 wireless access points would be very high. As a matter of fact, this is also not a good choice for vehicular communications.

Figure 4 shows the tentative comparison of data rates and mobility support in terms of communication range for different wireless technologies. Cellular mobile communications standards have emerged from first generation to the fourth generation standards. Wi-Fi has the highest data rate (approx.. 11Mbps using 802.11b, 54 Mbps using 802.11a/g, over 100 Mbps using 8021.11n) with low coverage and mobility support while cellular network such as Global Mobile System (GSM) has the good mobility support with data rates of up to 180 Kbps, Mobile Telecommunication System (UMTS), one of the third generation cellular telephone standards, could support mobility and data rates of up to 384 Kbps and fourth generation promises high data-rates with high mobility support and smooth handoff across heterogeneous networks. Furthermore, satellite based communication for a vehicular network is also not a suitable choice because of low data rate and the delay that is introduced when a message has to travel from a source vehicle to a satellite and back to destination vehicles. The delay in satellite communication would be higher than that in cellular and IEEE 802.11 wireless networks. Satellite communication uses licensed bands and vehicular network may also have to pay when they exchange information.

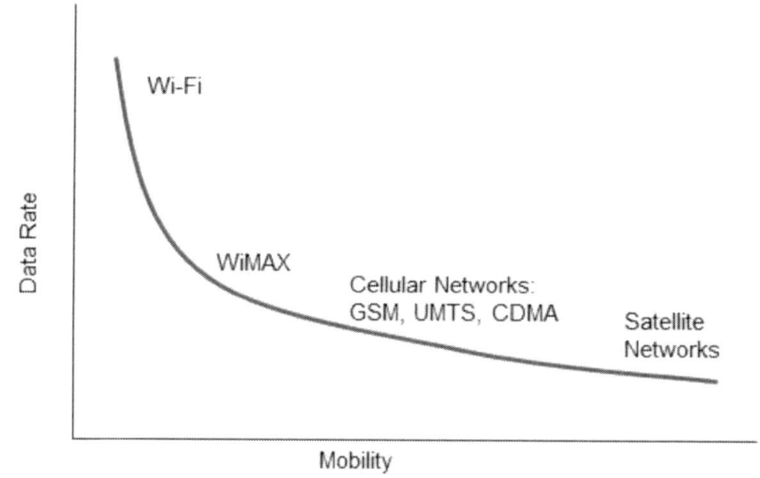

Figure 4. Comparison of data rate and mobility support of wireless technologies for vehicular communications.

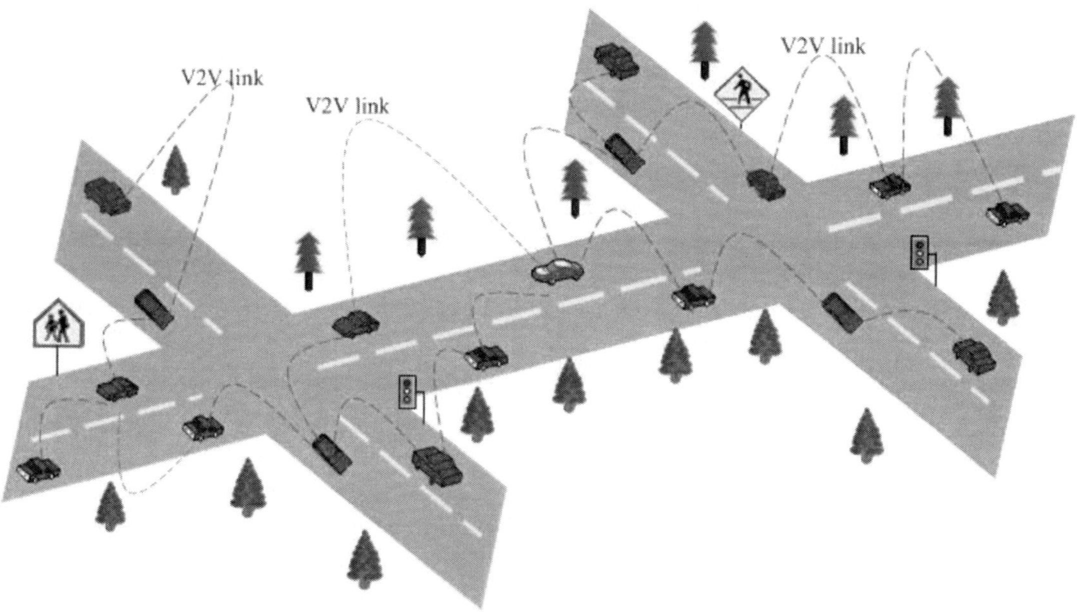

Figure 5. Vehicle-to-Vehicle communications using Single Hop and Multiple Hops.

Furthermore, the roadside units such as base stations or access points or satellites can be used to provide the information about participating vehicles to the government authorities and the information could be used to track the malicious vehicles. In this case privacy of vehicular users should not be compromised by wireless service providers.

Vehicle-to-Vehicle (V2V) Model

Another model for information dissemination in vehicular networks is V2V where vehicles directly communicate with each other through single hop or multiple hops by forming an ad hoc network of vehicles as shown in Figure 5. In this model, vehicles do not use any roadside communications and thus the vehicular network would need no cost for the installation of roadside units. Using direct communications, vehicular network could transmit the information more quickly than that in V2R based communications. This would be the best option for the emergency messages as they have to travel as quickly as possible towards the destination region. Furthermore, vehicles could use ISM bands for V2V communications without paying any licensing fees associated with RF spectrum. In addition, it is important to note that there are many technologies for V2V based communications such as Bluetooth, ZigBee, Wi-Fi technology in ad hoc mode, ultra wide band (UWB), etc. [22, 23].

However, in this model, as vehicles directly communicate with each other without using any roadside units to forward the traffic information, there are several challenges before implementing it. Vehicular users could pretend to be someone else or could insert malicious messages in the vehicular network to mislead the communications [10]. As there is no central unit to keep records of all participating vehicles, it would be almost impossible to track down malicious vehicles or vehicular users.

Most of the vehicles on the road are private properties and directly related to the privacy and security of the owners. To hide the actual identity of the vehicles, some mechanisms are needed to protect the privacy of participating users through some techniques that provide anonymity of participating vehicles or users [10]. When we use such mechanism for anonymity, malicious drivers or users could attack the network easily and could not be tracked back by concerned authorities.

We present the comparison in terms of delay introduced during message propagation using different wireless technologies as shown in Figure 6. V2V based communication will have the least delay in message propagation since vehicles directly communicate with each other without using any road side units. Satellite communication network will have highest delay as a message has to travel from a source vehicle to satellite and back from satellite to a destination vehicle.

It is important to note that the choice of the wireless technology depends on the application that the vehicular network is proposed to support. For time-sensitive emergency messages, V2V based communication would be suitable whereas V2R based communications could be used to transmit other types of messages. Most of the time vehicles would use combination of wireless technologies to communicate with each other depending on the availability and applications they are intended to support. When vehicles have choices of wireless technologies, they should be able to choose the best one using some best network selection methods which is discussed in the following sections.

For V2V based vehicular communication model, wireless devices mounted in vehicles should be associated through a connection setup procedure before ecahangeing their actual information. After sucessful connection setup, the two vehicles would be able to exchange information with each other. Association times needed for connection setup and other specifications for ZigBee, Bluetooth and Wi-Fi technologies are listed in Table 1 [22].

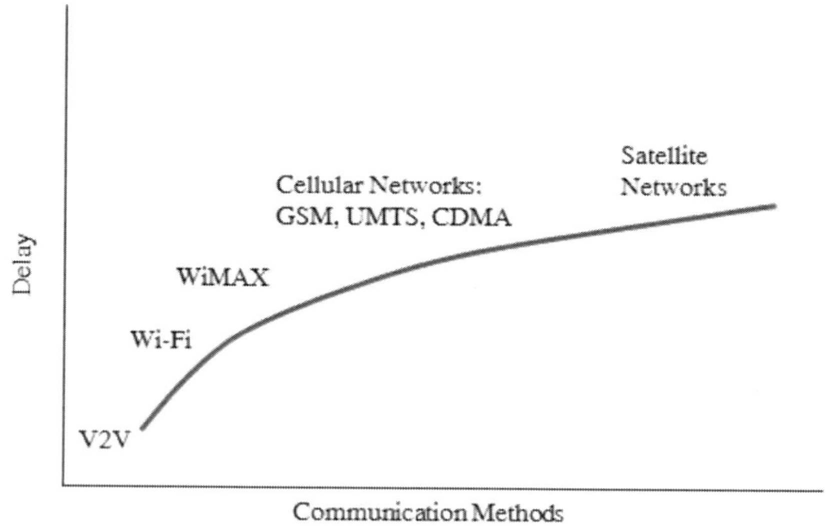

Figure 6. Comparison of delay introduced in message propagation in vehicular networks.

Table 1. Comparison Table for Different Wireless Technologies

Features \ Wireless device	ZigBee	Bluetooth	Wi-Fi/WLAN
New association Time	30 milliseconds	~4 seconds	500 milliseconds
Sleeping to active transition time	15 milliseconds	3 seconds	NA
Active slave channel access/scan time	15 milliseconds	2 milliseconds	100 milliseconds
Distance (meters)	1 – 100+	1-10 (with 0dB power) 100 (with 20dB power)	100+
Data Rate	20-250 Kb/s (Baseband)	720 Kb/s (Baseband) and 1, 2, 3 Mb/s (EDR)	11Mb/s (802.11b) 54Mb/s(802.11a/g)
Frequency	2.4 GHz (global), 902-928MHz (Americas), 868 MHz (Europe)	2.4 GHz	2.5 GHz, 5 GHz
Network Size	Unlimited (2^{64})	7	32
IEEE Standard	IEEE 802.15.4/4c	IEEE 802.15.1	802.11
Network Topology	Star/mesh	Star	Mesh/star
Transmission Technology	Direct Sequence Spread Spectrum (DSSS)	Frequency Hopping Spread Spectrum (FHSS)	DSSS/FHSS

Numerical Results and Discussion for V2V Model

In order to study the feasibility of different wireless technologies for real time wireless communications in vehicular networks, individual vehicles are considered to be equipped with communication devices (such as Wi-Fi, ZigBee, Bluetooth, etc.) in the simulation. Two different scenarios are considered:

- Scenario 1 (one-way-traffic, i.e., vehicles move in the same direction): In this scenario, vehicles move with almost constant speeds and the relative speed between the vehicles is very small. For instance, the relative speed of two vehicles moving with 70 miles/hour is zero and thus one vehicle could be seen as stationary to a vehicle moving with same speed in the same direction (same velocity). The smaller the relative speed, the longer the time for connection setup and data exchange between the vehicles will be.
- Scenario 2 (two-way-traffic, i.e., vehicles move in both directions): As noted, the relative speed between vehicles moving in the same direction will be small. However, the relative speed of two vehicles moving in opposite directions will be sum of the speeds of two vehicles. For instance, two vehicles travelling in opposite directions on a highway at speeds of 70 miles/hour will be moving at a relative speed of 140 miles/hour and these vehicles will have a very short time for connection setup and data exchange using wireless devices for a given transmission range.

Simulations are conducted to evaluate message delivery capabilities of individual vehicles equipped with ZigBee, WLAN or Bluetooth wireless devices for both scenario 1 and 2. It is considered that the communication/transmission range of wireless technologies (WLAN, ZigBee and Bluetooth) is 15 meters to compare them in identical simulation setups. If the transmission range is greater than 15 meters, roadside attackers may be able to insert malicious messages in the vehicular network. Thus, limiting the communication range to 15 meters should help provide increased security in vehicular networks. For a given relative speed (s) and transmission range of a wireless device, i.e., the distance (d), time (t) is computed using:

$$t = \frac{d}{s} \tag{1}$$

Eq. (1) calculates total time available used for connection setup and the subsequent data exchange between vehicles. For instance, two vehicles, with relative speed s = 70 miles/hour (i.e., 31.29 meters/second) and wireless device with a transmission range d = 15 meter, will remain within a communication range for t = 479.34 milliseconds. This time will be used for association and information exchange among vehicles.

For instance, when vehicles are within a communication range for 479.34 milliseconds, two vehicles with ZigBee devices will take about 30 milliseconds for connection setup leaving 249.34 milliseconds for actual message exchange between them, as shown in Figure 7. However, vehicles with Bluetooth or Wi-Fi devices would not be able to even connect with each other as the total available time (479.34 milliseconds) is less than the association time of Bluetooth (4 seconds) or Wi-Fi (600 milliseconds) and thus would not be able to exchange any information.

In order to compare the suitability of ZigBee, Wi-Fi and Bluetooth technologies for vehicular communications, it is considered that all the vehicles are equipped with these devices (one type at a time) and that the relative speed of vehicles ranges from 0 miles/hour to

150 miles/hour. Speed limits on typical US interstates are 70 miles/hour. However, we consider speeds of up to 75 miles/hour (150 miles/hour relative speed) for evaluating the performance of different communication technologies. Furthermore, using a given range for the relative speeds from 0 to 150 miles/hour represents vehicles that are at a complete stop or moving at the same speed and in the same directions; to vehicles travelling in opposite directions at the maximum stipulated speed. The total available time is computed that would be used for connection setup/association and message exchange between the vehicles. Then, the time duration left after successful association is computed for ZigBee, WLAN and Bluetooth devices and plotted the results in Figure 8. It is important to note that the available time for vehicles decreases with an increase in relative speed as shown in Figure 8. Vehicles with ZigBee devices have sufficient time (greater than 100 milliseconds) to transmit messages even with relative speed 150 miles/hour as shown in Figure 8. However, the time left after successful association for message exchange is not available for the vehicles with WLAN devices when their relative speed is greater than 130 miles/hour because the total available time is less than the connection setup time (600 milliseconds). Similarly, vehicles traveling with a relative speed greater than 10 miles/hour and using Bluetooth devices could not communicate with each other as Bluetooth devices could not establish network connection successfully because of their high connection setup time (~2 to 4 seconds) requirement.

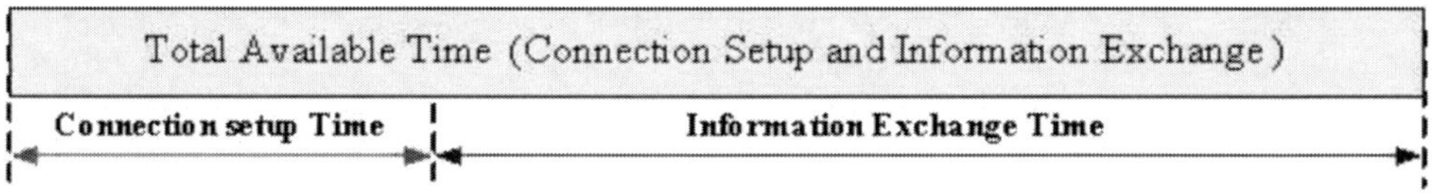

Figure 7. Total available time (connection setup with information exchange).

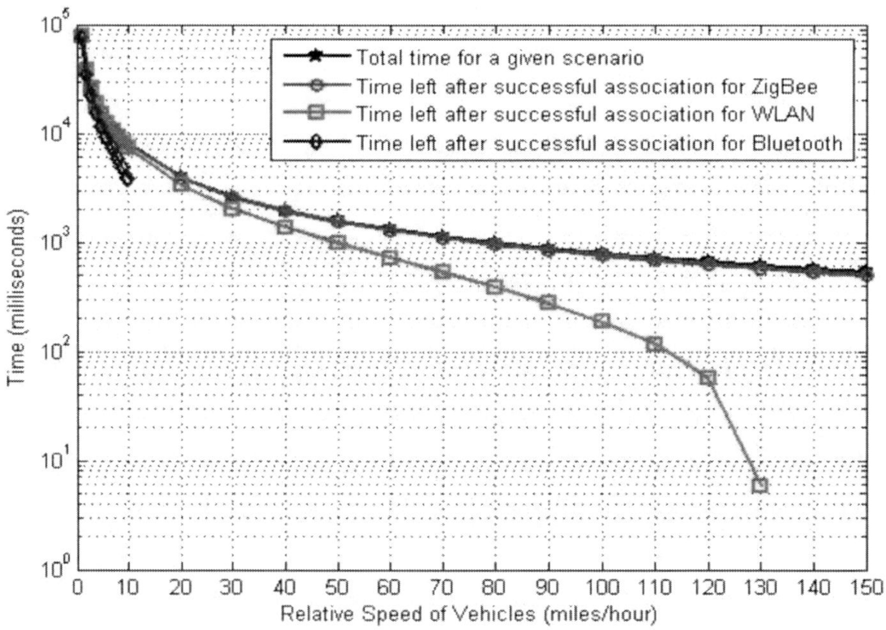

Figure 8. Total available time and data exchange time for ZigBee, Wireless LAN and Bluetooth.

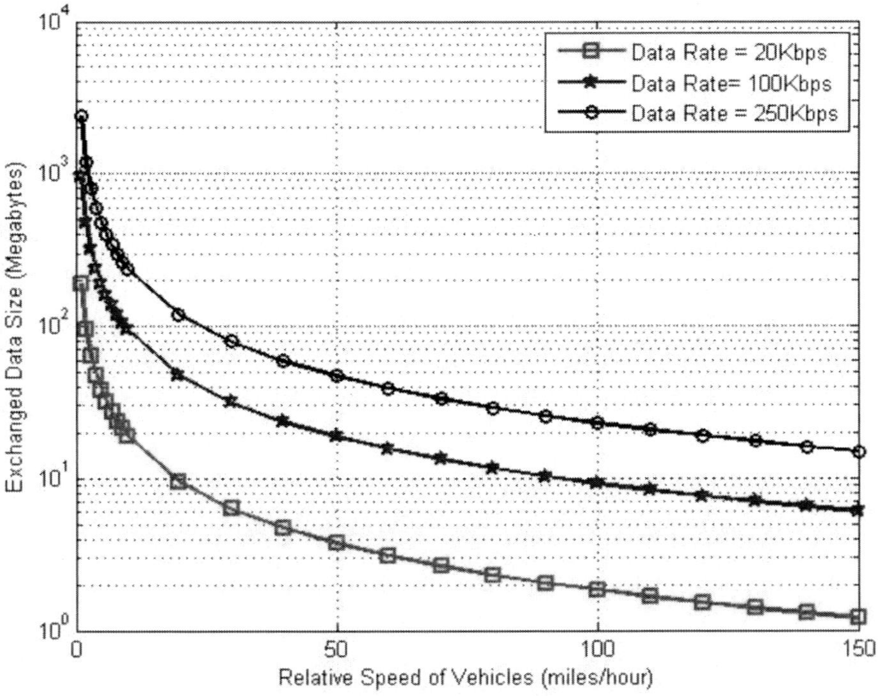

Figure 9. Data exchanged using ZigBee Networking after successful association.

Next, we examine the impact of the relative speed on the size of the data exchanged at different data rates supported by different communication technologies. Vehicular communication using ZigBee devices was simulated for transmission rates of 20 Kbps, 100 Kbps or 250 Kbps and different relative speeds. The simulation result is shown in Figure 9. Transmission rates in wireless communications vary with distance between the communicating devices. For the worst case scenario, which is the slowest transmission rate when vehicles are moving at the highest relative speed, 20 Kbps data rate for relative speed of 150 miles/hour, the size of the message that could be exchanged between vehicles is approx. 1.2 Megabytes as shown in Figure 9. It is important to point out that the size of a typical one page message with 568 words is about 5 Kilobytes. Thus, in the worst case scenario, vehicles could exchange 240 pages of messages (including header bits). In the best case (with high data rate and/or lower relative speed), more number of pages can be exchanged.

Next, we consider individual vehicles that are equipped with Wi-Fi devices for exchanging messages wirelessly. Figure 10 shows the size of the message exchanged using Wi-Fi devices at different relative speeds for different data transmission rates. Vehicular communications using Wi-Fi devices was simulated with transmission rates of 1 Mbps, 2 Mbps or 5.5 Mbps and 27 Mbps (data rates for 35 meter in 802.11b/g/n) considering different distances between communicating vehicles. In the worst case (1 Mbps data rate for 130 miles/hour relative speed), the size of the message that could be transferred between vehicles is approximately 0.71 Megabytes as shown in Figure 10. When the relative speed of participating vehicles decreases they could exchange bigger amount of data. Vehicles moving with the relative speed greater than 130 miles/hour could not exchange any message using Wi-Fi devices for a given transmission range of 35 m as shown in Figure 8 because there would be no time left for message to exchange between vehicles after successful association of Wi-Fi devices mounted in the vehicles.

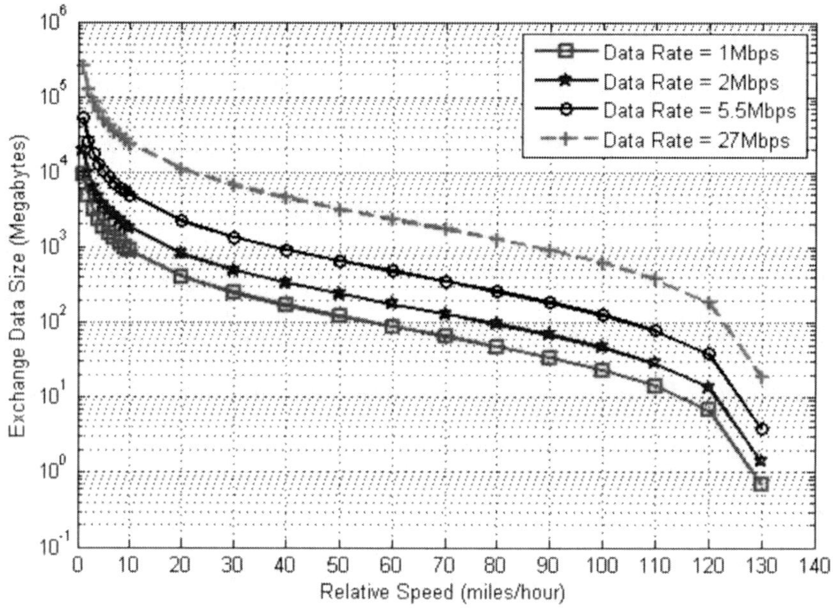

Figure 10. Data exchanged using WLAN Ad hoc networking after successful association.

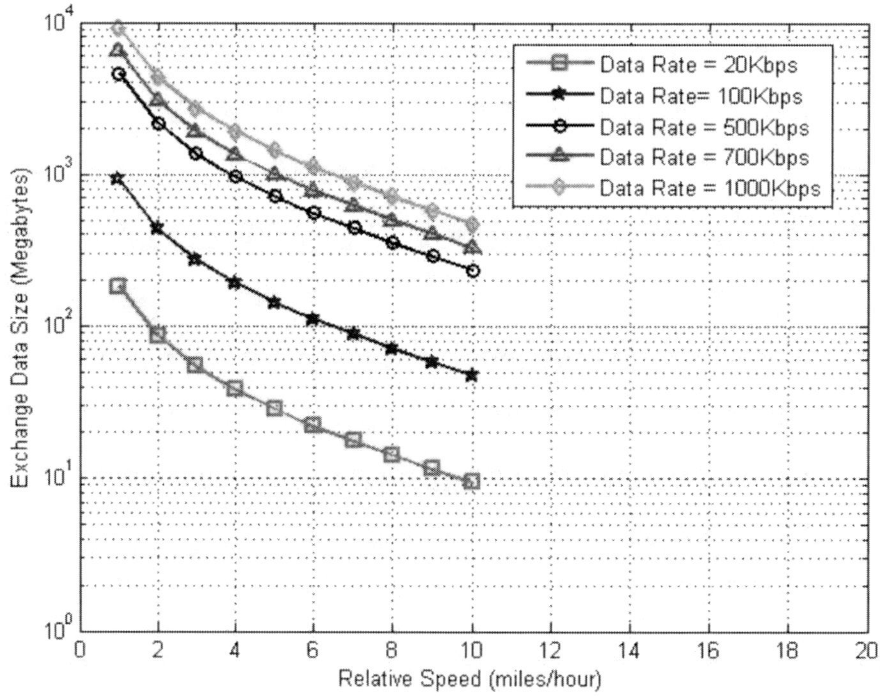

Figure 11. Data exchanged using Bluetooth networking after successful association.

Finally, we consider individual vehicles equipped with Bluetooth devices for exchanging traffic information. Figure 11 shows the size of the message exchanged using Bluetooth devices at different relative speeds for different transmission rates. As noted in Table 1, Bluetooth devices take about 4 seconds for connection setup. As a result vehicles moving with relative speed greater than 10 miles/hour could not establish the connection with another vehicle. This results in no message being exchanged between vehicles. Considering the worst case for Bluetooth-based vehicular communications, vehicles moving with a relative speed of 10 miles/hour could exchange 9.46 Megabytes of message using 20 Kbps data rate. As shown in Figures 11, vehicles moving with relative speed less than 10 miles could easily exchange messages using Bluetooth devices. However, vehicles moving in opposite directions could not use Bluetooth to exchange the message unless they travel with relative speed less than or equal to 10 miles per hour.

Based on the simulation results, it is concluded that the ZigBee technology is applicable for inter-vehicular communications for vehicles traveling with high relative speed since ZigBee has short association time (30 milliseconds). Wi-Fi can replace ZigBee only when a relative speed between vehicles is smaller and a high data rate is needed for bandwidth-hungry applications. Bluetooth can only be used if the relative speed is smaller than 10 miles/hour. However, when a message needs to be broadcast to a large geographic area the existing cellular network could be used for vehicular communications.

So Are We There Yet? Challenges in Deployment of the Wireless Framework for Transportation CPS

With the assumption that there are 346 million vehicles and 16 million built each year, Michael Cops [3], Program Manager of Vehicle infrastructure integration Consortium, has predicted that by 2020, 50% of vehicles on the road will have computing and communication equipment, and that by 2030 all vehicles will have the equipment and will be able to participate in vehicular communications. There are several challenges that still need to be addressed for fully realizing the capabilities of vehicular communication for intelligent transportation systems. These include:

- User Needs: Vehicular users would need communication with the least latency and reliable connectivity. This is very difficult to achieve because of the high mobility of vehicles and changes in network topology. Users would also expect high bandwidth for interactive multimedia applications which is hard to achieve in VANETs.
- Security and Privacy: Since most of the vehicles are privately owned, maintaining privacy and security using vehicular communications is important. Wireless mobile users of vehicular networks would expect the same level of privacy and security as they have with legacy road driving. To address these issues, vehicles' identities should be made anonymous.
- Authentication: Validation and authenticity of messages is also challenging when vehicle are made anonymous because of privacy and security concerns.
- Data Ownership: Messages containing identity of drivers should not be in the public domain so that no one can trace individual vehicles or drivers.

- Interference from other RF devices: In high density vehicular networks, RF interference would affect the performance of vehicular communications.
- Human Behaviors: Drivers can join the highway or take an exit at any time when it is possible for them to do so. This result in variation of network density and topology according to human behaviors.

It is anticipated that all of these issues will be addressed in near future and there will be true wireless communication over vehicular networks for forwarding emergency and upcoming traffic information, which will make the roads safer to travel.

Conclusion and Future Research

This chapter has presented vehicular communications for intelligent transportation cyber physical systems. Delivering real-time traffic information to drivers through wireless communication in vehicular network can assist in avoiding traffic accidents and congestions. The selection of wireless technology depends on the application that the vehicular network is envisioned to support. For time-sensitive emergency messages, V2V based communication is suitable whereas other messages could be transmitted using V2R communications. To fully realize the vehicular network for intelligent transportation cyber physical systems, several concerns and issues related to security, privacy and trust among others need to be addressed.

References

[1] Bluetooth Technology., 2012. Bluetooth Wireless Technology: Simple, Secure, Everywhere. https://www.bluetooth.org/Building/overview.htm, last accessed: May 1, 2014.

[2] Car-to-Car Communication Consortium., 2007. CAR 2 CAR Communication Consortium Manifesto, Overview of the C2C-CC System. http://www.car-to-car.org, last accessed: February 2, 2014.

[3] Cops, M., 2006. VII Strategy for Safety and Mobility Program. http://www.sigmobile.org/workshops/vanet2006/slides/Cops_VANET06.pdf, last accessed: May 1, 2014.

[4] Festag, A., Noecker, G., Strassberger, M., Lubke, A., Bochow, B., Torrent-Moreno, M., Schnaufer, S., Eigner, R., Catrinescu, C., Kunisch, J., 2008. NoW - Network on Wheels: Project Objectives, Technology and Achievements. *Proceedings of 5th International Workshop on Intelligent Transportation* (*WIT*). 211-216.

[5] De Fuentes, J., Gonzalez-Tables, A., Ribagorda, A., 2011. Overview of Security Issues in Vehicular Ad hoc Networks. *Handbook of Research on Mobility and Computing*: *Evolving Technologies and Ubiquitous Impacts*. 894-911.

[6] Hartenstein, H., Laberteaux, K., 2010. *VANET*: *Vehicular Applications and Inter-Networking Technologies*, 1st ed., John Wiley and Sons.

[7] IEEE 802.15.4., 2003. IEEE 802.15.4 ZigBee Standard, http://standards.ieee.org/, last accessed on: May 1, 2014.

[8] Little, T. D. C., Agarwal, A., 2005. An Information Propagation Scheme for VANETs. *Proceedings of the IEEE Conference on Intelligent Transportation Systems*. 155-160.

[9] Moskvitch, K., 2011. 'Talking' Cars could Reduce Motorway Pile-ups. http://www.bbc.com/news/technology-14125245, last accessed on: May 1, 2014.

[10] Rawat, D. B., Bista, B. B., Yan, G., Weigle, M. C., 2011. Securing Vehicular Ad hoc Networks against Malicious Drivers: A Probabilistic Approach. *Proceedings of the International Conference on Complex, Intelligent and Software Intensive Systems*. 146-151.

[11] Rawat, D. B., Popescu, D. C., Yan, G., Olariu, S., 2011. Enhancing VANET Performance by Joint Adaptation of Transmission Power and Contention Window Size. *IEEE Transactions on Parallel and Distributed Systems*, 22, *9*, 1528-1535.

[12] Rawat, D. B., Popescu, D. C., 2012. Precoder Adaptation and Power Control for Cognitive Radios in Dynamic Spectrum Access Environments. *IET Communications*, 6, *8*, 836-844.

[13] Rawat, D. B., Bista, B. B., Yan, G., 2012. CoR-VANETs: Game Theoretic Approach for Channel and Rate Selection in Cognitive Radio VANETs. *Proceedings of the 7th International Conference on Broadband, Wireless Computing, Communication and Applications*. 94-99.

[14] Smith, B. L., Zhang, H., Fontaine, M., Green, M., 2003. Cell Phone Probes as an ATMS Tool. *University of Virginia, Research Report No. UVACTS-15-5-79.*

[15] Santa, J., Moragon, A., Gomez-Skarmeta, A. F., 2008. Experimental Evaluation of a Novel Vehicular Communication Paradigm based on Cellular Networks. *Proceedings of the IEEE Intelligent Vehicles Symposium*. 198-203.

[16] Thiagarajan, A., Ravindranath, L., LaCurts, K., Madden, S., Balakrishnan, H., Toledo, S., Eriksson, J., 2009. VTrack: Accurate, Energy-aware Road Traffic Delay Estimation using Mobile Phones. *Proceedings of the 7th ACM Conference on Embedded Networked Sensor Systems*. 85-98.

[17] Trivedi, H., Verraraghavan, P., Loke, S., Desai, A., Singh, J., 2011. Routing Mechanisms and Cross-layer Design for Vehicular Ad hoc Networks: A Survey. *Proceedings of the IEEE Symposium on Computers and Informatics*. 243-248.

[18] U. S. Department of Transporation., 2005. Vehicle infrastructure integration. http://www.its.dot.gov/vii/, last accessed on: May 1, 2014.

[19] U.S. National Highway Traffic Safety Administration. (2012). Budget Overview of FY 2012 Congressional Submission. http://www.nhtsa.gov/, last accessed on: May 1, 2014.

[20] Wang, C. D., Thompson, J. P., (1997). Apparatus and Method for Motion Detection and Tracking of Objects in a Region for Collision Avoidance Utilizing a Real-time Adaptive Probabilistic Neural Network. US Patent No. 5613039.

[21] Wafta, M., 2010. Advances in Vehicular Ad hoc Networks: Developments and Challenges. 1st ed., IGI Publications.

[22] ZigBee Alliance., 2009. ZigBee Overview, https://docs.zigbee.org/zigbee-docs/dcn/07-5482.pdf, last accessed on: May 1, 2014.

[23] ZigBee Alliance., 2012. ZigBee Specification: Features at a glance, https://docs.zigbee.org/zigbee-docs/dcn/07-5299.pdf, last accessed on: May 1, 2014.

In: Recent Advances in Ad Hoc Networks Research
Editor: Natarajan Meghanathan
ISBN: 978-1-63321-337-1

Chapter 5

A SECURE DATA AGGREGATION FRAMEWORK FOR WIRELESS MOBILE SENSOR NETWORKS

Natarajan Meghanathan*
Jackson State University, Jackson, MS, US

ABSTRACT

The high-level contribution of this paper is an integrated framework for secure data aggregation (SDA) in mobile sensor networks whose topology changes dynamically with time. As part of this framework, we propose a pair-wise key establishment mechanism along the edges of a data gathering tree as well as a trust evaluation model that are tightly integrated with the data aggregation process itself. If an aggregator node already shares a secret key with its child node, the two nodes locally coordinate to refresh and establish a new pair-wise secret key; otherwise, the aggregator node requests the sink to send a seed-secret key message that is used as the basis to establish a new pair-wise secret key. The trust evaluation model uses the two-sided Grubbs' test to identify outlier data in both the periodic beacons collected from the child nodes/neighbor nodes as well as in the aggregated data collected from the sub trees rooted at the child nodes. The decision to flag a child node and/or its neighbors as Compromised or Faulty (CF) node(s) is taken based on an estimated average trust score (weighted average of the raw trust scores assigned for each beacon/round of data over a buffer window), kept track for each child node and its sub trees. We anticipate the proposed SDA framework to be resilient to both insider and outsider attacks, including network disruption and energy depletion denial of service attacks, as well as provide confidentiality, integrity and authentication of the aggregated data.

Keywords: Secure Framework, Data Aggregation, Trust Evaluation, Pair-wise Key Establishment, Mobile Sensor Networks

* Mailbox 18839, Jackson State University, Jackson, MS 39232, USA; Email: natarajan.meghanathan@jsums.edu.

Introduction

Wireless sensor networks (WSNs) are of much interest for critical applications like real-time traffic monitoring, military surveillance, natural disaster relief, health monitoring, homeland security and etc. [1]. A WSN comprises of hundreds to thousands of low-cost sensors that collect data from the environment for a given task, and one or more sinks (a.k.a. Base Station, BS) responsible for administering and collecting data from the sensor nodes either periodically or on-demand. WSNs are often deployed to detect a parameter or event of common interest (like temperature, humidity, fire, intrusion, etc) and the sink needs only one representative data of the entire area being monitored. Hence, instead of requiring the sensor nodes to individually send their data (either directly or through multi-hop paths), it would be more efficient (resource-wise) to gather data from all of these sensor nodes and send only one aggregated version of the data (say the minimum, maximum, sum, etc.) to the sink. In this context, several data aggregation protocols (e.g., [2,3,4]) have been proposed for WSNs to eliminate the redundancy in data transmission and thereby reduce the communication overhead and energy lost at the sensor nodes.

Data aggregation in WSNs is typically conducted using a tree topology, as it is the most energy-efficient in terms of the number of link transmissions; there is only one path from any node to the root leader node (no scope for duplicate packets). Each intermediate non-leaf node in a data aggregation tree (DA-tree) acts as an aggregator, fusing the data collected from its immediate child nodes and forwarding the aggregated data to its own upstream parent node in the tree. This way, data is processed and fused at several hops on the way to the leader node, which eventually forwards the aggregated data to the sink.

However, hop-by-hop aggregation of data along the tree is prone to false data injection attacks. With sensor nodes often deployed in the open, they are vulnerable to physical tampering and it is impossible to physically protect every individual node from being captured by an adversary. Once under his control, an adversary can reprogram a sensor node with malicious code to disrupt the normal functioning of the network. For example, a compromised sensor node could inject one or more spurious data packets that could corrupt the aggregated data that is on its way further up a DA-tree. Several works in the literature (e.g., [12,13]) have addressed the problem of secure data aggregation in WSNs. However, their focus had been on secure data aggregation in *static* sensor networks wherein the nodes do not move.

In this research, we focus on secure data aggregation in wireless mobile sensor networks (WMSNs) wherein the sensor nodes move randomly, independent of each other. Only in the past few years, research on WMSNs has started to gain momentum, with the proliferation of electronic devices like Smart Phones and Personal Digital Assistants that are embedded with sensors to measure the temperature, location, humidity and other vital parameters of interest. The WMSN nodes can exploit the memory and processing capacity of their associated devices for more complex processing and are also not severely energy-constrained, due to the flexibility to frequently recharge the battery of these devices. However, due to the dynamically changing topology, the communication protocols and their secure variants developed for static sensor networks are not directly applicable for WMSNs. Like during the initial days of its static counterpart, most of the research focus on WMSNs is currently on topology control [14], data aggregation [15], energy-efficient clustering [16], etc., and relatively very little focus is on secure communication. Nevertheless, like static sensor networks, several network disruption attacks (like node capture and false packet injection), packet interception attacks (due to the shared wireless medium) and denial of service attacks (like energy-depletion) are very much possible in WMSNs. In this context, we propose to develop a secure communication framework for data aggregation in WMSNs that is embedded with a rigorous trust evaluation model and pair-wise secret key establishment process for the mobile sensor nodes. Ours will be the first such comprehensive secure data aggregation framework for WMSNs. Existing work, if any exists, has dealt with the above three mechanisms only in an isolated fashion, and not together.

Objectives and Key Characteristics of the Secure Data Aggregation (SDA) Framework

The following are the objectives of the proposed secure data aggregation (SDA) framework for wireless mobile sensor networks (WMSNs): **(1)** Protect from outsider attacks through secure, energy-efficient in-network data aggregation that provides confidentiality, integrity and authentication; **(2)** Protect from insider attacks through an embedded trust-evaluation model that can be used to detect and mitigate network disruption and energy depletion attacks as well as identify malicious compromised nodes and faulty nodes; and **(3)** Maximize the number of pair-wise secret keys established between sensor nodes, facilitated through node mobility and communication as part of data aggregation.

The two key characteristic features that are embedded within the proposed SDA framework are: **(1)** ***Pair-wise Key Distribution***: SDA facilitates establishment of pair-wise secret keys between as many sensor nodes as possible; and to be robust from node capture and packet interception attacks, the pair-wise secret keys need to be refreshed by the concerned nodes every time a new data aggregation tree (DA-tree) is setup. With node mobility [11], we foresee frequent reconfiguration of the DA-trees and hence scope for establishment and renewal of pair-wise secret keys between several node pairs. **(2)** ***Trust Evaluation of Sensor Nodes***: With the trust-level of the sensor nodes evaluated as part of the data aggregation process itself, the SDA framework is robust to network disruption and denial of service attacks without any additional communication overhead other than those incurred for the secure data aggregation process designed to provide confidentiality, integrity and authentication.

Pair-Wise Key Establishment along a Data Aggregation Tree

Key Assumptions

The key assumptions are: (1) The sink BS is secure and it shares a secret key (128-bits long) with each of the sensor nodes. (2) The BS broadcasts any information to one or more sensor nodes in a secure fashion through the well-known μTESLA [5] protocol that also provides authentication. (3) We assume the sink BS and the sensor nodes are loosely synchronized with respect to time – this is a requirement to use the μTESLA protocol for authentic broadcast. (4) Each node stores a Key Cache in its memory. The Key Cache of a node consists of the 128-bit pair-wise secret keys the node shares with one or more of the other nodes in the network and the sink. The Key Cache is maintained in the main memory on a most recently used basis, and the unused ones are paged to the internal storage. (5) The data aggregation tree (DA-tree) is securely formed each time when needed. There is no scope for attack or impersonation during its construction.

Sequence of Steps in Pair-Wise Key Establishment

The following are the sequence of steps for pair-wise key establishment along a DA-tree.

1) *Construction of the DA-Tree:* The sink initiates the construction of the DA-tree by sending a trigger signal to the leader node (the node with the largest available energy) to broadcast a *Tree-Construction* message to its neighborhood. When a sensor node receives the *Tree-Construction* message for the first time, it sets the sender of the message as its predecessor upstream node in the tree and broadcasts the message further to its neighbors, and discards any further *Tree-Construction* messages received. This way, the *Tree-Construction* message is broadcast by every sensor node (but exactly once) so that it can propagate throughout the network to eventually establish a spanning topology tree rooted at the leader node. The child nodes send a *Parent-Update* message to inform their parent node that they have chosen the latter as their immediate upstream node in the DA-tree.
2) *Maintenance of the DA-Tree:* Each intermediate node of the DA-tree monitors the links to its downstream nodes (expecting periodic beacons from the neighbor nodes). When a downstream link breaks, the upstream node sends a secure *Tree-Error* message (encrypted and decrypted every hop on the path with the pair-wise secret keys that would have been established by then for the DA-tree using steps 3 through 5) to the leader node, which forwards the message further to the sink. The sink initiates another tree construction process (Step 1).
3) *DA-Notification Message from the Aggregator Node to the Sink:* After a new DA-tree is configured, each intermediate aggregator node checks its Key Cache to see if it shares a secret key with each of its child nodes. If the aggregator node does not share a secret key with one or more of the child nodes, then the aggregator node sends a *DA-Notification* message to the sink, containing the IDs of the child nodes with which it does not yet share a secret key. The DA-Notification message also contains a Nonce (randomly generated by the aggregator node) that needs to be incremented and included in the *Seed-Secret-Key* message sent as a response by the sink BS. The DA-Notification message is encrypted with the secret key that the aggregator node shares with the sink BS.
4) *Seed-Secret-Key Message from the Sink to the Aggregator Node:* The sink BS responds to the DA-Notification message with a Seed-Secret-Key message that contains different components – one for each of the aggregator node and the requested child nodes (with which the aggregator node needs to establish a new pair-wise secret key). The Seed-Secret-Key message component meant for the aggregator

node – contains 64-bit random numbers generated by the BS (one for each of the aggregator node and its requested child nodes) as well as the incremented value of the Nonce sent in the DA-Notification message. The Seed-Secret-Key message components meant for the individual child nodes include the random number generated for the aggregator node as well as the ID of the aggregator node and the random number generated for the individual child node. The Seed-Secret-Key message component meant for a node is encrypted using the secret key shared by the sink BS with the individual node.

5) *Agreement on a New Pair-wise Secret Key:* Upon the receipt of the Seed-Secret-Key message from the sink BS, an aggregator node forwards to the appropriate child nodes – their respective encrypted message components as it is. A child node decrements the Seed-Secret-Key component message (addressed for it) using the secret key shared with the BS and ensures that the message component includes the ID of the aggregator node that forwarded the Seed-Secret-Key message. The child node then generates a 128-bit pair-wise secret key (generated on the fly by the child node as well as a Nonce value (meant for the aggregator node to later send an incremented Nonce value in its response and get authenticated for receiving the new pair-wise secret key) and encrypts them using a temporary key, which is basically a product of the random numbers (generated by the sink BS and included in the Seed-Secret-Key message component) for the individual child node and the aggregator node. The child node sends this encrypted pair-wise secret key to the aggregator node as part of a *New Pair-wise Key Establishment* message. Upon receiving the New Pair-wise Key Establishment message from a child node, the aggregator node computes on its own the temporary key (product of the random number sent to it by the sink BS and the random number meant for the appropriate child node) and decrements the message to extract the new pair-wise secret key and the Nonce value. The aggregator node encrypts the incremented value of this Nonce with the pair-wise secret key and sends the encrypted value as part of the *New Pair-wise Key Acknowledgment* message to the child node. Upon decryption of this acknowledgment message with the new pair-wise secret key and validating the incremented Nonce value, the child node is convinced of the establishment of the pair-wise secret key with the aggregator node.
6) *Refreshment of a Pair-wise Secret Key:* If an aggregator node already shares a pair-wise secret key with a child node established earlier due to their association in some data gathering tree of the past, the aggregator node refreshes this association by establishing a new pair-wise secret key using the currently shared pair-wise secret key as the basis. In this pursuit, the aggregator node sends the child node a *Pair-wise Key Refresh Request* message that contains a randomly generated Nonce encrypted using the currently shared pair-wise secret key with the child node. The child node decrypts the message using the shared pair-wise secret key, and sends the following as part of a *Pair-wise Key Refresh Response* message: the incremented value of the Nonce received from the aggregator node, a new 128-bit pair-wise secret key (generated on the fly by the child node) as well as a new Nonce value (to be used to validate the aggregator node's receipt of the new pair-wise secret key) – all of these encrypted with the most recently shared pair-wise secret key. The aggregator node decrypts the Pair-wise Key Refresh Response message to extract the new pair-wise

secret key and confirms the receipt of the same by sending back (to the child node) an incremented value of the Nonce (generated and included by the child node in the Refresh Response message) encrypted with the new pair-wise secret key sent as part of a *Pair-wise Key Refresh Acknowledgment* message.

Example for Pair-Wise Key Establishment

We now illustrate below the contents of the DA-notification message, seed-secret-key message and the sequence of messages that will be exchanged to establish or refresh the pair-wise secret key between an aggregator node and its child nodes. Note that the DA-notification message contains only the IDs of those child nodes with which the aggregator node does not already share a pair-wise secret key. For the sake of illustration, we refer to the aggregator node as A and its child nodes as B, C and D. We also assume that node A already shares a pair-wise secret key with node B and the key is to be refreshed (Figure 2). Node A requests the BS for a seed-secret-key only to establish pair-wise secret keys with C and D (Figure 1 shows the message exchange between A and D to establish a pair-wise secret key).

DA-Notification Message: E[$K^{BS,A}_{Secret}$; $\{ID_A$ || Nonce (N_A) || Children$(ID_C, ID_D)\}$]

Seed-Secret-Key Message: E[$K^{BS,A}_{Secret}$; $\{BS$ || Nonce $(N_A + 1)$ || RN(A) || RN(C) || RN(D)$\}$] ||

E[$K^{BS,C}_{Secret}$; $\{BS$ || ID_A || RN(A) || RN(C)$\}$] ||

E[$K^{BS,D}_{Secret}$; $\{BS$ || ID_A || RN(A) || RN(D)$\}$]

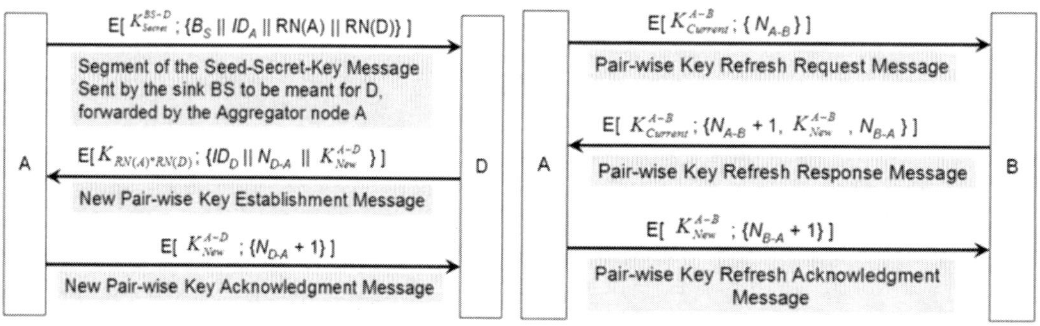

Message Exchange: Aggregator – Child Message Exchange: Aggregator - Child
Nodes to Establish a New Pair-wise Secret Key Nodes to Refresh/Renew a Pair-wise Secret Key

Figure 1. Example for Pair-wise Key Establishment.

TRUST EVALUATION MODEL

We will evaluate the genuineness of the data disseminated by the individual downstream child nodes and that of the aggregated data received from them (in case the child nodes are also intermediate nodes) through a comprehensive trust-evaluation model. The objective of the trust evaluation model is to eventually classify whether a node is a CF node (Compromised or Faulty node) or an N-node (Normal node).

Assumptions

We assume the range of a sensed value to be in a specific range [D_{min}, …, D_{max}] and that the sensed values are not typically expected to reach either of these two extremes under normal functioning of the nodes and the network. Each sensor node periodically disseminates its individual sensed data to its neighbors through beacon broadcasts. The time period between two successive rounds of data aggregation is the same as the time period between two beacon broadcasts. However, it is up to the individual sensor nodes to decide on the exact time they would broadcast their data to the neighborhood.

Beacon Buffer and Data Aggregation Buffer

An intermediate node maintains a maximum of two buffers per child node – one buffer (referred to as the *Beacon Buffer*) to analyze the trust-level of the raw sensed data collected from the periodic beacons disseminated by the child node (as a neighbor node) and another buffer (referred to as the *DA-Buffer*) to analyze the trust-level of the aggregated data sent by the child node if it is a non-leaf node (i.e., intermediate node). Since the network topology and the DA-tree change dynamically with time, we anticipate the sizes of the two buffers maintained per child node/neighbor node to be not too large.

With regards to the buffer size, we envision two parameters related for each buffer, the *maximum buffer size* and the *buffer window size* whose appropriate values will have to be evaluated to correctly identify the compromised and faulty nodes and reduce the number of false positives and false negatives as much as possible. Since we are assuming the frequencies of periodic beacon broadcast and data aggregation rounds to be the same, we hypothesize that the values for the above two parameters be the same for both the beacon-buffer and DA-buffer, and the uniformity in the window sizes for the two buffers especially helps to assign a node-centric trust score (rather than a buffer-centric trust score). For irregular data aggregation, we anticipate the sizes of the two buffers to be different and evaluation of the impact of variable-rate data aggregation on the trust-evaluation model will be part of our future work. If the number of data points collected from a child sensor node in a buffer exceeds the *buffer window size*, then we will use a moving window and only the last *buffer window size* amount of data points will be used for the statistical analysis (described below) and the prior data points falling outside this window will be still stored in the buffer if the total number of data points does not exceed *maximum buffer*. Overall, the two buffers would be filled in a FIFO (First-In First-Out) basis.

Statistical Test and Scores

We will use the well-known Grubbs' test [6] for detecting a single outlier (hypothesized to be the most recently added data to the buffer) for each of the two buffers (Beacon buffer and DA-buffer) maintained per child node at an aggregator node. We will conduct the two-sided version of Grubbs' testing as we consider an attacker or a faulty node to inject data that could be too low or too high than the regular value. Four possible outcomes (as shown in Table 1) are expected from the Grubbs' test conducted on a single child node. If there are no outliers detected in both the Beacon buffer and the DA-buffer, then we consider the child node and the nodes as part of the DA-tree rooted at the child node to be *Normal*; otherwise we consider one or more them to be *Suspect* as explained below.

Table 1. Possible Outcomes of an Outlier Test on the Buffers and the associated Trust Score

Result from Beacon buffer	Result from DA-buffer	Perceived Child Node Status	Perceived Status of the DA-tree rooted at Child Node	Trust score for the child node per test
No outlier	No outlier	Normal	Normal	4
One outlier	No outlier	Suspect	Normal	3
No outlier	One outlier	Normal	Suspect	2
One outlier	One outlier	Suspect	Suspect	1

We propose a 1-4 trust-score for a sensor node based on the results of an individual Grubbs' test conducted on the node. The higher the seriousness of the situation, the lower is the trust value. The logic behind the assignment of the trust scores is as follows:

- The highest trust score of 4 indicates everything is fine with both the child node and the sub tree of nodes rooted at the child node.
- If we detect an outlier in the Beacon buffer and no outlier is detected in the DA-buffer, it is an indication that the data disseminated by the particular child node has a problem, and the aggregated data from the sub tree rooted at the child node is not yet corrupted. This is an indication that the child node is likely to be either compromised or faulty, while the rest of the sub tree nodes are normal. A trust score of 3 is assigned to this situation to illustrate that the situation is not very serious and just one sensor node is likely to be compromised or faulty.
- If we detect an outlier in the DA-buffer and no outlier is detected in the Beacon buffer, it is an indication that the data disseminated by the particular child node is within the normal range, and the child node is not compromised or faulty; however, the aggregated data obtained from the sub tree and the individual child node's data turns out to be not normal. This is likely an indication that the aggregated data obtained from the downstream nodes of the sub tree is likely to be corrupt, rather than the individual data disseminated from the child node. We assign a trust score of 2 to this situation to indicate that it is relatively more serious as more than one sensor node is likely to have been affected by now.
- If we detect an outlier in both the Beacon buffer and the DA-buffer, it is an indication that both the child node as well as the downstream nodes that are part of the sub tree rooted at the child node are likely to have been compromised or faulty. This is the most serious situation, and a trust score of 1 is assigned to the child node.

Calculation of Estimated Average Trust Score

The method employed for computing the estimated average trust score (EA-Trust-Score) at the individual child nodes plays a significant role in our trust-evaluation model as it directly influences the crucial decisions taken regarding flagging the nodes as CF or Normal, as well as raising a Network Field Alert. We do not want to simply compute the average of all the trust-scores accumulated until the current time instant to raise the flags – because, a node could be functioning normally until it suddenly became compromised. Hence, we compute the average of the trust scores observed for the currently active buffer window size (Window Average Trust Score, WA-trust-score) and compute the estimated average of the trust score (i.e., the EA-trust-score, based on all the data points collected so far) as the weighted average of the EA-trust-score before the latest data point and that of the WA-trust-score computed including the latest data point. An aggregator node maintains an estimated average value of the trust scores observed per child node as the data points are accumulated over a period of time spanning the *buffer window size* and beyond. We propose to use the Internet re-transmission algorithm model (to detect and mitigate congestion control) [7] for maintaining the estimated average trust score at a child node, formulated as follows: EA-Trust-Score = α * EA-Trust-score + (1- α) * WA-Trust-Score.

Note that until the number of data points collected in the buffers exceeds the *Buffer Window Size*, the EA-Trust-Score would be the same as the WA-Trust-Score. The weighted average parameter (α) comes into picture only if the number of data points collected in the buffer exceeds the *Buffer Window Size*. A proper value of α needs to be chosen in order to balance the lack of importance given to temporary variations in the data points due to fluctuations in the underlying network field (i.e., situations that would require giving more importance to history, the EA-Trust-Score, rather than the temporary fluctuations) and the occurrence of sudden node captures (i.e., situations that would require giving more importance to the sudden fluctuations affecting the WA-Trust-Score).

Decision Taken Based on the Values of the Estimated Average Trust Scores

(a) If the EA-trust-score of each of the child nodes of an aggregator node is 3.5 or above – we conclude that everything is fine with all the downstream nodes of the DA-sub tree rooted at the aggregator node.

(b) If the EA-trust-score of a particular child node is between 2.5 to 3.5 and the rest of the child nodes have a score above 3.5, then the child node alone is considered to be either compromised or faulty, and a CF flag is raised for the node.

(c) If the EA-trust-score of a majority of the child nodes (> 1 child node) of the aggregator node is between 2.5 to 3.5, then there is likelihood of these child nodes being compromised or faulty, and a CF flag is raised on all of these immediate child nodes of the aggregator node.

(d) If the EA-trust-score of a particular child node is between 1 to 2.5 and the rest of the child nodes have a score 2.5 or above, then the sub tree rooted at the child node is considered to be probably under attack and all the downstream nodes, including the immediate downstream child node are flagged as CF nodes.

(e) If the EA-trust-score of a majority of the child nodes (> 1 child nodes) of an aggregator node is from 1 to 2.5, then the sub tree rooted at each of these child nodes (that have an EA-trust-score from 1 to 2.5) are considered to be probably under attack. Hence, we propose that all the child nodes of the aggregator node and the downstream nodes of the sub trees rooted at these child nodes be flagged as CF nodes.

Significance of the Trust Evaluation Model

Note that when we flag a sub tree, not all the sensor nodes need to have been actually compromised or faulty. But, since a sub tree comprises of sensor nodes that are in the vicinity of each other, the presence of even one compromised node under the control of an attacker, could put the nearby nodes under risk, and it would be better to flag all these nodes as under risk and take immediate action to prevent the further escalation of the attack. This way, we are able to detect the presence of a falsely injected data downstream at an intermediate node itself and prevent it from poisoning the aggregated data further upstream. Thus, our trust-evaluation model helps to prevent a denial of service attack by flagging one or more nodes in the vicinity as CF nodes and stops the suspicious data from propagating further up in the tree. The same logic applies for flagging a faulty node and its nearby nodes as CF nodes.

CONCLUSION AND FUTURE WORK

The proposed design for a secure data aggregation (SDA) framework will be the first such comprehensive framework for defense against network disruption attacks and energy depletion attacks for mobile sensor networks, a classical example for distributed sensing systems whose topology changes dynamically with time. With node mobility, the data gathering trees change with time, and we anticipate the SDA framework to establish as many pair-wise secret keys as possible between the sensor nodes just based on their association in a data aggregation tree. The integrated approach of evaluating the trust level of the nodes and regular refreshing of the pair-wise secret keys between the sensor nodes as part of the data aggregation process meets the need to: develop autonomic and innate defense (self-discovery and assessment) capabilities for sensor networks to detect adversarial actions and develop techniques that are resistant to detecting network disruption attacks (e.g., denial of service, false packet injection attacks). Every intermediate aggregator node of the data aggregation tree (DA-tree) keeps track of the trust level of each of its immediate child nodes and the rest of the nodes that are part of the sub tree rooted at each child node. The trust evaluation model uses the well-known statistically sound Grubbs' testing (for detecting two-sided outliers) and the TCP/IP model for maintaining an estimated weighted average of the trust scores based on a sliding buffer window. Note that when we flag a sub tree, not all the sensor nodes need to have been actually compromised or faulty. But, since a sub tree comprises of sensor nodes that are in the vicinity of each other, the presence of even one compromised node under the control of an attacker, could put the nearby nodes under risk, and it would be better to flag all these nodes as vulnerable and take immediate action to prevent further escalation of the attack. Thus, our integrated trust-evaluation model helps to prevent a denial of service attack by flagging one or more nodes in the vicinity as CF (Compromised or Faulty) nodes, and stops the erroneous or falsely injected data at a downstream node itself and prevents it from poisoning the aggregated data propagating further up in the tree.

Now that the design of the secure data aggregation (SDA) framework is completed, the next phase of our research will be to implement the framework in a discrete-event simulator in Java (e.g., [8,9]). This simulator, developed by the author, has already been successfully used for simulating several routing protocols and data aggregation algorithms for mobile ad hoc and sensor networks. We will investigate the impact of the use of data aggregation trees constructed with different algorithmic principles (shortest path, minimum-distance spanning tree, maximum leaf node spanning tree, etc.) on the performance of the SDA protocol, including the trust-evaluation model. We will compare the performance of the SDA protocol with that of the Secure Encrypted-data Aggregation (SEA) scheme [10], which is the only related data aggregation scheme that we could come across of mobile sensor networks. SEA forms a data aggregation tree of clusters (with a cluster head for each) that coordinate to transmit data to the sink; the sensor nodes within a cluster directly transmit data to their cluster head. We consider the sink node to be static and mobility is confined only to the sensor nodes. The results of the extensive simulations conducted in this research will quantify the effects of disruption attacks on data aggregation in terms of degradation to performance metrics such as the network throughput, network lifetime and node lifetime; in addition, the effectiveness of the trust-evaluation model built-in to the data aggregation framework will also be evaluated by measuring the number of false positives and the number of false negatives. In addition to the above quantitative simulations, we will also qualitatively (theoretically, with proofs wherever necessary) analyze the robustness of the proposed SDA framework against network disruption attacks, including warmhole attacks, sinkhole attacks and cybil attacks, and evaluate the confidentiality, integrity and authentication of data during data aggregation.

REFERENCES

[1] Akyildiz, I., Su, W., Sankarasubramaniam, Y., Cayirci, E., 2002. Wireless Sensor Networks: A Survey. *Computer Networks*. 38, *4*, 393-422.

[2] Heinzelman, W., Chandrakasan, A., Balakarishnan, H., 2000. Energy-Efficient Communication Protocols for Wireless Microsensor Networks. *Proceedings of the Hawaiian International Conference on Systems Science*. 1-10.

[3] Lindsey, S., Raghavendra, C., Sivalingam, K. M., 2002. Data Gathering Algorithms in Sensor Networks using Energy Metrics. *IEEE Transactions on Parallel and Distributed Systems*. 13, *9*, 924-935.

[4] Meghanathan, N., 2009. Grid Block Energy based Data Gathering Algorithm for Lower Energy Delay and Longer Lifetime in Wireless Sensor Networks. *Proceedings of the 1st ISCA International Conference on Sensor Networks and Applications*. 1-6.

[5] Perrig, A., Szewczyk, R., Wen, V., Culler, D., Tygar, J. D., 2001. SPINS: Security Protocols for Sensor Networks. *Proceedings of the 7th Annual International Conference on Mobile Computing and Networks*. 189-199.

[6] Frank, G., 1969. Procedures for Detecting Outlying Observations in Samples. *Technometrics*. 11, *1*, 1-21.

[7] Patterson, L. L., Davie, B. S., (2011). *Computer Networks: A Systems Approach*, 5th ed., Morgan Kaufmann, March 2011.

[8] Meghanathan, N., 2012. A Comprehensive Review and Performance Analysis of Data Gathering Algorithms for Wireless Sensor Networks. *International Journal of Interdisciplinary Telecommunications and Networking*, 4, *2*, 1-29.

[9] Meghanathan, N., 2010. An Algorithm to Determine Energy-aware Maximal Leaf Nodes Data Gathering Tree for Wireless Sensor Networks. *Journal of Theoretical and Applied Information Technology*. 15, *2*, 96-107.

[10] Huang, S-I., Shieh, S., 2007. SEA: Secure Encrypted-Data Aggregation in Mobile Wireless Sensor Networks. *Proceedings of the International Conference on Computational Intelligence and Security*. 848-852.

[11] Camp, T., Boleng, J., Davies, V., 2002. A Survey of Mobility Models for Ad hoc Network Research. *Wireless Communications and Mobile Computing*. 2, 483-502.

[12] Y. Yang, X. Wang, S. Zhu and G. Cao, SDAP: A Secure Hop-by-Hop Data Aggregation Protocol for Sensor Networks, *ACM Transactions on Information and System Security*, vol. 11, no. 4, article # 18, 43 pages, July 2008.

[13] Ozdemir, S., Xiao, Y., 2009. Secure Data Aggregation in Wireless Sensor Networks: A Comprehensive Overview, *Computer Networks*, 53, 2022-2037.

[14] Li, J., Huang, L., Xiao, M., 2008. Energy Efficient Topology Control Algorithms for Variant Rate Mobile Sensor Networks. *Proceedings of the 4th International Conference on Mobile Ad hoc and Sensor Networks*. 23-30.

[15] Santhosh Kumar, G., Vinu Paul, M. V., Jacob, K. P., 2008. Mobility Metric based LEACH-Mobile Protocol. *Proceedings of the 16th International Conference on Advanced Computing & Communications*, 248-253.

[16] Awwad, S. A. B., Ng, C. K., Noordin, N. K., Rasid, M. F. A., 2009. Cluster Based Routing Protocol for Mobile Nodes in Wireless Sensor Network. *Proceedings of the International Symposium on Collaborative Technologies and Systems*, 233-241.

In: Recent Advances in Ad Hoc Networks Research
Editor: Natarajan Meghanathan
ISBN: 978-1-63321-337-1

Chapter 6

DELAY-MINIMIZATION ROUTING IN HIERARCHICAL SENSOR NETWORKS

S. Narjes Khorashadizadeh and Hengameh Keshavarz*
University of Sistan and Baluchestan, Zahedan, Iran

ABSTRACT

Wireless Sensor Networks (WSNs) consist of a large number of sensor nodes that strongly interact with their physical environment. To evaluate performance of such networks, a number of parameters such as energy, lifetime, and capacity are used. There are some algorithms for reliable and effective delay-minimization routing in WSNs. One of the most important issues in wireless sensor networks is how to transfer data from sensor nodes to the control centre and to choose the best possible route for data transmission. Selecting the best route depends on several factors such as power consumption, throughput, transmission delay, and accuracy in data transmission. In this chapter, first of all, the concept of routing protocols is explained and then, some delay-minimization routing methods are briefly introduced. Finally, our proposed algorithm minimizing the number of hops is presented. In fact, some limitations such as nodes energy constraints and data transmission delay constraints for sending packets are two challenging parameters that should be addressed in this routing algorithm. Our energy-aware routing algorithm reduces delay and decreases energy consumption simultaneously.

Keywords: Hierarchical Wireless Sensor Networks, Routing Algorithms, Network Delay, Node Energy

* Department of Communication Engineering, University of Sistan & Baluchestan, Zahedan, Iran; Email: keshavarz@ece.usb.ac.ir.

INTRODUCTION

Wireless Sensor Networks (WSNs) consist of a large number of sensor nodes located in an area, and strongly interact with their physical environment. One of the simplest structures is the flat structure in which sensors perform as routers and transmitters of data through multipath routing. For better use of limited connections and sensors power, two or more layers may be applied, in which a stronger fixed relay is used for collecting and routing of sensor data [1]. Such structures are known as hierarchical structures. WSNs consist of a cluster head, command nodes and several sensor nodes grouped into clusters [2]. Each cluster in the hierarchical network structure has a leader which is called the cluster head (CH), typically performs special tasks such as data fusion and aggregation. There are also several common sensor nodes (SNs) as its members [3]. Clustering the sensor nodes makes it possible to minimize the data-collection time with the minimum energy consumption, and it reduces the processing time of the cluster head [4]. Sensors gather information from the environment and transmit them to the cluster head using single-hop or multi-hop transmissions. These networks have applications in various areas such as military, environment monitoring, health and medicine, traffic control etc., and different parameters such as energy, lifetime, capacity and delay have important roles in analyzing performance of WSNs.

Delay is one of the most important and critical parameters in WSNs. Many WSNs applications need to ensure low delay for time-sensitive applications. Delay arises when each node waits until the neighboring nodes within its communication range declare the situation. Delay time mostly depends on the number of hops to reach the cluster head and control centre. Providing a reliable context for data transmission is achieved by selecting the appropriate routing protocol in these networks. Moreover, some features like power constraints and limited acceptable delay for sending packets are challenges that must be addressed in WSNs. In this chapter, a hierarchical sensor network is considered and a routing algorithm is used to obtain the shortest path to the cluster head in each cluster.

CLASSIFICATION OF DELAY-MINIMIZATION PROTOCOLS

In recent years, many methods have been introduced to reduce delay in WSNs. These methods can be divided into sleep scheduling [4-10], data aggregation [11-13], routing and other way as shown in Figure 1. Since one of the most discussable issues in WSNs is focused on how to transfer data from the sensor nodes to the control centre and to choose the best possible route. Among various methods, we are focused on routing-based schemes reducing delay in WSNs. The best route can be selected according to several factors such as energy consumption, throughput, delay and accuracy of data transmission.

One of the critical issues in implementation of WSNs is on designing the routing protocols. Before introducing some routing protocols in WSNs, it is necessary to address some challenges in designing the routing protocols.

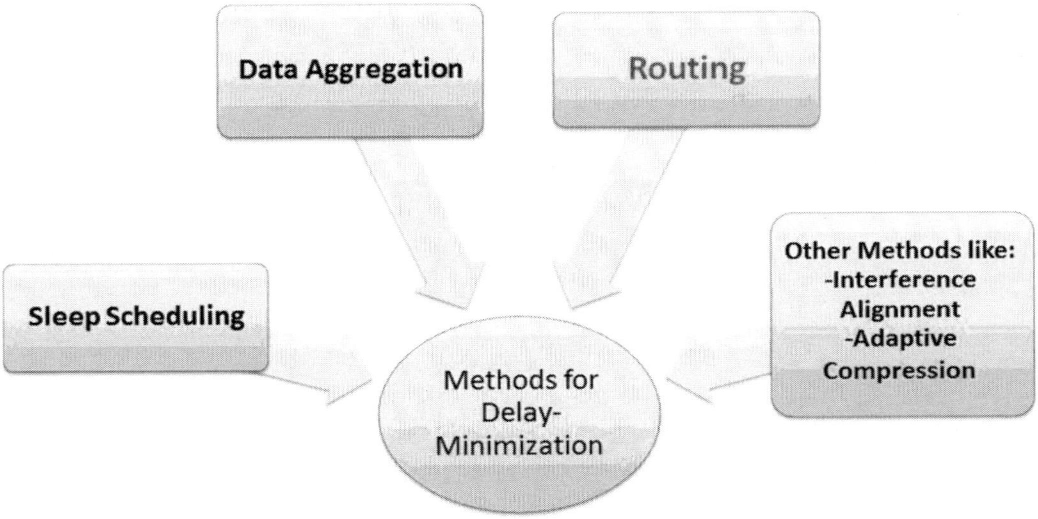

Figure 1. Classification Delay-Minimization Methods in WSNs.

ROUTING CHALLENGES IN WSNS

Routing protocols are affected by many challenging factors. Some major challenges are as follow [14]:

Dynamic Networks

Designing distributed efficient routing algorithms that dynamically update the routing structures is of crucial importance. Because geometric location information of nodes is more readily available, routing algorithms incorporating this information for effective routing form an increasingly important subject of study.

Replacement of Sensors

Replacement of sensors in different applications affects performance of the whole network. In some applications, each sensor location is predetermined and data is sent through predetermined routes. However, in most WSNs, sensors locations are not known a priori and routing is done automatically.

Energy Constraints

The main objective of routing protocols is efficient delivery of information between sensors and the sink node. To this end, energy consumption is the main interest in development of any routing protocol for WSNs. Because of limited energy resources of sensor nodes, data must be delivered in the most energy-efficient manner without losing QoS. So, many conventional routing metrics such as the shortest path algorithm may not be suitable.

Models of Information Transmission

Models of information transmission in WSNs are divided into time-based models, event detection, request-based models or a combination of them according to different applications. In the time-based model, each sensor gathers and sends information to the sink or the control centre. In the event detection model, whenever events occur in one part of the network, the event is reported. When information transmission is request-based, the control centre publishes a request and sensor nodes that have already been selected receive this message. Then, the sensor nodes transmit suitable responses to the control centre. For each model mentioned, some routing protocols have been proposed to achieve energy efficiency and stability.

Combining Data

Another important parameter in WSNs is the volume of time-sensitive information. Many sensors can produce redundant data increasing data traffic in WSNs. Combing data decreases this redundancy.

ROUTING PROTOCOLS IN WIRELESS SENSOR NETWORKS

Because of the unique characteristics of WSNs, routing is a challenging task in WSNs and makes it different from other wired or wireless networks like cellular or mobile ad-hoc networks [15]. First of all, since the number of sensor nodes is very large, building a global addressing scheme for the deployment of a large number of sensor nodes is not possible as the overhead of ID maintenance is high. Hence, traditional IP-based protocols may not be applied to WSNs [16]. Second, in contrast to other communication networks, almost all applications of sensor networks require the flow of sensed data from multiple sources to a particular base station [17]. Third, in terms of energy, processing, and storage capacities, sensor nodes are firmly constrained. So, they require precise resource management [18]. Fourth, in most application scenarios, nodes in WSNs are generally stationary after deployment except about a few mobile nodes. Nodes in other traditional wireless networks are free to move, which results in unpredictable and frequent topological changes [19]. However, in some applications, some sensor nodes may be allowed to move and change their location (although with very low mobility) [15].

Due to the limitations, many routing algorithms have been introduced over the past decades. According to the most popular algorithm classifications, routing methods can be divided into three main groups: flat networks routing, location-based routing and hierarchical networks routing [17].

Another classification of routing in sensor networks is: Negotiation-based routing, multipath-based routing, query-based routing, QoS-based routing consistency- and coherent-based routing [14]. This classification is shown in Figure 2. In the rest of this section, we present a detailed overview of the main routing paradigms in WSNs.

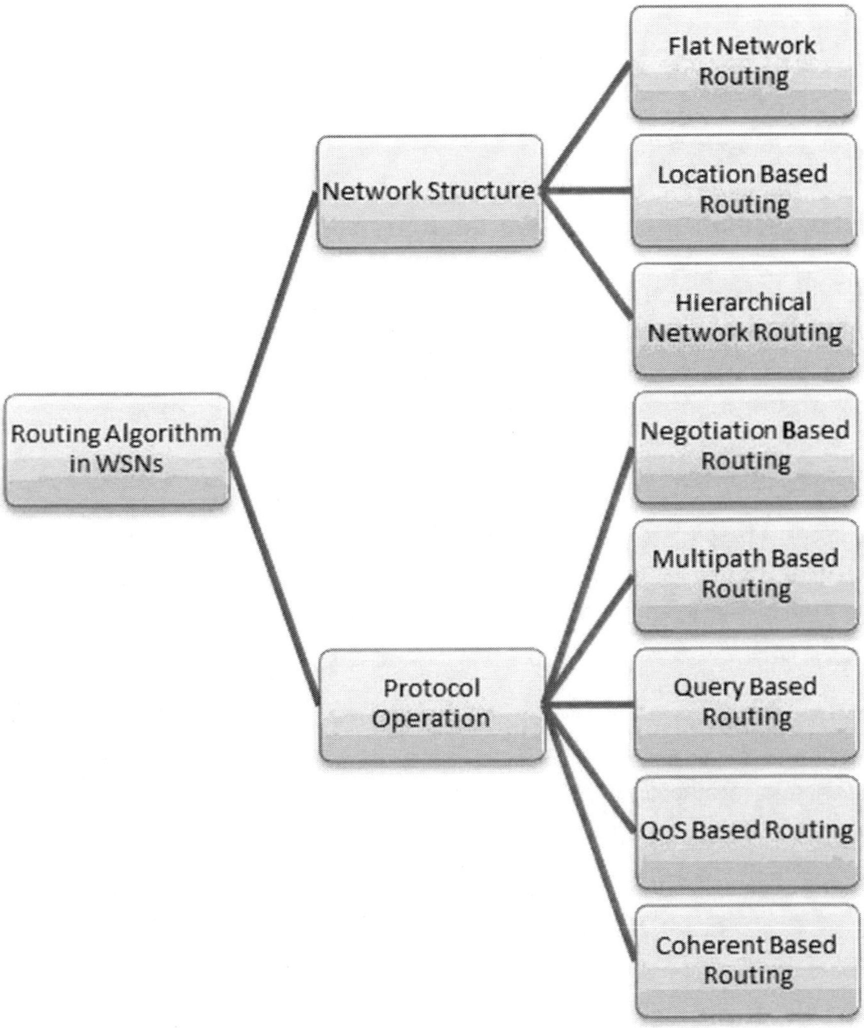

Figure 2. Classification of Routing Protocols.

OPERATION OF NETWORK STRUCTURE BASED PROTOCOLS

Negotiation-Based Protocols

Negotiation-based protocols want to omit redundant data by including high level data descriptors in the message exchanged. The sensor node can make communication decisions based on the data descriptors and energy of its battery such as SPIN [20] protocol.

Multipath-Based Routing Protocols

Multipath-based routing protocols want to increase the reliability to the use of multiple paths. The alternative path takes over the responsibility of relaying data when the main path stops functioning due to node failures or topology changes. However, extra energy is spent to maintain the alternative paths have priority in relation to the energy efficiency. The advantage of this routing can be considered to improve the reliability and tolerability against failures, distribution of load balancing, raised bandwidth and allocates the traffic rate to each path optimally.

Query-Based Routing Protocols

In query-based protocols, such as the directed diffusion, the communication is imported by the sink node broadcasting query for data over the network. If the source node has data that matches the query, it sends the data back to the sink node.

QoS-Based Routing Protocols

Before sensor nodes deliver the data to the sink node, the QoS-based protocols let sensor nodes to balance between the energy consumption and pre-determined QoS metrics. The Sequential Assignment Routing (SAR) is one of the QoS-based protocols.

Coherent-Based Routing Protocols

In this routing protocol, data will be sent to collectors after a minimal processing. For energy efficiency in routing, typically coherent-based routing is selected.

Network Structure Based Protocols

Flat Networks Routing

Flat networks routing algorithms act upon the query. Their useful feature is that a significant part of routing data redundancy can be eliminated [19]. In flat networks, each node typically plays the same role and sensor nodes collaborate together to perform the sensing task. Several protocols have been proposed that can be placed in the category of flat networks routing such as flooding, gossiping, security protocols for sensor networks (SPIN), directed diffusion, rumour routing, minimum cost forwarding algorithm (MCFA), gradient-based routing, information-driven sensor querying (IDSQ), constrained anisotropic diffusion routing (CADR), COUGAR and ACQUIRE [14].

Location Based Routing

Location based routing uses the exact position of the nodes, location information and their location factors. Most of routing protocols for WSNs need sensor location information. Some location-based routing protocols are SPEED [22], MMSPEED [23], HGR, and DHGR [21].

Hierarchical Networks Routing

Hierarchical networks routing divides the network into multiple zones, each managed by a cluster head. In this method, many ways of aggregating data in each cluster can be used. The routing protocols must ensure that the data packets are delivered to the sink in a fast and correct manner with very little or without loss. Hierarchical routing reduces energy consumption of a node. Each cluster is formed by considering remaining energy of nodes in each area. Some hierarchical routing protocols are LEACH [24], PEGASIS [25], TEEN [26]. In recent years, based on the aforementioned algorithms, some practical routing algorithms for WSNs have been proposed.

The graph theory can be used to create the sensor clusters and to identify the cluster heads. The graph-theory based routing uses the features of flat and hierarchical routing. In this scheme, routing is conducted by identifying the maximum energy possessing path links. This clustering scheme provides scalability [27].

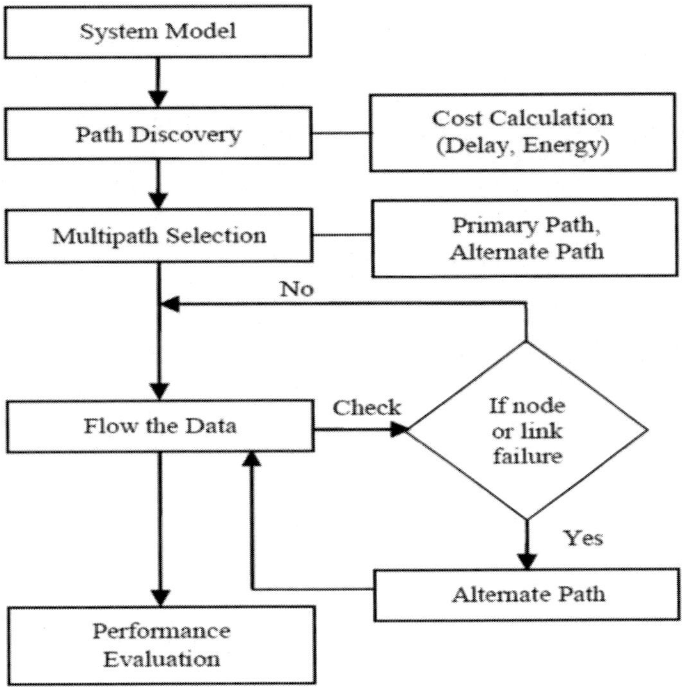

Figure 3. Flowchart of Mutipath-GT Routing.

Hybrid Reliable Routing technique (HRR) organizes the network into clusters and then, changes the cluster head at an appropriate time, and consumes least energy to perform routing through the cluster heads to the sink [28].

A hierarchy-based multipath routing protocol (HMRP) minimizes the path loading of the system by distributing the energy consumption among the nodes. The HMRP employs the hierarchical concept to construct the whole sensor network. The energy consumption is distributed and the network lifetime is prolonged. Finally, the HMRP can support the multiple sink nodes situation [29].

The Multipath-Generalized Topology (Multipath-GT) routing estimates delay due to the processing time at each node, packet loss rate, energy, and the delay history and finds the best possible route. In this routing, the graph theory can be used to create the sensor clusters and dynamic source algorithm can be used to provide QoS guarantees. The flow diagram of this routing scheme is shown in Figure 3. Each node broadcasts the Hello message when it is awake at the time. Finding neighborhood process then starts. Nodes located inside the communication range of the source node are able to receive messages. Thus, nodes find their neighborhood members and nodes located outside this communication range doesn't establish any connection with the source node. Using the tree-based search algorithm, the shortest path is determined and then, multipath routing is applied. For each sensor node, different routes are marked as main or alternate routes to be chosen for data delivery. In the case of link failure and retransmission, an alternate path is selected to transmit the data to the sink. This feature increases error tolerance and load adjustment on network paths. It is shown that as the network size varies, multipath-GT achieves better packet delivery ratio and throughput [30].

Proposed Hierarchical Routing Algorithm

Many routing algorithms have already been proposed to reduce end-to-end delay. Since energy efficiency is also an important factor in WSNs, the proposed routing algorithm aims to decrease delay and energy consumption simultaneously using a multipath routing technique.

Assumptions

Our assumptions in this hierarchical routing algorithm are as follow:

- The current network has asymmetric hierarchical structure consisting of clusters, control centre, and a large number of sensor nodes. The sensor nodes in this network have two types. The majority of nodes are similar (i.e., having the same type, same sensing and communication range together) and are called ordinary nodes used as relays for sensing the environment. These nodes are not used as cluster heads. The second types of the sensor nodes are called cluster heads. They have higher energy and communication range than ordinary sensors. It is assumed that all sensor nodes are randomly deployed in the two-dimensional environment.
- The point-to-point communications is considered for each transmitter-receiver pair in the network. In each cluster, there are single-hop and multi-hop data transmission, so

that the nodes which are farther away from the cluster head use multi-hop transfer to transmit sensed data and the single-hop transfer is used for the nodes closer to the cluster head.

- When an event occurs or data aggregates from all sensors in the sensor network, the collected data is sent to the cluster head and finally, to the control centre.

Energy Model

The energy model for transmitting and receiving one bit of data is assumed to be in accordance with the LEACH energy model [24]. Suppose the distance between the transmitter and the receiver is d in the energy model mentioned above. If the distance between the transmitter and the receiver (i.e., d) is more than d_0, the multi-path model (with path loss coefficient 4) will be used. Otherwise, the open space model (with pass loss coefficient 2) is used:

$$E_{TX}(l,d)=E_{TX-elec}(l)+E_{TX-apm}(l,d)=\begin{cases} lE_{TX-elec}+l\varepsilon_{mp}d^2; d\langle d_0 \\ lE_{TX-elec}+l\varepsilon_{fd}d^4; d\rangle d_d \end{cases} \tag{1}$$

Where $E_{TX\text{-}elec}$ is the required energy for activating the electrical circuit, ε_{mp} and ε_{fd} are the activating energy for power amplifiers in multi-path and open space cases, respectively. A more general form of (1) with constant coefficients p and q is represented as:

$$E_{TX}(l,d)=p+qd^{\alpha}. \tag{2}$$

At the receiver, the consumed energy for receiving one bit of information equals to:

$$E_{RX}(l)=E_{RX-elec}(l)=E_{elec}(l)=p. \tag{3}$$

In the asymmetrical networks, the initial energy of super nodes is assumed to be several times greater than the initial energy of typical or ordinary sensors.

Method of Clustering

In asymmetric hierarchical WSNs, many sensors with higher capabilities than the sensor network are distributed. The cluster heads choose can identify their location and give this information (i.e., their location information) to other network nodes. Each node relatively knows its area and this is due to the cluster heads in the network. Each non-cluster head node decides to which cluster it belongs by comparing the received signal strength from all neighboring cluster heads. Then, the number of hops is recorded in a look-up table. Now, every sensor knows its distance to the cluster head. Meanwhile, the sensor containing data must have information from other neighbour sensors to transmit data through the best and the shortest path. If the selected path is banned for any reason, an alternative route will be selected. This route must have the minimum number of hops. Figure 4 shows graphical examples of the clustering process for a network of size 50 and 100 nodes.

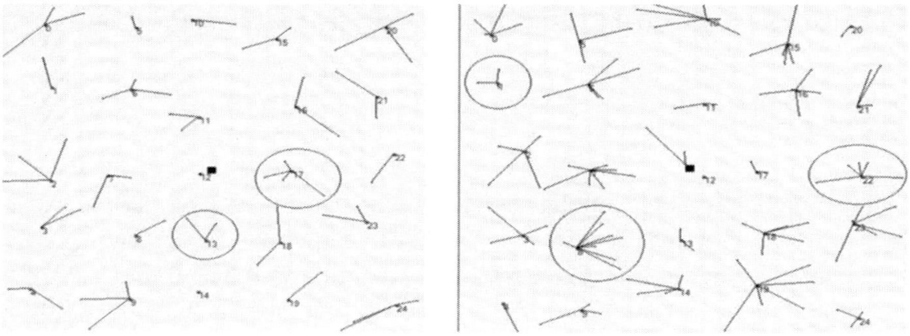

Network with 50 Nodes Network with 100 Nodes.

Figure 4. Graphical Examples of the Clustering Process.

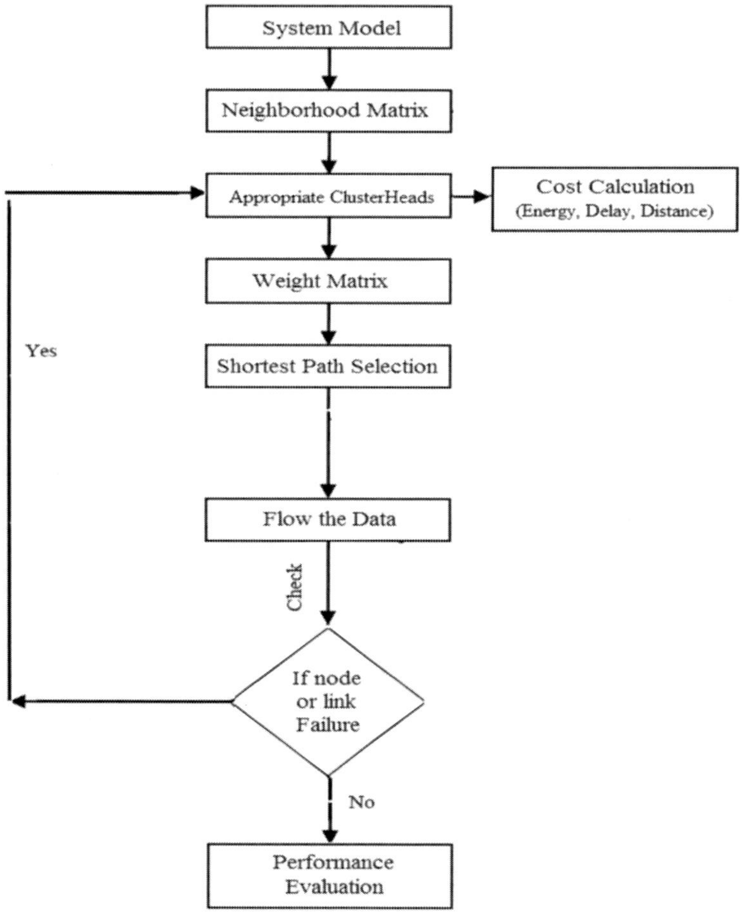

Figure 5. Flowchart of Mutipath-GT Routing.

The Proposed Routing Algorithm

Taking the paths weight matrix and path costs (based on the distance and energy) into account and applying the Floyd algorithm to build the shortest path matrix, the minimum delay for data transmission is achieved. This process continues until the remaining energy of sensor nodes in the selected path is not enough to participate in routing. In this condition, the proposed algorithm finds an alternate route to transmit information to the corresponding cluster head. Two types of WSNs can be considered according to their functionality: event-based and data aggregation WSNs. If a node dies, the network has to find an alternate route for data transmission to the cluster head. The goal of the proposed routing is not on delivering data to the cluster heads with the minimum number of hops. Although having an excess hop increases delay, this additional hop sometimes guarantees stability and network lifetime. The flowchart of the proposed routing algorithm is shown in Figure 5.

Performance Metrics

To evaluate performance of the routing algorithm in a WSN, the following parameters are chosen:

- *Delay:* The average number of hops required to transmit information from the sensor nodes to the cluster heads and finally to the control centre is defined as the delay. We have to follow the path with the minimum delay. It should be noted that averaging is done in each cluster.
- *Total Remaining Energy:* It is defined as the total unused energy level of nodes in the network.
- *Lifetime:* Network lifetime is the time in which all sensors in the network are connected. Hence, the sensed data can be transmitted from sensors to the cluster heads and finally, to the control centre.

CONCLUSION

In this chapter, some delay-minimization routing protocols in wireless sensor networks are studied. First, routing challenges in wireless sensor networks are presented. Then, routing algorithms are classified into different categories in terms of network structures and protocol operations. Finally, a routing algorithm minimizing end-to-end delay or the number of hops is proposed. In this algorithm, nodes energy constraints and data transmission delay constraints for sending packets are considered. In the data aggregation case, energy-aware routing algorithm reduces delay and decreases energy consumption simultaneously. In event detection case, the routing algorithm in which the nodes energy constraint is not considered, the delay minimization and optimizes energy consumption; however, it reduces the network lifetime. Hence in delay-sensitive applications, the energy-aware routing algorithm can be used with some acceptable delay.

REFERENCES

[1] Khan, Z.H., Catalot, D. G., Thiriet, J.M., 2009. Hierarchical Wireless Network Architecture for Distributed Application. *Proceedings of the 5th International Conference on Wireless and Mobile Communications*. 70-75.

[2] Zhang, J., Shankaran, R., Orgun, M. A., Varadharajan, V., Sattar, A., 2010. A Trust Management Architecture for Hierarchical Wireless Sensor Networks. *Proceedings of the 35th Annual IEEE Conference on Local Computer Networks*. 264-267.

[3] Zhang, Y., Yang, L. T., Chen, J., (2010). *RFID and Sensor Networks: Architectures, Protocols, Security and Integrations*. 1st ed., Taylor & Francis Group.

[4] Quan, S. G., Kim, Y. Y., 2008. Fast Data Aggregation Algorithm for Minimum Delay in Clustered Ubiquitous Sensor Networks. *Proceedings of the International Conference on Convergence and Hybrid Information Technology*. 327-333.

[5] Banu, A. J., Velayutham, R., 2013. Secure Communication in Wireless Sensor Networks using AES Algorithm with Delay Efficient Sleep Scheduling, *Proceedings of the International Conference on Emerging Trends in Computing, Communication and Nanotechnology*, 706-711.

[6] Kanhere, S. K., Goudar, M., Wadhai V. M., 2012. End-To-End Delay Optimization in Wireless Sensor Network (WSN). *International Journal of Smart Sensors and Ad Hoc Networks*. 1, *3*, 2248-9738.

[7] Guo, P., Jiang, T., Zhang, Q., Zhang, K., 2012. Sleep Scheduling for Critical Event Monitoring in Wireless Sensor Networks. *IEEE Transactions on Parallel and Distributed Systems*. 23, 2, 345-352.

[8] Kim, J., Lin, X., Shroff, N. B., Sinha, P., 2010. Minimizing Delay and Maximizing Lifetime for Wireless Sensor Networks with Anycast, *IEEE/ACM Transactions on Networking*. 18, *2*, 515-528.

[9] Kher, A., Khatavkar, A., Bamb, S., Sadaphal, V. P., 2010. Efficient Algorithms to Compute Sleep Schedules Resulting in Minimum Delay Routes in Sensor Networks. *Proceedings of the International Conference on High Performance Computing*. 1-9.

[10] Jiang, Z., Wu, J., Ito, R., 2010. A Metric for Routing in Delay-Sensitive Wireless Sensor Networks. *Proceedings of the 7th International Conference on Mobile Ad hoc and Sensor Systems*. 272-281.

[11] Lu, G., Sadagopan, N., Krishnamachari, B., Goel, A., 2005. Delay Efficient Sleep Scheduling in Wireless Sensor Networks. *Proceedings of the 24th Annual Joint Conference of the IEEE Computer and Communications Societies*. 4, 2470-2481.

[12] Yao, M., Chuang, L., Tian, Y., Wu, L., Chen, Y., 2012. Energy and Delay Minimization in Cluster-Based Wireless Sensor Networks. *Proceedings of the International Conference on Green Computing and Communications*. 588-594.

[13] Xu, X. H., Li, M., Mao, X. F., Tang, S., Wang, S. G., 2010. A Delay Efficient Algorithm for Data Aggregation in Multi-hop Wireless Sensor Networks. *IEEE Transactions on Parallel and Distributed Systems*. 22, *1*, 163-175.

[14] Al-Karaki, J. N., Kamal, A. E., 2004. Routing Techniques in Wireless Sensor Networks: A Survey. *IEEE Transactions on Wireless Communications*. 11, *6*, 6-28.

[15] Abbasi, A. A., Younis, M., 2007. A Survey on Clustering Algorithms for Wireless Sensor Networks. *Computer Communications Journal*. 30, *14*, 2826-2841.

[16] Culler, D., Estrin, D., Srivastava, M., 2004. Overview of Sensor Networks. *IEEE Computer*. 37, *8*, 41-49.

[17] Akyildiz, I. F., Su, Y., Sankarasubramaniam, Y., Cayirci, E., 2002. Wireless Sensor Networks: A Survey. *The International Journal of Computer and Telecommunications Networking*. 38, *4*, 393-422.

[18] Heinzelman, W. R., Kulik, J., Balakrishnan, H., 1999. Adaptive Protocols for Information Dissemination in Wireless Sensor Networks. *Proceedings of the 5th Annual ACM/IEEE International Conference on Mobile Computing and Networking*. 174-185.

[19] Stojmenovic, I., Olariu, S., (2005). Data-centric Protocols for Wireless Sensor Networks. Handbook of Sensor Networks. 1st ed., Wiley & Sons. Inc.

[20] Perrig, A., Szewczyk, R., Wen, V., Culler, D., Tygar, J.D., 2002. SPINS: Security Protocols for Sensor Network. *Wireless Networks*. 8, *5*, 521-534.

[21] Chen, M., Leung, V. C. M., Mao, S., Xiao, Y., Chlamtac, I., 2009. Hybrid Geographic Routing for Flexible Energy-Delay Tradeoff. *IEEE Transactions on Vehicular Technology*. 58, *9*, 4976-4988.

[22] He, T., Stankovic, J., Lu, C., Abdelzaher, T., 2003. SPEED: A Stateless Protocol for Real-time Communication in Sensor Networks. *Proceedings of the 23rd International Conference on Distributed Computing System*. 46-55.

[23] Felemban, E., Lee, C. G., Ekici, E., 2006. MMSPEED: Multipath Multi-SPEED Protocol for QoS Guarantee of Reliability and Timeliness in Wireless Sensor Networks. *IEEE Transactions on Mobile Computing*. 5, *6*, 738–754.

[24] Heinzelman, W. R., Chandrakasan, A., Balakrishnan, H., 2000. Energy-efficient Communication Protocol for Wireless Microsensor Networ*ks. Proceedings of the 33rd Annual Hawaii International Conference on System Sciences.*

[25]] Lindsey, S., Raghavendra, C. S., 2002. PEGASIS: Power Efficient Gathering in Sensor Information Systems. *Proceedings of the IEEE Aerospace Conference*, 3, 1125-1130.

[26] Manjeshwar, A., Agrawal, D. P., 2001. TEEN: A Routing Protocol for Enhanced Efficiency in Wireless Sensor Networks. *Proceedings of the 15th International Parallel and Distributed Processing Symposium*. 2009-2015.

[27] Chen, Y., Nasser, N., 2008. Enabling QoS Multipath Routing Protocol for Wireless Sensor Networks. *Proceedings of the IEEE International Conference on Communication.* 2421-2425.

[28] Kavitha, C., Viswanatha, K. V., 2009. A Hybrid Reliable Routing Technique (HRR) for Wireless Sensor Network. *International Journal of Computer Sciences and Network Security*. 9, *3*, 35-39.

[29] Wang, Y. H., Tsai, C. H., Mao, H. J., 2006. HMRP: Hierarchy-Based Multipath Routing Protocol for Wireless Sensor Networks. *Tamkang Journal of Sciences and Engineering*. 9, *3*, 255-264.

[30] Pratheema, S., Srinivasagan, K.G., Naskath, J., 2011. Minimizing End-to-End Delay using Multipath Routing in Wireless Sensor Networks. *International Journal of Computer Application*. 21, *5*, 20-26.

In: Recent Advances in Ad Hoc Networks Research
Editor: Natarajan Meghanathan
ISBN: 978-1-63321-337-1

Chapter 7

TARGET COVERAGE IN WIRELESS SENSOR NETWORKS

Ali Shokouhi Rostami[1]***, Farahnaz Mohanna***[2]***, Hengameh Keshavarz***[3,*] ***and Marzieh Badkoobe***[4]
[1,2,3] University of Sistan and Baluchestan, Zahedan, Iran
[4] Science and Research Branch, Islamic Azad University, Kerman, Iran

ABSTRACT

One of the most important goals in sensor networks is to prolong the network life time by maintaining quality of service, such as maintaining network connectivity and target coverage. Target coverage algorithms ensure all separate targets are covered by the sensor network. In this chapter, the coverage problem in sensor networks is introduced and different coverage algorithms are classified and explained. Then, performance of some point coverage algorithms are analyzed and compared with each other in terms of energy consumption and network lifetime.

Keywords: Target Coverage, Energy Efficiency, Lifetime

INTRODUCTION

The interest in wireless sensor networks (WSNs) has been increased in the recent years. A wireless sensor network consists of many (even thousands) small sensor nodes. These sensors have great capabilities, despite the small size and limited energy that are often applied with irreplaceable batteries. Sensor networks are used to monitor an area in order to detect mobility, record changes in temperature, pollution and so on [1].

A wireless sensor node is a small electronic device having a limited energy source and generally, it is not possible to replace or to recharge the batteries. The main goal in sensor

* Department of Communication Engineering, University of Sistan & Baluchestan, Zahedan, Iran; Email: keshavarz@ece.usb.ac.ir.

networks is on maintaining coverage and network connectivity. Given resource constraints and environmental conditions, Nodes arrangement strategies have a great impact in efficient energy consumption, computation complexity reduction and provide high degrees of coverage. Another important issue in coverage is on maintaining connectivity. In other words, at least one single-hop direct connection or multi-hop indirect connection should exist between any two sensors [2].

One of the critical issues in wireless sensor networks is the network lifetime because the sensor network is usable until the sensor nodes are able to communicate sensed data. Much of the energy is consumed during the sensing and communications, so balanced management of energy and sensors scheduling are effective in extend network lifetime. In some situations, the nodes are located in the environment by plane because there is no physical access to the environment; therefore, the nodes are placed in the environment completely random. This random deployment makes the coverage problem difficult [3].

In this chapter, first of all, the coverage problem in WSNs is introduced and its challenges are discussed. Second, the network coverage is mathematically presented and classified. Then, point coverage is addressed and energy-aware point coverage algorithms are studied in homogeneous and heterogeneous networks respectively. Finally, performance of some point coverage algorithms is compared with each other.

COVERAGE IN WIRELESS SENSOR NETWORKS

There are different views about the quality of service in WSNs. From the viewpoints of majority, service quality has been divided into two categories: application-specific quality of service and network quality of service [4]. In application-specific quality of service, parameters such as coverage, measurement error, and optimal number of active sensors are considered as the parameters of quality of service. Due to variation in the number and types of sensors and their applications, several concepts are presented for coverage. In WSNs, sensors are deployed in the network in a specific way in order to provide the maximum coverage and an acceptable quality of service. Possibly, there are a number of blind spots in the network that are not monitored by any sensor. These points can be identified easily by measuring the coverage of the network. Hence, evaluation criteria of controlling coverage are essential for checking optimality and effectiveness of coverage algorithms. In this section, challenges of coverage algorithms will briefly be described from different perspectives [5].

Challenges of the Coverage Problem

Coverage Ability

The size of coverage area and the target points are main criteria to measure coverage control algorithms. The main purpose of the sensor network is to understand environment, monitor environment, and acquire and transmit data efficiently. The sensor network can explore the coverage ability of the area and the target using these data [5].

Network Connectivity

As the sensor network is non-infrastructure and is constructed of a large number of sensor nodes, nodes are self-organized (nodes are separately organized). Each node collects data by itself and sends them to the base station in a single hop or multiple hops (directly or indirectly). Nodes connectivity ensures that each node is by itself able to communicate with other nodes. It also determines the monitoring, sensing, communicating and other standards of the QOS accurately [5].

Network Survival Time

In sensor networks, sensors have resource constraint. As there is huge number of nodes in a network and environmental conditions are very sophisticated, there is no possibility to replace or recharge batteries of failure nodes. Therefore, optimum usage of limited energy and extend of the network lifetime are important indicators for evaluating the performance of the coverage algorithms [5].

Algorithm Complexity

One of the most important standards in determining optimality of the coverage control algorithm is complexity of the algorithm. The more appropriate complexity of algorithm can lead to more positive effects on the optimality of the algorithm [5].

Network Dynamics

In some of the applications of sensor networks such as the monitoring of the moving targets, dynamic characteristics of the network should be considered in the algorithm. These characteristics are one of the main standards in evaluating coverage control algorithm [5].

Scientific and Mathematical Models of Coverage in WSNs

In order to understand the physical system of a sensor network in the field of coverage, its scientific model will be presented [6].

Sensing Model

Experimental observations show that the quality of the sensed data by the sensors will gradually be increased with reducing distance. The sensitivityof a sensor S_i at the point P can be modelled as follows:

$$P(S_i, P) = \frac{\lambda}{d(S_i, P)^{\alpha}} \quad (1)$$

λ and α are parameters depending on the sensor and $d(S_i, P)$ is the Euclidean distance between the node and the target point. As the sensitivity rate of sensors is quickly decreasing with increasing distance, a sensing range is defined for each sensor. A simple model is the binary disc model by which a node can only observe points that lie within its sensing range and doesn't have access to any other point beyond this range. In this model, the sensing range of each node is confined a circle around the node with the radius of R_s that is usually referred to as the sensing radius.

Another model is the probabilistic sensing model shown in Figure 1 that is the advanced version of the previous model. In this model, the quantity R_u is defined. When $R_u < R_s$, the probability of detection of a target that is in the distance less than or equal $(R_s - R_u)$ by a node is 1. (i.e., a target whose distance to the node is less than $(R_s - R_u)$ will definitely be detected by the node). Targets that are in the distance greater than or equal to (R_s+R_u) cannot be identified. If targets are in the range of (R_s+R_u, R_s-R_u) they can be detected by the probability of P. The quantity R_u is a measure of uncertainty in detecting the sensor [6].

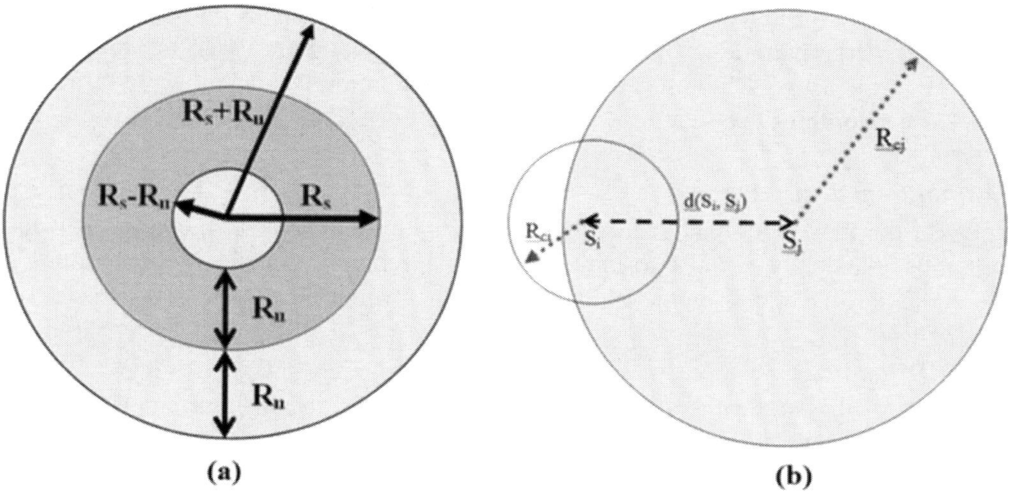

Probabilistic Sensing Model Communication Model.

Figure 1. Probabilistic Sensing Model and Communication Model.

Let $X = \{S_i, i = 1, 2, 3, \ldots, k\}$ be the set of the network nodes whose sensing ranges cover the point $P(x_i, y_i)$.The total coverage of the point P can be defined as follows:

$$C_{x_1y_1}(x) = 1 - \prod_{i=1}^{k}\left(1 - C_{x_1y_1}(S_i)\right) \tag{2}$$

As the amount of C_{x1y1} presents the probability of point coverage, $1-C_{x1y1}(S_i)$ shows the probability of the point not covered by S_i. The coverage probability can be calculated using the following formula:

$$C_{x1y1}(S_i) = \begin{cases} 0 & R_s + R_u \le d(S_i, P) \\ e^{-\omega\alpha^{\beta}} & R_s - R_u \le d(S_i, P) < R_s + R_u \\ 1 & R_s - R_u \ge d(S_i, P) \end{cases} \tag{3}$$

In the above formula, $\alpha = d(S_i, P) - (R_s - R_u)$, ω and β are parameters measuring the probability of target detection that is located in a definite distance from the sensor node.

Communication Model

Experimental studies show that radio links between sensors that have a low-power sensing is extremely unreliable. Thus, it is very challenging to provide a realistic modeling of radio communication channels. The simplest of communication models referred to as the binary disk model, it is assumed that each node S_i can only able to communicate with sensors whose distance from itself is less than a certain threshold. This threshold is referred to as communication radius and is shown by R_{ci}.

The power of the received signal of the sensors can be calculated using the following formula:

$$P_r = \frac{P_S}{d(S_i, S_j)^\eta} \quad (4)$$

where P_r is the power of the received signal, P_s is the power of the transmitted signal, $d(S_i, S_j)$ is the Euclidean distance between sender and receiver, and η is the path-loss exponent lying between 2 to 6 based on environmental conditions [4].

COVERAGE CLASSIFICATION IN WIRELESS SENSOR NETWORKS

In wireless sensor networks, coverage is one of the fundamental issues related to the quality of the service in the network. Sensors are shown to achieve the maximum coverage of the network. The coverage problem in sensor networks can be classified as follow [5]:

Classification Based on Applications

The sensor network has extreme applications in military and non-military forces. Thus, coverage is used for a wide range of applications. The coverage control problem not only includes the meaning of a simple coverage but also relates closely to energy saving in communications, path planning, reliable communications, and special applied targeting specific applications. Based on the application attributes of the sensing, a novel classification can be used for the network coverage.

Energy Saving Coverage

Sensors of the sensing network are very small and have limited resources of energy. That is why in large scale networks, the optimal use of energy is one of the most important research issues that can directly affect the overall survival of the network. In this model, in order to increase the lifetime of the network, nodes are rotated between active and sleep modes (they rotate between these two states). Additionally, one of the requirements of the coverage condition in the network is maximizing the number of nodes rotating between these two states [3].

The Fence Coverage

One of the problems in the coverage of the sensing network is the fence coverage. The goal in such a coverage control is on finding one or more of the path which is from the start position of *S* to the left position recorded as *D*, so that each path has sensors with different capabilities or different coverage models to monitor targets. Based on these different models, fence coverage is divided into two categories: "the worst coverage and best-case situation" and "exposed through" [5].

Connectivity Coverage

Connectivity coverage is one of the most important issues related to coverage in WSNs. Connectivity coverage problem aims to solve how it is possible to satisfy a certain degree of coverage and communication connectivity requirements simultaneously [7]. Based on the connectivity requirements, connectivity coverage are divided into two categories:

- Connectivity coverage in the set of active sensors. In this case, the rotation mechanism of active nodes is used.
- The network connectivity

CLASSIFICATION BASED ON TARGET CHARACTERISTICS

Static Target Coverage

The coverage problem in this state is very common and simple. For example, monitoring forest fire or controlling temperature are of most important considerations in designing comprehensiveness of coverage and in processing the coverage of the redundant sensors [8].

Dynamic Target Coverage

In this case, targets are able to move and replace and the sensing network is constructed to cover these targets. Due to the complexity of the target movement including uniform motion, variable, linear motion, and curvilinear motion, the capability of the node and the ability to cover the region and targets need different requirements. In algorithms designed for coverage, all these requirements should be considered [5].

Classification Based on Coverage Types

Different applied programs require different degrees of coverage. In a simple word, the coverage degree at a specific point depends on the number of the sensors whose coverage range involves that coverage point. There are different factors that should be considered in network coverage.

Different types of network coverage shown in Figure 2 are as follow [9]:

- ***Area coverage***: The main aim of the sensor network in the area coverage is the monitoring and the full coverage of an area. All points of the area should be covered.
- ***Point coverage***: The aim of this model is to monitor a set of points whose location is known. In the model of the point coverage, the exact position of sensors should be determined in order to ensure that a finite number of static targets can be efficiently covered. In general, it is a specific case of the region coverage in which there may be a large number of sensor nodes.
- ***Target coverage***: There are a number of targets with known positions which are continuously monitored. A large number of sensors are located near the target.
- ***Barrier coverage***: This coverage is related to detection of sensors movement across a barrier. This coverage has many applications in applied programs to detect the intruder in crossing a barrier or entering into a protected area.

Point Coverage

In point coverage, the goal is on covering a set of points. The coverage approach can be divided into two groups based on the sensors deployment: random and deterministic which a represented as model 1 and model 2 respectively [9]:

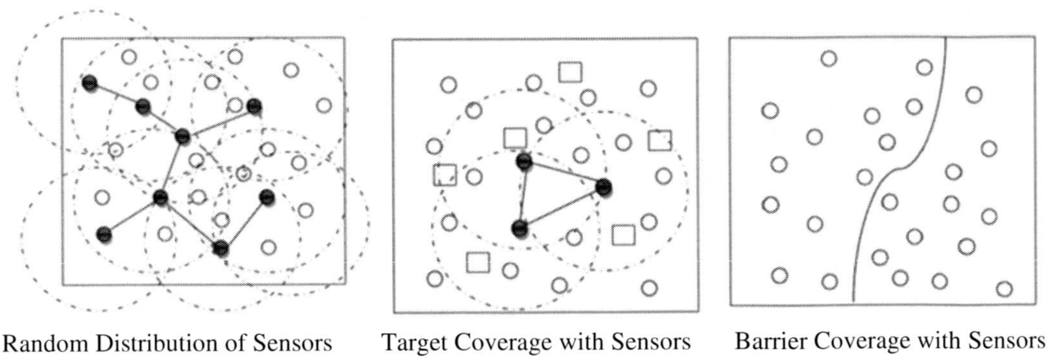

Figure 2. Different Types of Coverage with Sensors.

- ***Model 1***: In this model, nodes are randomly deployed in the area and have no prior knowledge about their position. This model can be used in cases where the availability of the area is very difficult such as the battlefield or the dangerous regions [10]. In this model, the aim is to find the maximum disjoint sets. Finding such a set is of meta-heuristic problems. Here, we have a limited number of targets whose positions are known. These targets should be covered [9].
- ***Model 2***: If sensors are located exactly in the desired position, the deployment method will be deterministic. In this model, the minimum number of sensors is determined and their positions are specified [11]. These sensors are deployed in the

area to cover all targets. A probabilistic algorithm is the use of the minimum spanning tree with target points. Then, the position of these nodes will be determined based on this tree [9]. Issues relating to point coverage will be investigated in greater detail in the next section.

Target Coverage

Target coverage problem can be divided into several categories:

1. Target coverage problem with a fixed sensing range
2. Target coverage problem with different sensing range
3. Target coverage problem in directional sensor networks
4. Target area coverage in which sensors not only cover a set of targets, but they can cover a small area coverage and Q-coverage in which each target should be monitored and covered by at least Q sensors [12].

For non-mobile nodes with the uniform distribution, if the probability of detecting a target by a sensor is P_{min}, then the probability of target detection is calculated by n Sensors that are placed around it:

$$P_n = 1 - (1 - p_1)^n \tag{5}$$

where n is the number of sensors deployed around the target and P_1 is the probability of target coverage by a sensor node. P_1 is calculated according to the following formula [13]:

$$P_1 = \frac{\pi d^2}{terrainarea} \tag{6}$$

Definitions of Target Coverage in Symmetrical Sensor Networks

Target Coverage Problem

Assume the positions of some targets are well known for all sensors and these targets should be properly covered and monitored. Many sensors with a random distribution are deployed around these targets. Also there is a base station that collects the sensors data. The information sensed by the sensor is either locally processed by aggregated, sent to the base station. Also assume that the sensors are capable of detecting their locations (GPS) in the network [3].

Assume that s_1, s_2, … s_n, N are the Sensors that are randomly deployed in the environment and s_0 is the position of the base station. Let M targets t_1, t_2, …, t_m that are located in the environment to be covered continuously. Each sensor has an initial energy E and has multiple sensing range r_0, …, r_p in terms of energy consumption e_0, …, e_p. If the Euclidean distance between the sensor s_i and the target t_j is larger than a predefined Sensing range r, we say that s_i can cover the target t_j [14].

The initial energy of sensors is E and its communication radius is R_c and the sensing range is R_s where $R_c \leq R_s$. One sensor uses the amount of e_1 units of energy for sensing and the amount of e_2 units of energy for data transmission and communication per time unit. The base station is located in position S_0 such that it is placed at least in the communication range of one sensor. When sensors are deployed in the environment, they are scheduled for being active and sending their sensed data to the base station. The goal of this network is that the targets are consistently covered.

A sensor node covers a target if the Euclidean distance between the target and sensor node is less than or equal to sensing range of that node, also two sensor nodes can communicate with each other if the Euclidean distance between them is less than or equal to their communication range. One approach to reduce energy consumption and prolong the network lifetime is to divide the sensors into sets such that the sensors of each set cover all targets and there is a path between a sensor Su And the base station for each active sensor node S_u within this set. The network activity is organized into rounds and each set is activated in one round. The length of each round is as long as δ and in each round, only the sensors of the active set are responsible for monitoring targets and transmission sensed data to the base station and the rest of sensors are in the sleep mode [15].

Figure 3 shows an example where there are four sensors and three targets. In this example, assume that the sensing area of each sensor is a disc which the sensor is located in center of it and its radius is equal to the sensing range of the sensor [3]. Coverage communication between sensors and targets are defined as: $S_1 = \{R_1, R_2\}$, $S_2 = \{R_2, R_3\}$, $S_3 = \{R_3, R_1\}$ and $S_4 = \{R_1, R_2, R_3\}$.

Suppose that all sensors have the same energy and In order to model the network lifetime assume that each sensor can be active in a unit time of 1. By this definition, if all sensors are active continuously, the lifetime of network would be 1. The sensors are divided into sets, such as $S_1 = \{S_1, S_2\}$ and $S_1 = \{S_3, S_4\}$. As a result, the network lifetime will be equal to 2.

MSC (Maximum Set Cover)

The set C which is a finite subset of the set R is given. The total is to find the number of subsets cover S_1, S_2, ..., S_p with the time weights t_1 , t_2 , … , t_p in the interval [0 1] such that t_1, t_2, …, t_p is maximized and for each subset S in C, the total weight is at most 1, where 1 is the lifetime of each sensor node. In MSC definition, C is a subset of the sensors and R is a subset of the targets in which each sensor monitors (covering) a set of targets. We want to find the number of sets cover S_1, S_2, …, S_p so that each set cover should be able to cover all the targets itself and maximize the network lifetime $t_1 + t_2 + \ldots + t_p$, where t_j, $j = 1$, ..., p represents the time interval in which the set cover S_j is active. One should keep in mind that even if a sensor node belongs to more than one set, the total time interval of that set cannot be greater than 1. It happens because each sensor node cannot be activated more than once [3].

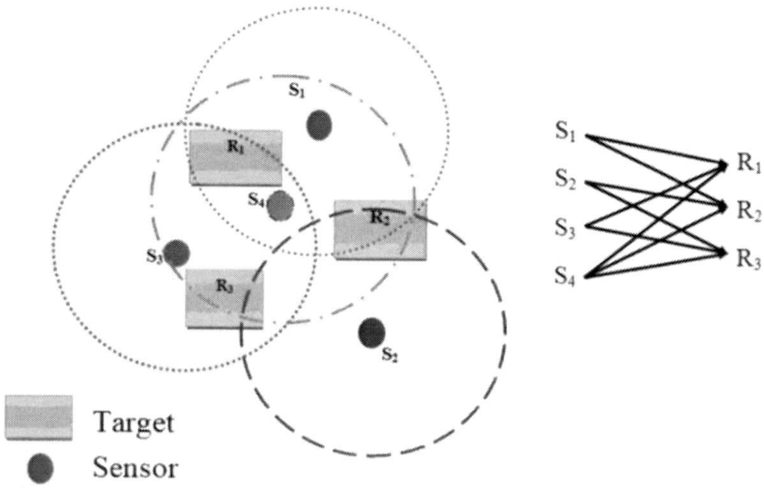

Figure 3. Example of three targets and four sensors.

1-Connected Target Coverage Problem

Assume that *M* targets with known locations are located in an energy constrained sensor network with *N* Sensors. The Sensor Activities must be scheduled because 1) each target at a moment must be covered by at least one sensor 2) There should be a path between each active node to the base station 3) to maximize the network lifetime [15].

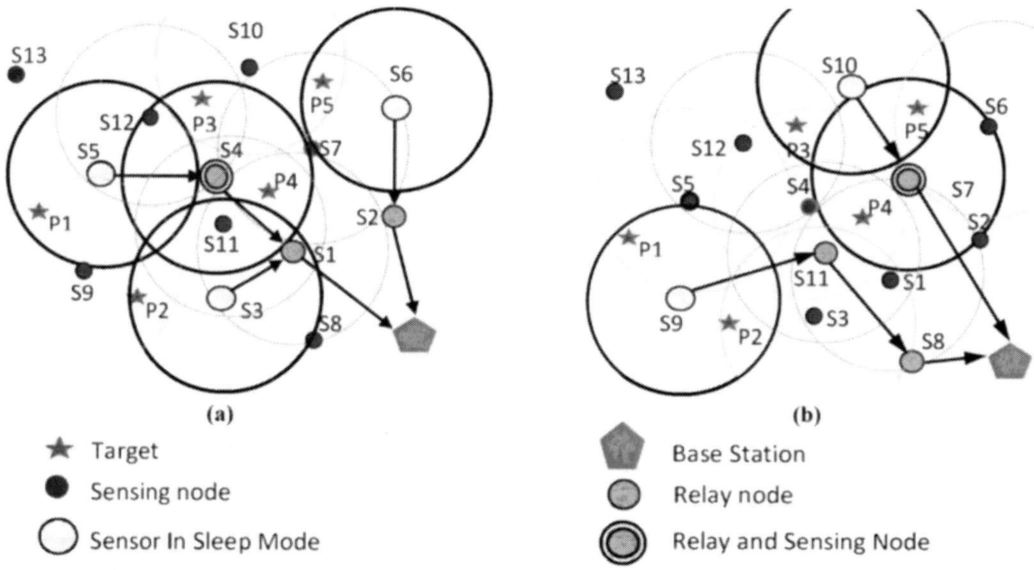

Figure 4. Illustration of the CTC problem. (a) Solution 1; (b) Solution 2.

The CTC problem is shown in Figure 4. In this Figure, there are 13 sensors, 5 targets and 1 sink. The sensors that can cover more than one target are marked with their circle. The solid circles represent active sensors and the rest indicate inactive or relays sensors. The arrow lines show the paths between the sensors and the base station. Two solution (a) and (b) are illustrated in Figures 4 (a) and 4 (b) respectively. In both solutions all the targets are covered by the sensors and there is a path between each active sensor and the base station (each sensor is connected to the BS). This figure shows that only a subset of deployed nodes is sufficient to cover all the targets and different subsets can be used in different rounds [15].

DEFINITIONS OF TARGET COVERAGE IN SENSOR NETWORKS WITH MULTIPLE SENSING RANGES

Each sensor has *P* sensing range. In order to solve this problem, a set cover model is used and only one set at each time are responsible for monitoring targets and the remaining sensors are in sleep mode [14]. We want to express it as a mathematical formula.

1-Multiple Sensing Ranges-Set Cover Problems (MSR-SC)

We have *M* target and *N* sensor nodes with sensing range *P*. We want to determine C_1, C_2, ..., C_k sets which dedicate the sensors and their sensing ranges in each set such that the conditions 1) *K* is maximized and 2) the sensors of each set can cover all of targets [14].

Participation of sensor s_i with sensing range r_k is defined as:

$$B_{ik} = \begin{cases} \dfrac{\theta_{ik}}{e_k} & E_i \geq e_k \\ 0 & E_i < e_k \end{cases} \tag{7}$$

In (7), e_k denotes the energy consumed by a sensor in a round in the sensing range r_k. θ_{ik} is the number of targets that are not covered and the sensor s_i in the sensing range r_k can cover those targets. E_i is the residual energy of the sensor s_i [15].

DEFINITIONS OF TARGET COVERAGE IN ASYMMETRICAL SENSOR NETWORKS

In heterogeneous sensor networks sensors have different capabilities, the sensors may be equipped with more than one sensing unit and the characteristics of each sensing range are different from each other [16].

For example, Figure 5 (a) shows a heterogeneous sensor network. Figure 5 (a) indicates two targets and six sensors that each sensor has a different sensing range. The sensing area of each sensor is shown as circular shape that sensor is placed in the center, with radius is as much as the sensing ranges of the sensor. Figure 5 (b) shows the coverage relationship between the sensing ranges of the sensor and the targets' characteristics.

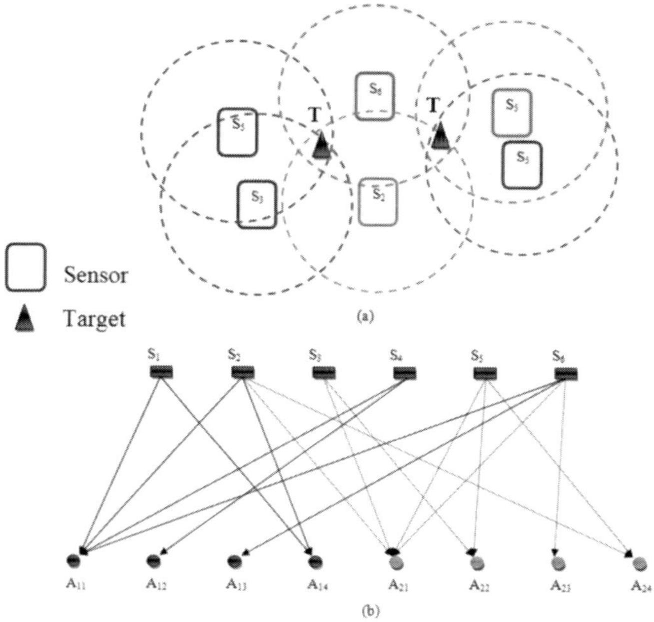

Figure 5. Two Targets and Six Sensors with Multiple Sensing Ranges.

TARGET COVERAGE IN PRIORITY SENSOR NETWORKS

A set of n sensors $S = \{S_1, S_2, \ldots, S_N\}$ have been deployed in the environment to cover m targets $R = \{r_1, r_2, \ldots, r_m\}$ with priority vector $Q = \{q_1, q_2, \ldots, q_m\}$. Priority vector at any moment indicates that the target r_k must be covered by k active sensors $k \geq 1$. Initially, each sensor node S_i has the primary energy i.e., $i = 1, \ldots, n$ [17].

Target Coverage Graph

Target Coverage Graph is a bidirectional graph; TCG = $\{S, L, R\}$, where if the sensor S_i for all $S_i \subseteq S$ is able to cover target r_k for all $r_k \subseteq R$, there is a link between them. The requirements of target Q-Coverage is as follows [17].

At any time, the target r_k should be covered at least by k sensors, $k = 1, 2, \ldots, m$. Figure 6 (a) shows five sensors that are deployed to cover five targets with priority vector $Q = \{1, 1, 1, 1, 1\}$. The initial energy of the set is 100 units for all five sensors and one second coverage of each target costs 1 unit of energy for each sensor. In the beginning (Figure 9 (b)) the nodes S_5 and S_2 are chosen that S_2 see targets R_2, R_3, R_4, R_5 and S_5 covers target R_1. If the coverage is allowed to use coverage pattern 1, S_2 dies after 25 seconds and R_2, R_3, R_4, r_5 lose their coverage, so the network lifetime would be 25 seconds. Similarly, according to pattern 2 (Figure 9 (c)) S_1 covers target R_2, S_3 covers target R_4, S_4 covers target R_5 and S_5 covers targets R_1 and R_3. If we use only the pattern 2, S_5 dies after 50 seconds and targets R_1 and R_3 are removed from the coverage and the network lifetime will be 50 seconds. As shown in Figure 9 (d), we can use both coverage patterns respectively, as follows:

In the first 25 seconds we use pattern 1, if that happens, S_2 is died and S_5 has 75 units of energy. Then, we will continue the coverage based on pattern 2, which does not include sensor S_2. We can use this pattern from 25th to 57.5th second. Then the energy of R_5 is ended and died and R_2 and R_3 lose their coverage. Therefore, the network lifetime will be increased as much as 57.5 seconds. Also after death of S_5, since R_2 and R_3 can be monitored by S_1, we can increase the network lifetime up to 62.5 seconds. Thus, we have shown that with proper scheduling between the patterns, the energy consumption can be reduced, as a result the network lifetime is extended [17].

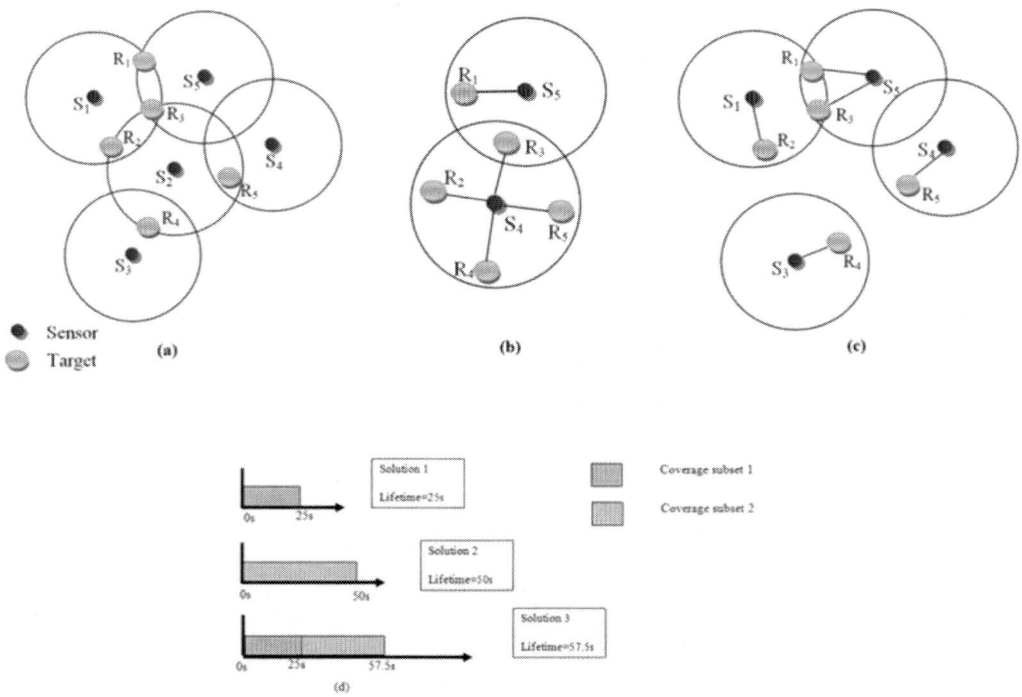

Figure 6. Example to show coverage pattern and use of multiple coverage patterns to extend lifetime.

Definitions of Target Coverage in Directional Sensor Networks

There are many challenges in the protocol design for directional sensor networks. One of the main problems is in monitoring all targets in the environment and forwarding the sensed data to the sink and also maximizing the network lifetime. This problem is known as connected target coverage (CTC) problem [18]. There are two important issues in this problem: First, the sensing angle of the sensors is limited and cannot fully sense the circular area. This feature has created methods to deal with this problem in WSNs [19].

Second, the energy of the sensors is limited and they cannot charge their battery [19, 20]. So a solution is needed while maintaining coverage and network connectivity, considering the energy constraint of the sensors and their sensing limitation. The issue is realized using scheduling algorithms in which a subset of the sensors is active and the rest are inactive and asleep. The sensors that are placed in active set should be connected to the sink and cover all the targets [21]. Figure 7 shows a scheme of scheduling for CTC problem (Connected Target Coverage). Figure 7 shows a network consisting of 11 sensors, 4 targets and one sink. If the sensor covers a target, a sensing link is made between the sensor and the target. In addition, there is a communication link between any two connected sensors [21].

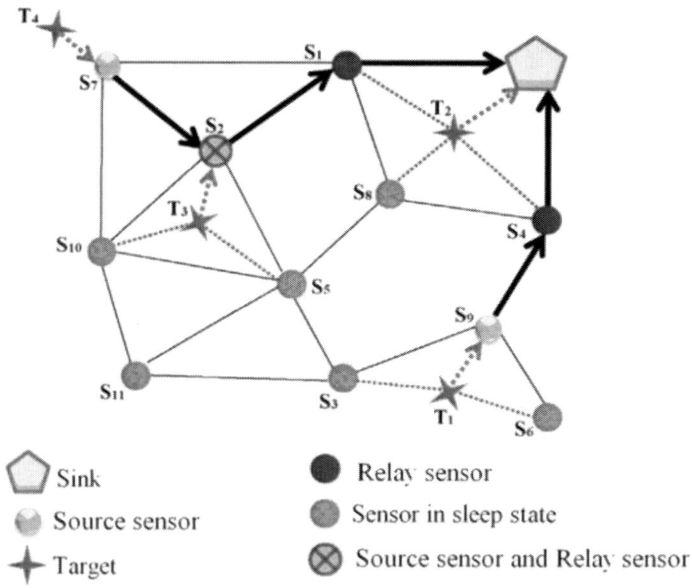

Figure 7. Connected coverage problem.

TARGET COVERAGE IN K-COVERAGE NETWORKS

Consider the following assumption in the network [22]: *Assumption* 1: The interest area is a unit square i.e., its area is equal to 1. *Assumption* 2: All sensors are homogeneous. *Assumption* 3: Boolean sensing model and the sensing radius r is adopted. *Assumption* 4: Sensing radius r is less than 1. *Assumption* 5: Sensors are identically and independently distributed in the area with a uniform distribution.

Based on the above assumptions, each point in the area is covered by K Sensors with the same probability (K-Coverage), so this possibility is named as the possibility of K-Coverage point coverage. The concept of the point coverage can be demonstrated by the following example.

The amount of P_{a1} Shows that the probability of each point is 1-coverage If $P_{a1} = 0.99$. In this situation, if we randomly select 100 points in the area, none of these points will be covered or generally the sensors will cover 99% of the total area. If a point is 1-covarge, there is at least one sensor that monitors the point in its sensing range (or the target is placed within sensors sensing range).

Therefore, $P_{a1} = 1 - \left(1 - \frac{S}{A}\right)^N = 1 - (1 - S)^N$. In general form, P_{ak} shows the probability of being in the *K*-coverage of the area [33].

$$P_{ak} = 1 - \sum_{i=0}^{k-1} C_N^i (S)^i (1 - S)^{N-i} \tag{8}$$

If the sensors are randomly activated with a certain probability P, the following theorem is used to illustrate the probability of being K-coverage of the point [22]:

Theorem: If P is the probability that a sensor is activated and $P_{Ik}(p)$ is the probability that a target is *K*-coverage then we have:

$$P_{ak}(p) = 1 - \sum_{i=0}^{k-1} C_N^i (S)^i (1 - S)^{N-i} \quad k = 1, 2, ..., \ s = \pi r^2. \tag{9}$$

After the sensors were deployed in the environment, these questions must be answered that whether the full coverage is in type of the Boolean? If the entire area is covered, the answer is yes, and if the area is not fully covered, the answer is no. This problem is for point coverage of the number between 0 and 1 (The more covered area to total area, this number would be closer to 1). Thus, the area coverage has a higher sensitivity than the sensor's location [22].

Energy Efficient Algorithms in Point Coverage

Point coverage algorithms can be categorized from different aspects. In some of the algorithms, all sensors have similar conditions, initial energy, sensing ranges and communication ranges. In some algorithms, sensors are hierarchically and with different conditions, energies, and sensing ranges. As a result, point coverage algorithms are classified into point coverage algorithms in homogeneous network and point coverage algorithms in heterogeneous networks [23].

From another perspective, in some algorithms, all sensors are static and stationary in the environment but in some other algorithms, some of the sensors can consume their energy and move toward uncovered targets to cover better, maintain connectivity and standards of service quality. Hence, point coverage algorithms can also be classified as static point coverage algorithms and mobile point coverage algorithms. In some algorithms, all coverage operations are performed locally and in a distributed way. In others, coverage operations are monitored and controlled by a central station. From this perspective, point coverage algorithms can be divided as distributed point coverage algorithms and centralized point coverage algorithms [24].

In this section, some of the point coverage algorithms are presented and dividing theses algorithms as homogeneous and heterogeneous networks.

Point Coverage Algorithms in Homogeneous Networks

In homogeneous sensing networks, all sensors are similar. Sensors are able to sense, process and transmit sensed data.

Energy Aware Trust Coverage Algorithm

In this method, nodes are formed sets so that nodes of a set can cover all targets of the environment. These sets are successively activated. This method prolongs the network lifetime by maximizing the number of these sets [3]. Only sensors of the active set are responsible for monitoring targets and transmitting collected data. Other sensors go into sleep mode to consume less energy. In this method, sensors are allowed to participate in several sets [25].

Network activities are divided into different periods. At the beginning of each period, active nodes are determined based on requirements of the network including area coverage, connectivity maintenance, and optimal energy consumption and so on [3].

Linear Programming Algorithm

The time complexity of this algorithm is $O(N^3)$ where N represents the number of variables. In this method [3]:

C is the set of all n nodes of the network. $C = \{S_1, S_2, \ldots, S_n\}$
R is the set of m targets. $R = \{r_1, r_2, \ldots, r_m\}$

The relation between sensors and targets is as follows: Each sensor that is in a set of targets should be covered. For this purpose, each component of C is modelled as a finite subset of R:

$$C_k = \{\, i \mid sensor\ S_i\ covers\ target\ T_k\}$$

For $j = 1, 2, \ldots, p$ and $i = 1, 2, \ldots, n$
$X_{ij} = 1$ if sensor s_i is in the coverage set of t_j
0 otherwise.
$t_j \in \mathbf{R}$ $0 \le t_j \le 1$; for $j = 1, 2, \ldots, p$ represents the allocated time to each coverage set of S_j.
The optimizing problem can be expressed as follows:
Maximize $t_1 + t_2 + \ldots + t_p$ such that

$$\sum_{j=1}^{p} X_{ij} t_j \le 1 \qquad (10)$$

And for all $r_k \in R$ and $j = 1, 2, \ldots, p$, the following condition should be met.

$$\sum_{i \in C_k} X_{ij} \geq t_j \tag{11}$$

If $s_i \in S_j$, then $X_{ij} = 1$; otherwise $X_{ij} = 0$.

The first condition is based on this principle that dedicated time for each sensor S_i in the coverage set is less than 1 as the lifetime of each sensor is 1. The second condition is based on this principle that each r_k target is covered at least by one s_i in the coverage set. Thus, X_{ij} is not linear, and by introducing Y_{ij}, the problem is formulated again: $Y_{ij} = X_{ij}\, t_j$.

The objective is to maximize $t_1 + t_2 + \ldots + t_p$ such that for all $S_i \in C$, there is

$$\sum_{j=1}^{p} y_{ij} \leq 1 \tag{12}$$

For all $r_k \in R$ and $j = 1, 2, ..., p$, there is:

$\sum_{i \in C_k} y_{ij} \geq t_j$ $Y_{ij} = 0$, or t_j and $Y_{ij} \leq 1$ [3].

The Greedy Meta-Heuristic Algorithm of MSC

In [3], a greedy approach is presented to solve the problem of the smallest coverage set of MSC. In this algorithm, the set of sensors C, the set of targets R and lifetime W are given; $\omega \in (0, 1]$. The algorithm output will be the number of coverage sets.

In this algorithm, a coverage set is constructed at the first step. Then, nodes with remaining energy more than zero are saved in the set of sensors. These sensors can exist in more than one set. In the target set, there are targets that aren't covered and should be covered by coverage set of C_i. At every step, one of the targets of this set should be chosen and should be covered at that step. Contribution rate of sensors can be defined based by several functions. For example, the node covering more uncovered targets and having more remaining energy have largest contribution, nodes with highest contribution are selected. When a sensor is chosen, it will be added to the current coverage set and other targets existing in the set of target will be deleted for the attend at the next step then the next step is started. When all targets are covered, a new coverage set is formed. Using the parameter of W, it will be determined which coverage set is activated. Time complexity of this algorithm is O (im^2n) where i indicate the number of coverage set, n shows the number of sensors, and m is the number of targets.

α-RMSC Algorithm

One important aspect of wireless sensor network's application (WSNs) is the network lifetime. In WSNs, sensors operate under energy constraints and they are usable as long as nodes can sense and communicate. Poor communication links and dangerous environments cause the WSNs to be unreliable [26]. Existing schemes are based on this assumption that the covering state of a sensor is binary: success (covering the targets) or failure (not covering the targets). However, in real WSNs, a sensor can covers targets with a specified probability. In order to improve WSNs reliability, it should be considered that a sensor covers targets with the probability of satisfying the user. In order to solve this problem, the present paper introduces the probability of failure in the target coverage problem to improve and control the system reliability. Additionally, we model this solution as the α-Reliable Maximum Sensor Covers (α-RMSC) problem and design a heuristic greedy algorithm that efficiently calculates the maximal number of α-Reliable sensor covers. To efficiently extend the WSNs lifetime with the predefined probability of failure, only active sensors are responsible to monitor the targets and other sensors go into a low-energy sleep mode. The results of simulation confirm that this algorithm can increase the system reliability without increasing energy consumption [12].

Dynamic Point Coverage in Wireless Sensor Networks

The problem of dynamic point coverage in the wireless sensor network is detecting some moving target points. In this network, nodes are relatively small. In order to accomplish this goal, dynamic scheduling should be run in which nodes are active in some intervals and deactivate in other intervals. Only nodes that can sense target nodes will active at that interval.

This problem can be investigated in different ways. For example, a deployment strategy which with the minimum number of required nodes can be designed [27, 28, and 29]. In rearranging nodes it is assumed that sensors have movement ability [30, 31, 32] and a suitable scheduling strategy is designed to activate and deactivate sensors in different intervals and each sensor can sense its environment only when it is active [33, 34, 35]. The last solution is more efficient than previous algorithms and can deal with changes occurred in the topology of the network. In the algorithm, in each interval, only some sensors are active that leads to prolonging the network lifetime. In all the time of decentralized scheduling, a number of notification messages are exchanged between nodes in on and off states. This approach has two problems: 1. Overhead of sent messages are very high; 2. Massages in the off state should have the ability to receive messages i.e., they cannot turn their receiving antenna off. This makes sensors consume energy even when they are not active [36].

Coverage Based on Learning Automaton

A novel and different solution for the coverage problem of dynamic point in sensing network is presented in [37]. Previous solutions were based on using notification messages that should have been exchanged between nodes in the on and off states. This is required the nodes in off state to have their receiving units cause them to consume high energy. But the proposed method uses a learning automaton in each node to make it capable of learning it's off and on periods based on the target path. There is no need for notification messages.

At the beginning, the algorithm is off for one interval. Learning automaton of each node can perform three actions; Extending, shortening at the interval when the node is off and no change action. At the beginning, extending action has a high probability near to 1. Both shortening and no change actions have a low probability near to 0. As the algorithm goes on, the off period is gradually increased. Therefore, the probability of extending action is reduced to near 0 while the probability of no change action is increased to near 1.

The proposed algorithm works as follows: each node starts its work in on state and senses its environment to detect whether it can sense a target or not. If it doesn't sense any target, it will still remain in the on state until it senses a target in its sensing range. When a target is sensed, the node remains in on state and goes on monitoring. When it cannot sense the target any more, it changes into off state. But before getting off, the algorithm approximates the time of being off using learning automata algorithm. Learning automata of a node chooses one of the operations. Based on the operations chosen, the off time of the node either is increased or is decreased. It may also remain unchanged. Node becomes off for the specified duration and then turns into on. Then, it examines its environment for a short time. Based on the obtained results, the learning automata are either encouraged or punished [37].

Connected Set Covers Algorithms

One of the most important goals in sensor network is to rise Network lifetime while maintaining quality of service, such as maintaining network connectivity and target coverage. Energy consumption occurs in communication and sensing so we can increase the lifetime by energy management [38]. In [39], there are a large number of static and fixed sensor nodes that are deployed in the environment to take care of a few target points. Each of target points can be covered by multiple nodes [39].

[40] and [41] are the first articles in the field of target coverage problem in which the set of sensors must be Disjoint and each sensor only can be a member of one set cover called DSC (Disjoint Set Cover), such that each set can cover all targets. It has been proven that DSC Problem is in class of NP-Complete Problems and its time complexity is 2 or polynomials.

In [41] an algorithm is presented, in which each node can be a member of more than one set. Algorithm in [42] is the first article that provides an approximation algorithm for point coverage. These works only have examined and maintained the coverage and they do not address the connectivity issue.

In [43] the lifetime of algorithm described in [41] is improved, such that maintaining connectivity with the base station is added to the algorithm. They Expressed connected set cover (CSC) problem and showed that it is an NP-Complete algorithm. Then they stated three solutions to solve the problem. The first two solutions are in centralized manner; the former uses integer programming and the latter utilizes a greedy algorithm. The third approach is distributed and centralized.

TPICSC Algorithm

In [39] heuristic method is expressed for solving CSC problem. The time complexity of proposed algorithm was polynomial and it improves the performance compared with greedy-CSC and IP-CSC heuristic methods.

In [39], an algorithm with three phases iterative called TPICSC is provided to solve the CSC problem. This algorithm is implemented in multiple rounds. In each round, the algorithm finds a CSC among available set of sensors. The proposed algorithm consists of three phases in each round: coverage Phase, Connectivity phase, redundancy Reduction phase.

Coverage Phase

The input of coverage Phase is the sets of available sensors and targets. In this phase, the set cover is calculated. The sensors that are placed in this set will cover all targets. The Greedy algorithm is used to calculate the set cover.

Connectivity Phase

After all targets have been covered, this guarantee must be established that all sensors of a set are connected to the base station. The input of this phase is the previous phase set cover and connectivity Graph of network nodes. The goal of this phase is to calculate how the nodes of a set are connected to the base station. If the distance from the node to the base station is less than communication radius of a node, the connection is done in a single hop manner. Otherwise, the interface nodes will be used. The shortest path tree (SPT) is used to solve this problem. If the number of interface nodes is less, data aggregation is increased in the network.

Redundancy Reduction Phase

The input of this phase is computed set that shows the connected set cover. The purpose of this phase is to reduce redundant nodes as far as possible to form the minimum nodes that maintain coverage and establish the connection.

MVRST Algorithm

Coverage Mechanisms are trying to cover an area using the least possible number of sensors. Many of area Coverage mechanisms are addressed the network connectivity issue, however there are limited mechanisms in maintaining network connectivity in field of point coverage [44]. In point coverage mechanism, method to calculate the waiting time that reduces the number of required sensors is provided in [32]. A virtual robust spanning tree (VRST) and a modified virtual robust spanning tree (MVRST) are introduced to maintain connectivity.

In these mechanisms a virtual spanning tree is constructed then the resulting virtual tree is converted to a physical tree. There are different ways to send the sensed data to the base station. Nodes and targets are fixed and we assume that all nodes know the location of all targets and the sink. The algorithm is implemented in multiple rounds. Each round begins with an initial phase. In this phase, each sensor decides whether to be active or inactive until the end of the round. This phase is divided into two stages.

The first stage is the sensing nodes selection. At this stage the Sensors are selected and finally sum of them covers all the targets in the network. The second stage is the relay nodes selection, in this stage some relay nodes are selected to ensure that all chosen nodes have a path to the sink and the network connectivity is established. We explain these two sections in the following [44].

Sensing Nodes Selection

In this phase, a set of efficient nodes is selected to cover all the targets. As this issue is regarded as NP-hard problem, we use a distributed heuristic greedy algorithm to solve it. To convert this algorithm into a distributed heuristic algorithm, each sensor calculates the waiting time based on the residual energy and the number of uncovered targets that this sensor can cover it. This waiting time is used for prioritization and selection of active sensor nodes. The sensors that cover uncovered targets and have more residual energy will get less waiting time and therefore have higher priority. The waiting time for each sensor is calculated according to the following equation:

$$T_u = \left(1 - \alpha \times \frac{E'_u}{E} - \beta \times \frac{|TargetS_u|}{M} \times W_1 - T'_u\right) \tag{13}$$

In the above equation:

E'_u: the residual energy of the sensor S_u; E: the initial energy of the sensors; M: the number of available targets in the network; W_1: the maximum waiting time; α and β: the weights that are assigned to the residual energy and the number of uncovered targets; T'_u: the waiting time that the sensor S_u has passed it; $TargetS_u$: the targets that are located in the sensing rage of a sensor S_u but are still not covered by any other sensor.

When the waiting time of sensor S_u is expired, it is selected as active node and monitors all the targets in set $TargetS_u$. Then, it sends a notification message to its neighbors and informs the targets that will cover. A sensor that passes its waiting time, when receive a notification message from its neighbors, it will update the waiting time and the set $TargetS_u$, if there is at least one common target in their sensing range and the target that entered in the notification message of its neighbors.

Relay Node Selection

After selecting active sensors and covering all the targets, relay nodes should be selected to preserve node connectivity and the sink. VSRT algorithm is similar to prim algorithm, but instead of using edge's cost, it applies a combination of the edge's cost and the vertex's depth (Hop count). Here we suppose that the edge's costs are equal to the Euclidean distance between connecting points. In this algorithm the cost is calculated as follows:

$$Cost = \lambda * hop\ count + (1\text{-}\lambda) * (weight\ of\ path_i) \quad (14)$$

$$\lambda_i = 1 - (h_i/\varepsilon_1) \text{ and } weight\ of\ path_i = weight\ of\ path_j + z_{ij} \quad (15)$$

Hop count: The number of hops to the sink; *weight of path*$_i$: the sum of edge's costs that are connected to the vertex i; ε_1: the depth of the minimum spanning tree, MST (with the maximum hop count); h_i: the depth of vertex i; z_{ij}: the cost of edges between vertices i and j.

In relay node selection, initially we must build a MST based on the targets set and the sink and using Prim algorithm. Consider ε_1 as the depth of the tree. Subsequently the cost of each edge is calculated according to equation 15. For each vertex, the edge with the lowest cost is selected and added to the edge of spanning tree. If the vertex is closer to the sink, its λ value will increase. Vertices that are closer to the sink directly connected to it. In other words, the vertices that are far away from the sink have more options for connecting; as a result the depth of tree will fall [44].

Multiple Target Coverage Algorithms

In sensor networks, scheduling and energy management are as one of the key techniques to extend a network lifetime. In MCTP the target may also be monitored at the same time by multiple nodes, this will result in energy wastage. In [45], an energy-efficient model is provided for scheduling sensors in multiple target coverage and considering the number of targets covered by each node and the redundancy of Overlapped targets, the network lifetime is enhanced. Two scheduling models are offered in this model: optimization and heuristic models [45]. This algorithm works in this way; first the sensors are classified based on the coverage relationship between nodes and targets. Each node can be a member of more than one group and each group consists of minimum nodes that are sufficient to cover all the targets. Then redundancy is disappeared, the redundancy occurs when each target is covered by multiple nodes. This redundancies lead to wasting energy and bandwidth. Finally, the active time of each set is calculated so that the network lifetime is maximized. When active time of a set was determined, each connected set is activated in order. As a result, the network lifetime will be the total active time of all the sets [45].

Coverage Algorithms in Target Tracking

Coverage control is one of the basic technologies in wireless sensor networks. An incomplete coverage Control based on target tracking is called mobile constrained optimal target tracking coverage algorithm (MCOTT) and presented in [46]. In this approach, some of the sensors that were static and already deployed in environment, cooperate with mobile sensors to get optimal coverage based on target trajectory prediction.

In [47], Kumar has provided an optimization algorithm called Prehari that not only is used in the same lifetime, but also applied in more complex cases when the sensors have different lifetimes. However, because the nodes are deployed randomly there may not have enough time in sleep mode to achieve effective full coverage of the nodes that are placed around a moving object. Coverage efficiency in this algorithm depends heavily on the number and location of sensors that are placed in sleep mode.

In [48] static and mobile nodes work together to achieve the required detection performance. Specifically, mobile sensors initially remain stationary, and then when they come to consensus in target detection, the sensors move to the possible target. However, they do not predict the eventual area and as a result there will be a great delay.

A new algorithm named ISOGRID (isometric algorithm based on the GRID) is presented in [54] to deploy mobile nodes. First, after the random deployment of nodes, the algorithm calculates the sensor movement continuously to enhance the coverage and avoids obstacles. It calculates the movement in a way that maintains the connection of the nodes in each iteration. Since nodes are mobile, the network operating cost is high, and when all the nodes are moved together, they cause traffic (congestion).

Coverage Control MCOTT Algorithm

This algorithm takes place in two stages [46]: mobile nodes pre-deployment phase and movable cover adjustment phase.

Nodes Pre-Deployment Phase

We use nodes pre-deployment strategy to use the minimum number of nodes to provide the best coverage for the prediction. Under the conditions of the history mobile trajectory we place further nodes in reasonable conditions to implement more mobile nodes and save more energy.

Definition 1: T is a path to the target $T = (T_0(x_0, y_0) \ldots. T_{i\text{-}1}(x_{i\text{-}1}, y_{i\text{-}1}))$ where $T_i(x_i, y_i)$ is the position coordinates of the target at time i.

Definition 2: The monitored region G is divided into multiple hexagonal grid, each of these grids is called a cell and different cells are labelled as (i, j). $G(i, j)$ is to indicate the number of paths across the cell or area density.

Definition 3: When a cell density is greater than the average density of δ region, it is called a hot spot.

Specifically, for each region we consider the average density of its cell instead of overall density (which is usually higher). Finally, using different cell densities, we assign different colors to each of them. And we show fixed nodes in each cell with red and yellow colors which represents the area's hot spot. Here we introduce an algorithm to calculate the set of hot spot areas:

The region where the density is greater than the average density of δ is added to the set of hot spot areas. After calculating the hot spot regions we deploy the static nodes in a designated coordinates. The history trajectory for deploying static nodes is shown in Figures 8 and 9.

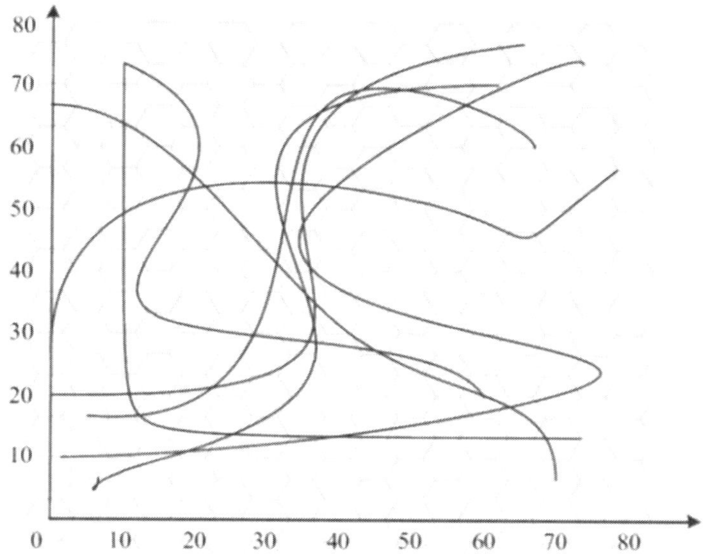

Figure 8. History trajectory for target.

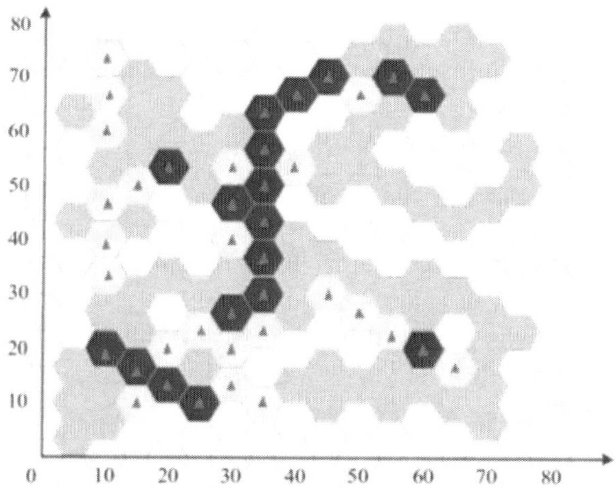

Figure 9. Static nodes deployment.

Mobile Coverage Adjustment

In this approach, the static nodes are pre-deployed and cooperate with mobile nodes to obtain optimize coverage based on the anticipated direction. Simulation results show that this method has a higher coverage rate and lower energy consumption and greater longevity in comparison with previous methods.

Target Coverage in Wireless Mobile Sensor Networks

The detection accuracy can be demonstrated by a probability distribution. Since the nodes are randomly deployed in the environment, some goals are supervised by a small number of sensors, while some other targets are monitored by a large number of sensors [49]. In applications that require full coverage and least accuracy, one node may not be able to fully cover an event. In this case, two or three nodes are needed to work together and completely cover the target. In addition, all nodes must be connected to the base station and send its data to the base station. This algorithm sacrifices part of the energy to move nodes to new locations, this causes the accuracy to reach the desired level. In order to extend longevity, the monitoring will be divided into several rounds and in each round there is a need to ensure that the network connection will be maintained. Furthermore, since the network lifetime is strongly dependent on the number of rounds, we present two models for reintegration of the nodes which improves the performance by balancing the number of sensors in high-density areas (areas that have been heavily covered) and a low - density areas (areas that are poorly covered [13].

A comparison between the model and the binary detection has been made in [50]. Through stimulating the authors concluded that in the region coverage using probabilistic models, there is greater accuracy than the binary models.

A protocol based on maximizing the degree of coverage is presented in [51] which could be achieved by minimizing the number of active nodes. Finding the minimum number of nodes for complete coverage as desired for each region is presented in [52]. The authors also presented a formula to describe the likelihood of favorable coverage by k sensors. In [53] the goal is to deploy the minimum number of sensors so that they are deployed in a distributed manner and increase the possibility of coverage. A number of possible approaches for solving the coverage problem are presented in [54]. This approach divided the sensors into two categories: active and inactive which are aimed to reduce the number of activated sensors.

Point Coverage Algorithms in Heterogeneous Networks

In asymmetric networks, the sensors have lower communication radius that is why they cannot directly send their data to the base station, so we use the super nodes [55].

Super nodes have more energy, processing power and wider communication radius than ordinary nodes. All nodes cannot be connected directly to super nodes, in such conditions; they send their data through relay nodes. Optimal selection of relay nodes and considering the residual energy of relay nodes are one of the most important parts in network design. By optimal selection of nodes the number of transmissions is reduced and the network lifetime increased.

For this purpose, in [55], an energy aware routing algorithm is presented in sensor networks. Many researchers have been done in the field of energy-aware algorithms and power consumption optimization. B. Carbunar and colleagues developed a method that decreases energy consumption by finding location of the sensors and reducing their overlap areas [56]. In [57], an approach is proposed to access to coverage that is used when there is an overhead and high computational cost to increase productivity. In [58], an approach is provided that reduces energy consumption at the border of covered area In order to decrease energy consumption.

In [59], an approach is mentioned based on genetic algorithm to reduce the number of active nodes and therefore decrease energy consumption. Uniform distribution of the nodes in this approach is one advantage of this approach compared with other approaches. In [46], an approach is suggested that increases the number of clusters in order to extend the energy lifetime. In this approach, each node can be a member of more than one cluster in order to increase the network lifetime.

In [60], a clustering approach is presented based on the maximum delay, power consumption in relay nodes and the cluster size. In This algorithm an overlap tree is built and the cluster head is its root. In [61], a sensor network is hierarchically clustered in order to reduce energy consumption in which the consumed energy of data transmission and communication between nodes and the base station is going down by allocation of a cluster heads.

Point Coverage Energy Aware Algorithms

In [62], a hierarchical clustering algorithm called DEEG is proposed which aims to reduce energy consumption caused by communication within the network and balancing “load” among the nodes. System energy consumption is composed of 3 parts 1 - sensor 2 - process 3 - send and receive. Among these, sending and receiving usually is accounted for greater part of energy consumption. In [62], by data aggregation technique using hierarchical clustering, the amount of data sent into the network is reduced which in results energy consumption is decreased.

This algorithm is based on three principles. 1 - Selecting the cluster heads with the network uniform distribution. 2 - Reducing energy consumption in each round. 3 - Ability to handle asymmetric networks. In [62], each node saves its single hop neighbors and their residual energy in each round. It gets a relation of possibility of being a cluster heads based on the average energies of the neighbors and sensor nodes and network coverage. In some cases in does not lead to balancing energy in network and some of the nodes may quickly use their energy up.

In [63], the EDTC method is provided. EDTC is based on the nodes priority. This priority is based on the sensing Capability of the node including the location and the number of monitored targets and the Residual energy. According to the authors these two parameters have not been evaluated logically.

In [64], the ILP method is described. This method is a way to solve a NP-Complete problem that requires a lot of computations and almost it is not feasible. Thus, some innovative methods are used to achieve its solution. Each round has two phases; initial phase and sensing phase. At first, active sensors are chosen in each round and do sensing until the end of the round.

The telecommunication complexity is defined as the number of packets transmitted by telecommunication. If W is the maximum number of single hop neighbors and N is the Number of sensors, the telecommunication complexity of the algorithm is $O(NW)$. The time of initial phase is 8 seconds and the time of sensing phase is ten in a round. The results is averaged in several iterations. The power consumption in communication and computation has been ignored.

As clearly stated, the residual energy and the sensing capability are two remarkable parameters in selection of on nodes sets in each round. The sensing capability is calculated equation 16.

$$SA_i = \sum_{m=1}^{1\sigma il} \frac{N}{NS(\sigma_i^m)} \tag{16}$$

In this equation, N is the total number of the sensors; M is the total number of the targets and $NS(\sigma_i^m)$ shows the number of sensors which are common in detection of the target m with node i. The priority p is determined through relation 17.

$$E_i = \left\lceil \frac{\in_i - 2}{\sigma} \right\rceil \quad Z = NS(\sigma_i^m)$$

$$p_i = \frac{(SA_i + \in_i) \times \left[(SA_i - 1 - \in_i) \times \sigma + 2(E_i - 1)\right]}{2} + SA_i \tag{17}$$

where E_i is the residual energy of the node and indicate the effectiveness of sensing capability in determining priority. This relation is based on the following assumptions.

First assumption: the more sensing capability and the residual energy, the higher priority level. ***Second assumption***: for each two sensors that have different sensing capability and Residual energy, they will have a different priority level. Indeed, if the target m is seen only by sensor i, the amount of is zero and regardless of other sum values, the sensing capability is infinite. This value represents the necessity for the nodes i to stay on in current round.

If the node i have more sensors to detect various targets, the amount of $\propto$ is larger and reduces the sensing capability and priority of a node. How priority parameter (P) influence on node selection as active node in each round is so that a time is calculated for each node at the beginning of initial phase. Each node waits until the time DT_i is passed. This time is obtained from equation 18.

$$DT_i = \left(1 - \frac{p_i}{p_{\max}}\right) DT \tag{18}$$

where p_i is the node priority, p_{max} is the maximum priority of this node and all of its single hop neighbor nodes. DT is a fixed time and its size is equal to the initial phase [63].

The Coverage and Routing Algorithm

In [55], the network is divided into time intervals called rounds and in each round the selected node are active and the rest are in sleep mode. The duration of each round can be calculated due to network requirements and physical parameters of the nodes used in the network. In each round, the following conditions must be established in selection of active nodes. In [55], the selection of relay node and the route is performed separately. In selection of relay nodes the entire network will be used, in contrast to previous works in which the specification and the location of nodes are considered. Using the network means that none of the nodes leads exclusively to save the data transmission that is associated with its own relay area. The traffic and processing volume is much less than other routing algorithms in selection of relay nodes. Another benefit of this algorithm is that you don't need to find the route for selected node. Each node which is selected as a sensor in a network will find the shortest route for relay in data transmission. The following figures show how to select the relay nodes.

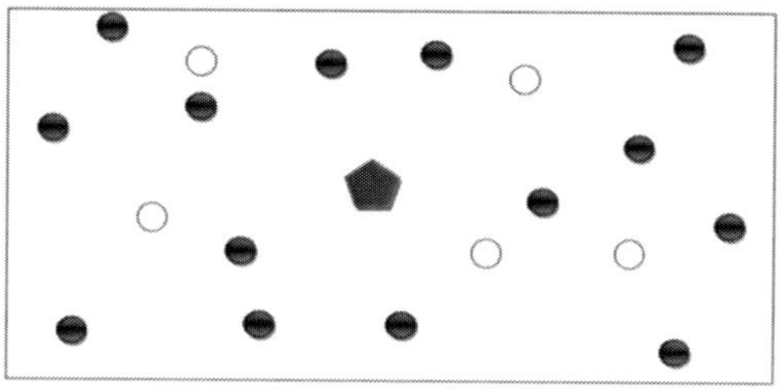

Figure 10. White Circles are Nodes and Blue Hexagons are Super Nodes.

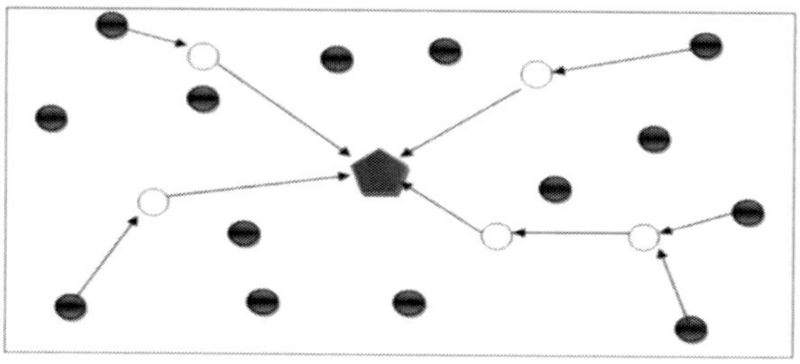

Figure 11. Selection of Relay Node for Transmission.

In figures 10 and 11, the route for relay should be chosen from selected nodes (white circles) to super node (blue circle). Two parameters *Relay-Value* and *Pre-Relay Value* calculate the relay amount of the node and the relay amount of previous node (in route between each node and the nearest super node) respectively.

Each node should have possessed at least desired Characteristics to be selected as relay node. In general, the nodes that receive the relay-update message from its neighbors and became aware of its relay amount ,compare it with relay amount of other neighbors who are placed in on step distance, then each node calculates its relay amount based on pre-relay value and sends it to its one hop neighbors. The relay value that is used to find a route is calculated by the following formula: E_r and E_i are the residual energy and the initial energy of the node respectively; N_c shows the density of super nodes in the network and depends on the number of super nodes to all nodes in the network.

$$\mathrm{Re}\,layValue = \mathrm{Pr}\,e\,\mathrm{Re}\,layValue \times \frac{E_r}{E_i} \times e^{-\frac{1}{n_c}} \tag{19}$$

Each node calculates its relay value and sends it to its neighbors and the neighbors update their Relay value based on perceived levels. This process is continued until each node chooses a relay node that use it to send data to super node [55].

The Optimal Sensor Selection Algorithm for Reducing Energy Consumption

This algorithm [65] consists of two stages: in first stage active nodes are selected and in second stage the data are collected from the nodes and sent via Interface nodes. In the first stage, the waiting time is calculated for each node. The waiting time can be expressed as a ratio of the total time of one round using parameters such as residual energy, initial energy and the number of targets that are located in the scope of sensor.

After passing waiting time, the sensor decides to stay awake or falling asleep. After ordering the nodes in the network, each node initially detects its single hop neighbor. In detection phase of each node, all nodes that their distance to desired node is less than the communication radius are considered as single hop neighbor. Then two hop neighbors of the nodes are determined. Indeed, two hop neighbors are the one hop neighbor of desired node. The node that must be active in each round is determined. This fitness is performed based on the function that is defined. Initially, each node stores a list of targets that sees. A waiting time is estimated for each node Based on this value and other factors, including Residual energy and the node must wait until this time is finished.

$$P_j = \sum_{i=1}^{n} \frac{1}{(nTari-1)\left(1-e^{\frac{-E_{remainj}}{E_{avi}}}\right)} \tag{20}$$

In the above equation, $T = 1/P$ is the waiting time for deciding each node. n_{Tari} is the number of nodes that the target i is seen by a few nodes. E_{avi} is the average energy of the nodes that see the mentioned target [65].

Point Coverage with Multiple Sensing Ranges

There are several sensing ranges and this means that the sensors can have several sensing range according to its residual energy and consumed energy [15].

Contribution of each sensor: the number of not covered targets that a sensor can cover them by using one unit of energy.

In this network, the sensors can be divided into sets, provided that first the number of these sets is maximum and second all targets are covered by the sensors in each set. To increase the network lifetime, the number of nodes within each set should be minimal [15].

In order to maximize the network lifetime in target coverage, we study the target coverage problem with multiple sensing ranges. This problem is in type of NP-complete. In CGH [66] that introduces a lot of extra nodes in each round, we have introduced energy - efficient centralized greedy and heuristic algorithm (ECGH).

The ECGH algorithm is dependent on General information that is why we introduce energy - efficient distributed localized greedy and heuristic algorithm (EDLGH). EDLGH algorithm schedules the sensors in a more energy-efficient manner. Also, in this method, an efficient method is presented for removal of additional sensors. In this method, the Sensors that possess more contribution or higher priority are selected.

ECGH Algorithm

In many applications, the nodes of sensor network are fixed and the probability of sensors fail is very low. In these situations a sink can collect all the network information including the location of sensors and the remaining of the energy and so on [67]. In [15], a localized model called ECGH is introduced that is implemented in the sink. In this algorithm a very important concept "remote target" is introduced. The remote target is a target that can be covered by minimum number of sensors and In fact, it is a target that possesses the less chance to cover compared to other targets.

In this algorithm, first, the remote targets are determined and then the sensor that has the greatest contributions is selected to cover the remote target. ECGH algorithm is not appropriate for applications in harsh and critical environments because the sink cannot collect the geographic information of all sensors, For this reason, we develop the algorithm and introduce it as a distributed and iterative algorithm named EDLGH, in which each node decides to stay in active mode or sleep mode based on information received from its neighbors [15].

ETCA Algorithm

In [68], we review the target coverage problem in heterogeneous networks in which each sensor has multiple sensing range and therefore they can cover several targets.

The ETCA algorithm is proposed based on a clustering architecture. Each sensor node sends its status to its cluster heads in the form of *m*COVER message. The status Information of each sensor includes node's ID, residual energy of the node and its sensing capability. Any cluster head sort the messages received from the cluster members after a waiting time, initially based on the Residual energy and then based on the sensor capability, next Sends its arranged list in the form of a NOTICE message to the cluster members. By receiving this message from the cluster members, each node is aware of its active or inactive status. This algorithm runs in multiple rounds [68].

The following are the symbols used by the algorithm: t_w: the time it takes to get the message of all nodes in cluster. This time is less than the running time of a round; E_i: the residual Energy of S_i; E_{thr}: the energy threshold of a sensor node. If the residual energy of a node is less than this threshold, it cannot attend in scheduling; β_i: The sensing capability of nodes S_i. It is the amount of sensing capability to the total amount of sensing capability that the node S_i is equipped with it and can cover different targets; *CL*: A list that the cluster head receive from the nodes in cluster. The status information of a node in cluster as node's ID, residual energy and the sensing capability are placed in this list. *m*COVER: A message that contains the residual energy of the node, sensing capability and other information. NOTICE: A message that is sent to the cluster nodes by cluster heads. It schedules Cluster nodes and determines the amount of their sensing capability. Each sensor can cover the corresponding targets based on determined sensing capability.

This algorithm is implemented in 4 steps [68]:

Step 1) each sensor determines its sensing capability.

$$\beta_i = \cup_{t=1}^{T}\{(u^t, T_j) | \delta_i^t \varphi_i^j = 1\} \tag{21}$$

Step 2) each sensor sends a *m*COVER message to its cluster head in which it dispatches the user ID, residual energy and sensing capability. Then the cluster head receives this information and stores in *CL* list.

Step 3) after the time t_w expires, the cluster head save its completed list and keeps the coverage Information of all or part of the sensor nodes that are able to cover all the targets within the cluster in this list. The cluster head sort the Information received from sensors of cluster that has stored in *CL* based on their residual energy of the nodes and energy capability.

Step 4) after completing step 3, the cluster head will review *CL* list and evaluate that which sensing range of a sensor must be scheduled to cover the targets within the cluster. This step consists of three subsections:

Step 4-1) the cluster head compares the residual energy of sensors within *CL* list with energy threshold E_{thr}. If the residual energy of a node is not less than the threshold value, the cluster head sends *m*NOTICE message to its cluster members. After receiving this message the nodes are on and cover the targets with respect to determined sensing range.

Step 4-2) since a node may be covered by several nodes in a round; the cluster head eliminate the covered targets from its list. This step ensures that (that each target is not covered by more than one node) each target is covered by one node.

Step 4-3) If all targets are covered, the algorithm is terminated; otherwise it continues to complete coverage of all targets.

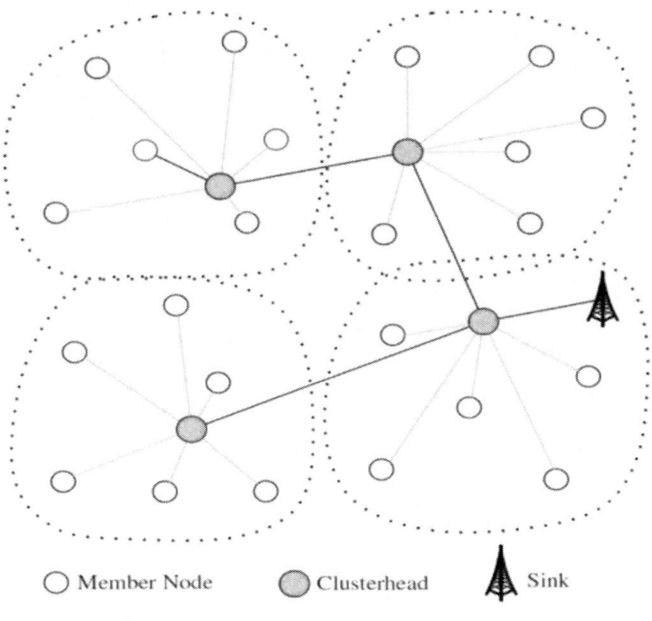

Figure 12. Topology of ETCA Model.

Point Coverage Algorithms Based on Population

Choosing Optimal Sensors with Genetic Algorithm

This algorithm [68] consists of two stages: the first stage is to select active nodes and the second stage is to collect data from nodes and send the data via interface nodes. In the first stage, a set of C_j is formed. When this set is active, the other nodes are inactive and in sleep mode. They consume very little energy and will be fitted and evaluated in the next phase. This evaluation is done during the running of the same period considering some of the physical factors of the sensors. We called the initial energy of the ordinary sensors E, energy consumption of the sensor in each period E_{s1} and the communication energy consumption in each period E_{c1}.

After elapsing this waiting time, the sensor decides to stay awake or falling asleep. This decision is done to assess the target coverage based on the above parameters. How to calculate the waiting time is considered in this protocol based on the relationship of instantaneous energy of the sensor, the initial energy of the sensor, the number of targets covered by each sensor, the total number of targets in the network and the coefficients to optimize the function. In [70], a function is provided for this purpose:

$$T_i = \left(1 - \frac{\alpha E_i}{E} + \beta \frac{\mathrm{Tarsi}}{m}\right).w \tag{22}$$

where E_i is the energy of the fitted sensor, *Tarsi* is the number of targets that the sensor *i* sees.

In (22), two coefficients α and β are presented. These two parameters form the chromosome structure for the algorithm that gives the best answer for these two parameters. By running this genetic algorithm, an appropriate combination of these two parameters α and β is achieved So that the network lifetime is maximized. Finding the optimal route of the relays by genetic algorithms should be such that the best choice of the monitoring sensors occurs in each period.

$E_{Network}^{TOTAL}$ is the total energy of the network . Reducing energy consumption and increasing residual energy throughout the network must be done during running COA algorithm. The residual energy in the network is obtained in equation (23).

$$E_{Remain} = | E_{Network}^{TOTAL} - \ldots - E_{Network}^{k-1} - E_{Network}^{k} | \tag{23}$$

where |.| represents the absolute value. Active sensor nodes should be selected in a manner to ensure that all parts needed for monitoring are covered by these sensors and also there is a route from these nodes to the sink. The following parameters are used in the problem formulation.

The objective function of this algorithm is defined as:

$$F = \sum_{i \in S}(AE_i + PC_i).y_i + \sum_{i \in S} NC_j.h_j \tag{24}$$

In the above equation, AE is the energy needed for a sensor to be on. Additionally, the problem constraints are shown in the following equation.

$$\sum_{ij} x_{ij} + h_j \geq 1 \qquad \forall j \in D \text{ and } \forall i \in S \tag{25}$$

Variable Pci is the route cost of the sensor i to sink nodes, cluster heads or manager node that the monitoring sensor pay it via selected nodes to relay. This variable is used as a surcharge for the nodes that have high-cost routes to the sink node.

X_{ij}: If the sensor i covers sensor j, its value will be one otherwise it will be zero.

Y_{ij}: design variable, if the sensor i is active, its value is 1, and otherwise it will be zero.

h_j: If it is one indicate that the required point jth has not been covered.

E_i: The amount of energy consumed by the sensor i.

NC_j: deliberate surcharge of required point coverage j [68].

Choosing Optimal Sensors with Simulated Annealing

This algorithm uses simulated annealing to optimize the algorithm and the parameters for choosing monitoring sensors in a point coverage network for each running period [71].

Finding an optimal set of monitoring sensors in point coverage is done using the effective removal of additional nodes, taking into account the cost of data transmission and the energy of interface nodes for the entire previous lifetime of the network. By optimizing and reducing the number of active sensors in a set that covers the desired points, more energy is saved and therefore the network lifetime is increased [72].

This algorithm in performed in three phases: the setup phase in which the suitable sensing ranges are determined for any specific target. The selection phase in which the appropriate active node is selected.

The steady-state phase in which the data transmission is done from the target to the monitoring node and from the monitoring node to the base station. Sensing range forming phase is performed only once, but the monitoring sensor selection and steady state phases are repeated in each round.

We show the total energy of the network with $E_{Network}^{TOTAL}$. Reducing energy consumption and increasing residual energy in network must be done during running COA algorithm. The residual energy in the network is obtained in equation (26).

$$E_{Remain} = \left| E_{Network}^{TOTAL} - \ldots - E_{Network}^{k-1} - E_{Network}^{k} \right| \tag{26}$$

where |.| represents the absolute value. Active sensor nodes should be selected in a manner to ensure that all parts needed for monitoring are covered by these sensors and also there is a route from these nodes to the sink. The following parameters are used in the problem formulation [15]. The objective function of this algorithm is similar to the algorithm presented earlier.

Comparison

In Tables 2 and 3, aforementioned algorithms are compared.

Table 2. Comparison of Point Coverage Algorithms - Part 1

Algorithm	Homogeneous/ Heterogeneous	Stationary/Mobility	Distributed/ Centralized
Integer programming	Homogeneous	stationary	Centralized
Meta heuristic IP	Homogeneous	stationary	Centralized
MSCmeta heuristic	Homogeneous	stationary	Distributed
Learning automaton	Homogeneous	mobility	Distributed
The coverage and routing algorithm	Heterogeneous	stationary	Distributed
The optimal sensor selection algorithm	Homogeneous	stationary	Distributed
Algorithm TPICSC	Homogeneous	stationary	Distributed
Algorithm ECGH	Homogeneous	stationary	Centralized
Algorithm EDLGH	Homogeneous	stationary	Distributed
Algorithm EDTC	Homogeneous	stationary	Distributed
Algorithm ETCA	Heterogeneous	stationary	Distributed
MCOTT	Heterogeneous	stationary and mobility	Distributed
MVRST	Homogeneous	stationary	Distributed
Choosing optimal sensors with Genetic Algorithm	Heterogeneous	stationary	Distributed

Table 3. Comparison point coverage algorithms - Part 2

Algorithm	Heuristic	Energy Efficiency	One Sensing Range/ Multiple Sensing Range	Connectivity
Integer programming	-	has	One sensing range	hasn't
Meta heuristic IP	Greedy	has	One sensing range	hasn't
MSCmeta heuristic	Greedy	has	One sensing range	hasn't
learning automaton	Learning automaton	has	One sensing range	hasn't
The coverage and routing algorithm	-	Has	One sensing range	hasn't
The optimal sensor selection algorithm	-	has	One sensing range	hasn't
Algorithm	Heuristic	Energy Efficiency	One Sensing Range/ Multiple Sensing Range	Connectivity
Algorithm TPICSC	Greedy	has	One sensing range	Has
Algorithm ECGH	Greedy	has	multiple sensing range	hasn't
Algorithm EDLGH	Greedy	has	One sensing range	hasn't
Algorithm EDTC	innovative	has	One sensing range	hasn't
Algorithm ETCA	Integer programming	has	One sensing range	hasn't
MCOTT	Greedy		One sensing range	Has
MVRST	Spanning tree	hasn't	One sensing range	Has
Choosing optimal sensors with Genetic Algorithm	Genetic algorithm	has	One sensing range	hasn't

CONCLUSION

In this chapter, the problem of coverage in wireless sensor network is introduced and challenges which exist in coverage are presented. Then, the problem of overage is formulated. Coverage is also classified regarding different aspects including applications, the target characteristics and the type of coverage. Definitions and explanations are presented for each of these classifications.

Additionally, the problem of target coverage is presented and is classified based on different conditions such as being mobile or stationary, having multiple sensing ranges, coverage with connectivity maintenance, and coverage in symmetric and asymmetric networks and so on. In each case, the problem of target coverage is formulated mathematically and is defined. Then, the algorithms of target coverage in sensing networks are investigated. Before investigating algorithms, they (algorithms) are classified based on this point that whether they are presented in homogeneous networks or in heterogeneous networks. In homogeneous networks, all nodes are in the same conditions but in heterogeneous networks, some nodes have different initial energy and sensing range in comparison with other nodes. The main point in both models of network is energy efficiency of algorithms. In classifying algorithms, the problem of energy efficiency is taken into account. Finally, the presented algorithms are compared in terms of time complexity, optimality of energy consumption, moveability, connectivity maintenance, and other cases.

REFERENCES

[1] Akyildiz, W. S., Sankarasubramaniam, Y., Cayirci, E., 2002. Wireless Sensor Networks: A Survey. *Journal of Computer.* 38, 4, 393-422.

[2] Rabaey, J. M., Ammer, M. J., da Silva, J. L., Patel, D., Roundy, S., 2000. PicoRadio Supports Ad hoc Ultra-low Power Wireless Networking. *IEEE Computer.* 33, 7, 42-48.

[3] Cardei, M., Thai, M. T., Li, Yingshu, Wu, W., 2005. Energy-Efficient Target Coverage in Wireless Sensor Networks. *Proceedings of the IEEE 24th Annual Joint Conference of the Computer and Communications Societies.* 3, 1976-1984.

[4] Chen, D., Varshney, P. K., 2004. QoS Support in Wireless Sensor Network: A Survey. *Proceedings of the IEEE International Conference on Wireless Networks.* 227-233.

[5] Lei, Y.., Zhang, Y., Zhao, Y., 2009. The Research of Coverage Problems in Wireless Sensor Network. *Proceedings of the International Conference on Wireless Networks and Information Systems.* 31-34.

[6] Ghosha, A., Dasb, S. K., 2008. Coverage and Connectivity Issues in Wireless Sensor Networks: A Survey. *Pervasive and Mobile Computing.* 4, 3, 303-334.

[7] Zhao, Q., Gurusamy, M., 2006. Maximizing Network Lifetime for Connected Target Coverage in Wireless Sensor Networks. Proceedings of the IEEE International Conference on Wireless and Mobile Computing Networking and Communications. 91-101.

[8] Li, X., Hunter, D. K., Zuyev, S., 2012. Coverage Properties of the Target Area in Wireless Sensor Networks. *IEEE Transaction on Information Theory.* 58, 1, 430-437.

[9] Bisht, M., Chhetri, S., 2013. A Survey on the Coverage of Wireless Sensor Networks. *International Journal of Advanced Research in Computer Science and Software Engineering.* 3, 3, 295-300.

[10] Cardei, M., Du, D-Z., 2005. Improving Wireless Sensor Network Lifetime through Power Aware Organization. *ACM Wireless Networks,* 11, 3, 333-340.

[11] Kar, K., Banerjee, S., 2003. Node Placement for Connected Coverage in Sensor Networks. Proceedings of the Workshop on Modeling and Optimization in Mobile, *Ad hoc and Wireless Networks.*

[12] He, J., Ji, S., Pan, Y., Li, Y., 2011. Reliable and Energy Efficient Target Coverage for Wireless Sensor Networks. *TSINGHUA Science and Technology.* 16, 5, 464-474.

[13] Zorbas, D., Razafindralambo, T., 2013. Prolonging Network Lifetime under Probabilistic Target Coverage in Wireless Mobile Sensor networks. *Computer Communications.* 36, 9, 1039-1053.

[14] Yang, S., Dai, F., Cardei, M., Wu, J., 2005. On Multiple Point Coverage in Wireless Sensor Networks. *Proceedings of the IEEE International Conference on Mobile Adhoc and Sensor Systems,* 756-764.

[15] Wang, J., Liu, M., Lu, M., Zhang. X., 2010. Target Coverage Algorithms with Multiple Sensing Ranges in Wireless Sensor Networks. *Proceedings of the IEEE Military Communications Conference.* 130-135.

[16] Jamali, M. A., Bakhshivand, N., Easmaeilpour, M., Salami, D., 2010. An Energy-Efficient Algorithm for Connected Target Coverage Problem in Wireless Sensor Networks. *Proceedings of the 3rd IEEE International Conference on Computer Science and Information Technology.* 9, 249-254.

[17] Gu, Y., Li, J., Zhao, B., Ji, Y., 2009. Target Coverage Problem in Wireless Sensor Networks: A Column Generation Based Approach. Proceedings of the 6th IEEE International Conference on Mobile Adhoc and Sensor Systems. 486-495.

[18] Shimokawa. T., Fujiwara, A., 2012. Centralized Algorithms for the Connected Target Coverage in Wireless Sensor Networks. *Proceedings of the International Conference on Networking and Computing.* 307-310.

[19] Ai, J., Abouzeid, A., 2006. Coverage by Directional Sensors in Randomly Deployed Wireless Sensor Networks. *Journal of Combinatorial Optimization.* 11, 1, 21-41.

[20] Kim, Y., Han, Y-H., Jeong, Y-S., Park, D-S., 2013. Lifetime Maximization Considering Target Coverage and Connectivity in Directional Image/Video Sensor Networks. *The Journal of Supercomputing,* 65, 1, 365-382.

[21] Mohamadi, H., Ismail, A. S., Salleh, S., 2013. Utilizing Distributed Learning Automata to Solve the Connected Target Coverage Problem in Directional Sensor Networks. *Sensors and Actuators A: Physical.* 198, 21-30.

[22] Chen, X., Ho, Y-C., Bai, H., 2009. Complete Coverage and Point Coverage in Randomly Distributed Sensor Networks. *Automatica,* 45, 6, 1549-1553.

[23] Huang, C-F., Tseng, Y-C., 2003. The Coverage Problem in a Wireless Sensor Network. *Proceedings of the 2nd ACM International Conference on Wireless Sensor Networks and Applications.* 115-121.

[24] Zhang, H., Hou, J. C., 2005. Maintaining Sensing Coverage and Connectivity in Large Sensor Networks. *Ad Hoc & Sensor Wireless Networks.* 1, 89-124.

[25] Carle, J., Simplot, D., 2001. Energy Efficient Area Monitoring by Sensor Networks. *IEEE Computer.* 37, 11, 40-46.

[26] Tian, D., Georganas, N. D., 2002. A Coverage-Preserving Node Scheduling Scheme for Large Wireless Sensor Networks. *Proceedings of the 1st ACM International Workshop on Wireless Sensor Networks and Applications.* 32-41.

[27] Dhillon, S. S., Chakrabarty, K., Iyengar, S. S., 2002. Sensor Placement for Grid Coverage under Imprecise Detections. *Proceedings of the International Conference on Information Fusion,* 1581-1587.

[28] Zou, Y., Chakrabarty, K., 2004. Uncertainty-aware and Coverage-oriented Deployment for Sensor Networks. *Journal of Parallel and Distributed Computing,* 64, 7, 788-798.

[29] Chen, H., Wu, H., Tzeng, N-F., 2004. Grid-Based Approach for Working Node Selection in Wireless Sensor Networks. *Proceedings of the IEEE International Conference on Communications,* 6, 3673-3678.

[30] Schwager, M., McLurkin, J., Rus, D., 2006. Distributed Coverage Control with Sensor y Feedback for Networked Robots. *Proceedings of the Conference on Robotics: Science and Systems.*

[31] Batalin, M. A., Sukhatme, G. S., 2002. Multi-Robot Dynamic Coverage of a Planar Bounded Environment. *Proceedings of the IEEE/RSJ International Conference on Intelligent Robots and Systems.*

[32] Prasetya, D. A., Yasuno, T., 2012. Cooperative Control of Multiple Mobile Robot using Particle Swarm Optimization for Tracking Two Passive Target. *Proceedings of the SICE Annual Conference,* 1751-1754.

[33] Gupta, R., Das, S. R., 2003. Tracking Moving Targets in a Smart Sensor Network. *Proceedings of the IEEE Vehicular Technology Conference,* 3035-3039.

[34] Gui, C., Mohapatra, P., 2004. Power Conservation and Quality of Surveillance in Target Tracking Sensor Networks. *Proceedings of the 10th Annual International Conference on Mobile Computing and Networking,* 129-143.

[35] Jeong, J., Sharafkandi, S., Du, D. H. C., 2006. Energy-aware Scheduling with Quality of Surveillance Guarantee in Wireless Sensor Networks. *Proceedings of teh 2006 Workshop on Dependability Issues in Wireless Ad hoc Networks and SEnsor NEtworks,* 55-64.

[36] Raghunathan, V., Schurgers, C., Park, S., Srivastava, M. B., 2002. Energy-Aware Wireless Microsensor Networks. *IEEE Signal Processing Magazine,* 19, 2, 40-50.

[37] Esnaashari, M., Meybodi, M. R., 2009. Dynamic Point Coverage in Wireless Sensor Networks: A Learning Automata Approach. *Communications in Computer and Information Science,* 6, 758-762.

[38] Wang, X., Xnp, G., Zhang, Y., Lu, C., Pless, R., Gill, C. D., 2003. Integrated Coverage and Connectivity Configuration in Wireless Sensor Networks. *Proceedings of the 1st International Conference on Embedded Networked Sensor Systems,* 28-39.

[39] Lu, M., Wu, J., Cardei, M., Li, M., 2005. Energy-Efficient Connected Coverage of Discrete Targets in Wireless Sensor Networks. *Lecture Notes in Computer Science,* 3619. 43-52.

[40] Cardei, M., Du, D-Z., Improving Wireless Sensor Network Lifetime through Power-Aware Organization. *Wireless Networks.* 11, 3, 333-340.

[41] Cardei, M., Thai, M. T., Li, Yingshu, Wu, W., 2005. Energy-Efficient Target Coverage in Wireless Sensor Networks. *Proceedings of the IEEE 24th Annual Joint Conference of the Computer and Communications Societies.* 3, 1976-1984.

[42] Berman, P., Calinescu, G., Shah, C., Zelikovsky, A., 2004. Power Efficient Monitoring Management in Sensor Networks. *Proceedings of the IEEE International Wireless Communications and Networking Conference.* 4, 2329-2334.

[43] Cardei, M., Cardei, I., 2008. Energy-Efficient Connected-Coverage in Wireless Sensor Networks. *International Journal of Sensor Networks.* 3, 3, 201-210.

[44] Ostovari, P., Dehghan, M., Wu, J., 2011. Connected Point Coverage in Wireless Sensor Networks using Robust Spanning Trees. *Proceedings of the 31st International Conference on Distributed Computing Systems,* 287-293.

[45] Pyun, S-Y., Cho, D-H., 2010. Energy-Efficient Scheduling for Multiple-Target Coverage in Wireless Sensor Networks. *Proceedings of the 71st IEEE Vehicular Technology Conference.* 1-5.

[46] Jin, M., Gao, Z., Huang, R., Chang, X., Qi, F., 2011. An Incomplete Coverage Control Based on Target Tracking Wireless Sensor Network. *Proceedings of the 7th International Conference on Mobile Ad hoc and Sensor Networks.* 15-19.

[47] Kumar, S., Ten, L., Posner, M. E., Sinha, P., 2007. Optimal Slee-Wakeup Algorithms for Barriers of Wireless Sensors. *Proceedings of the 4th International Conference on Broadband Communications, Networks and Systems.* 327-336.

[48] Tan, R., Xing, G., Wang, J., So, H. C., 2010. Exploiting Reactive Mobility for Collaborative Target Detection in Wireless Sensor Networks. *IEEE Transactions on Mobile Computing,* 9, 3, 317-332.

[49] Lam, M., Liu, Y-H., 2006. ISOGRID: An Efficient Algorithm for Coverage Enhancement in Mobile Sensor Networks. *Proceedings of the IEEE/RSJ International Conference on Intelligent Robots and Systems,* 1458-1463.

[50] Ahmed, N., Kanhere, S. S., Jha, S., 2005. Probabilistic Coverage in Wireless Sensor Networks. *Proceedings of the IEEE Conference on Local Computer Networks.* 672-681.

[51] Hefeeda, M., Ahmadi, H., 2007. A Probabilistic Coverage Protocol for Wireless Sensor Networks. *Proceedings of the IEEE International Conference on Network Protocols.* 41-50.

[52] Zaidi, S. A. R., Hafeez, M., McLernon, D. C., Ghogho, M., 2008. A Probabilistic Model of k-Coverage in Minimum Cost Wireless Sensor Networks. *Proceedings of the ACM CoNEXT Conference.* 33.

[53] Carter, B., Ragade, R., 2009. A Probabilistic Model for the Deployment of Sensors. *Proceedings of the IEEE Sensors Applications Symposium,* 7-12.

[54] Xing, G., Chang, X., Lu, C., Wang, J., Shen, K., Pless, R., O'Sullivan, A., 2010. Efficient Coverage Maintenance Based on Probabilistic Distributed Detection. *IEEE Transactions on Mobile Computing,* 9, 9, 1346-1360.

[55] Rostami, A. S., Tanhatalab, M. R., Bernety, H. M., Nosrati, K., 2011. Novel Algorithm of Energy-Aware Asymmetric Wireless Sensor Networks Routing for In-Point Coverage. *Proceedings of the International Conference on Computational Intelligence and Communication Networks.* 308-313.

[56] Carbunar, B., Grama, A., Vitek, J., 2004. Distributed and Dynamic Voronoi Overlays for Coverage Detection and Distributed Hash Tables in Ad hoc Networks. *Proceedings of the 10th International Conference on Parallel and Distributed Systems.* 549-556.

[57] Lu, J., Wang, J., Suda, T., 2006. Scalable Coverage Maintenance for Dense Wireless Sensor Networks. *Proceedings of the 3rd Annual IEEE Conference on Sensor and Ad hoc Communications and Networks.* 651-660.

[58] Watfa, M., Commuri, S., 2007. Boundary Coverage and Coverage Boundary Problems in Wireless Sensor Networks. *International Journal of Sensor Networks*. 2, 3-4, 273-283.

[59] Xu, Y., Yao, Xin, 2006. A GA Approach to the Optimal Placement of Sensors in Wireless Sensor Networks with Obstacles and Preferences. *Proceedings of the IEEE Consumer Communications and Networking Conference*. 127-131.

[60] Aoun, B., Boutaba, R., 2006. Clustering in WSN with Latency and Energy Consumption Constraints. *Journal of Network and Systems Management,* 14, 3, 415-439.

[61] Bandyopadhyay, S., Coyle, E. J., 2003. An Energy Efficient Hierarchical Clustering Algorithm for Wireless Sensor Networks. *Proceedings of the 22nd IEEE International Conference on Computer Communications*. 3, 1713-1723.

[62] Anisi, M. H., Abdullah, A. H., Razak, S. A., 2011. Energy-Efficient Data Collection in Wireless Sensor Networks. *Wireless Sensor Network*. 3, 329-333.

[63] Liu, Z., 2007. Maximizing Network Lifetime for Target Coverage PRoblem in Heterogeneous Wireless Sensor Networks. *Mobile Ad hoc and Sensor Networks, Lecture Notes in Computer Science,* 4864, 457-468.

[64] Yang, S., Dai, F., Cardei, M., Wu, J., 2005. On Multiple Point Coverage in Wireless Sensor Networks. *Proceedings of the IEEE International Conference on Mobile Ad hoc and Sensor System,* 757-767.

[65] Rostami, A. S., Tanhatalab, M. R., Bernety, H. M., Naghibi, S. E., 2011. Decreasing the Energy Consumption by a New Algorithm in Choosing the Best Sensor Node in Wireless Sensor Network with Point Coverage. *Proceedings of the International Conference on Computational Intelligence and Communication Networks*. 269-274.

[66] Cardei, M., Wu, J., Lu. M., 2006. Improving Network Lifetime using Sensors with Adjustable Sensing Ranges. *International Journal of Sensor Networks*. 42, 1, 163-174.

[67] Cardei, M., Du, D-Z., 2005. Improving Wireless Sensor Network Lifetime through Power Aware Organization. *ACM Wireless Networks,* 11, 3, 333-340.

[68] Xing, X., Wang, G., Li, J., 2012. Polytype Target Coverage Scheme for Heterogeneous Wireless Sensor Networks using Linear Programming. *Wireless Communications and Mobile Computing*.

[69] Rostami, A. S., Nosrati, K., Bernety, H. M., 2010. Optimizing the Parameters of Active Sensor Selection and using GA to Decrease Energy Consumption in Point Coverage Wireless Sensor Networks. *Proceedings of the 6th International Conference on Wireless Communication and Sensor Networks*. 1-6.

[70] Awada, W., Cardei, M., 2006. Energy-Efficient Data Gathering in Heterogeneous Wireless Sensor Networks. *Proceedings of the IEEE International Conference on Wireless and Mobile Computing, Networking and Communications*. 53-60.

[71] Azami, M., Ranjbar, M., Rostami, A. S., Amiri, A. J., 2013. Increasing the Network Lifetime by Simulated Annealing Algorithm in Wireless Sensor Network with Point. *International Journal of Ad hoc, Sensor and Ubiquitous Computing,* 4, 2, 31-45.

[72] Slijipcevic, S., Potkonjak, M., 2001. Power Efficient ORganization of Wireless Sensor Networks. *Proceedings of the IEEE International Conference on Communications*. 2, 472-476.

In: Recent Advances in Ad Hoc Networks Research
Editor: Natarajan Meghanathan
ISBN: 978-1-63321-337-1

Chapter 8

LOCALIZATION OF SUBMERGED SENSORS

Anisur Rahman*[*]*, Vallipuram Muthukkumarasamy and Elankayer Sithirasenan
Griffith University, Gold Coast, QLD, Australia

ABSTRACT

Underwater wireless sensor networks (UWSN) are envisioned to enable applications for oceanographic data collection, pollution monitoring, offshore exploration, disaster prevention, assisted navigation and tactical surveillance applications. Despite varieties of UWSN applications, the idea of submerged wireless communication may still seem far-fetched and attracted researchers in the last decades. As location of submerged sensors play a vital role in the significance of data validity, determining the coordinates precisely is very crucial. There are many distance measurement techniques for terrestrial application based on signal strength but those algorithms are not readily suitable for underwater environment because of a number of factors associated with it.

While various localization algorithms have been proposed for terrestrial wireless sensor networks (WSN), there are relatively a few efficient localization schemes for UWSNs. The characteristics of underwater sensor networks are fundamentally different from that of terrestrial networks. Conventional localization in underwater mainly performed with the use acoustic signal as radio waves do not propagate well; despite the fact that acoustic channel is characterized by harsh physical environments with stringent bandwidth limitations. Moreover, the variable speed of sound and the long propagation delays pose a unique set of challenges for localization in UWSN.

This chapter will explore the status-quo localization scheme as well as localization schemes that can exploit radio signal underwater despite its limited range. This chapter will also investigate the challenges in underwater wireless sensor networks and will elaborate on new mechanism to determine the coordinates of sensors minimizing multipath effects with as low as single mobile beacon (i.e., boat or buoy); having a mobile beacon is more pragmatic than having multiple beacons in the localization process.

Keywords: Underwater Sensor Network, Localization, Acoustic Signals, Radio Signals

[*] Griffith University, Parklands Dr., QLD 4222, Australia. Email: anis.rahman@griffithuni.edu.au.

INTRODUCTION

Wireless communication applications have become more prominent in terrestrial than underwater. However, in the recent years, there has been a growing interest to explore and fulfil the needs of a multitude of underwater applications. For example, marine life is a vast resource, providing food, medicine and raw materials, in addition to helping to support recreation and tourism all over the world. In fact marine life helps determine the very nature of our planet at a fundamental level. So, it becomes crucial to obtain accurate environmental data using underwater sensors, to provide and maintain sanctuary for the marine life. Besides, advanced robot navigation, autonomous control, find lost object, estuary monitoring and pollutant tracking also requires accurate localization [1]. In addition to underwater sensors, UWSNs may also comprise of surface stations and autonomous underwater vehicles. Therefore, regardless of the type of deployment (outdoor, indoor, underground or underwater), the location of sensors needs to be determined for meaningful interpretation of the sensed data [2].

Localization is a method of determining the location of an entity, e.g., a node (mostly mobile) in a network and self-localization capability is a highly desirable characteristic of wireless sensor networks. Sensors localization algorithms estimate the locations of sensors with initially unknown location information by using knowledge of the absolute positions of a few sensors and inter-sensor measurements such as distance and bearing measurements. Sensors with known location information are called anchors and their locations can be obtained by using a global positioning system (GPS), or by installing anchors at points with known coordinates. In applications requiring a global coordinate system, these anchors will determine the location of the sensors in the global coordinate system. In applications where a local coordinate system suffices (e.g., smart homes), these anchors define the local coordinate system to which all other sensors are referred. Because of constraints on the cost and size of sensors, energy consumption, implementation environment (e.g., GPS is not accessible in some environments) and the deployment of sensors (e.g., sensor nodes may be randomly scattered in the region), most sensors do not know their locations. These sensors with unknown location information are called non-anchor nodes and their coordinates will be estimated by the sensor network localization algorithm. The localization schemes that use reference nodes can be broadly classified into two categories: range-based schemes (schemes that use range or bearing information), and range-free schemes (schemes that do not use range or bearing information). Following sections elaborate on underwater wireless sensor networks, underwater signals propagation and localization techniques.

UNDERWATER WIRELESS SENSOR NETWORKS

Underwater Wireless Sensor Networks (UWSNs) are expected to support a variety of civilian and military applications. Sensed data can only be interpreted meaningfully when referenced to the location of the sensor, making localization an important problem. While global positioning system (GPS) receivers are commonly used in terrestrial WSNs to achieve this, this is infeasible in UWSNs as GPS signals do not propagate through water. Acoustic communications is the most promising mode of communication underwater. However, under water acoustic channels are characterized by harsh physical layer conditions with low band width, high propagation delay and high bit error rate. Here, we provide the techniques and challenges in localization specifically for UWSNs and categorize them into (i) range- based vs. range-free techniques (ii) techniques that rely on static reference nodes vs. those who also rely on mobile reference nodes, and (iii) single-stage vs. multi-stage schemes.

In addition to underwater sensor nodes, the network may also comprise surface stations and Autonomous Underwater Vehicles (AUVs). Regardless of the type of deployment (outdoor, indoor, underground or underwater), the location of the sensors needs to be determined for meaningful interpretation of the sensed data. Since radio signals are significantly attenuated underwater, the use of the well-known global positioning system (GPS) is restricted to surface nodes. Hence, message exchanges between submerged UWSN nodes and surface nodes (or other reference nodes with known locations) needed for localization must be carried out, usually using acoustic communications. Unfortunately, underwater acoustic channels are characterized by long propagation delays, limited bandwidth, motion-induced Doppler shift, phase and amplitude fluctuations, multipath interference, etc. [3]. These characteristics pose severe challenges towards designing localization schemes that fulfil the following desirable properties:

- High accuracy: The location of the sensor for which sensed data is derived should be accurate and unambiguous for meaningful interpretation of data. Localization protocols usually minimize the distance between the estimated and true locations.
- Fast convergence: Since nodes may drift due to water currents, the localization procedure should be fast so that it reports the actual location when data is sensed.
- Low communication costs: Since the nodes are battery-powered and may be deployed for long durations, communication overhead should be minimized.
- Good scalability: The long propagation delay and relatively high power attenuation in the underwater acoustic channel pose a scalability problem where performance is highly affected by the number of nodes in the network. Consequently, an underwater acoustic localization protocol should be distributed, rely on as few reference nodes as possible and the algorithm complexity at each node should be invariant with the network size.
- Wide coverage: The localization scheme should ensure that most of the nodes in the network can be localized.

In addition to the above quantifiable properties, practical considerations such as ease and cost of deploying reference nodes and other required infrastructure should be taken into account too.

UNDERWATER SIGNALS PROPAGATION

Most underwater wireless networks use acoustic wave as the transmission medium nowadays, which is a proven technology for underwater sensor applications with a long transmission range, but the chances of getting much more out of acoustic modems are quite remote. Another option that may be used for underwater transmission is optical wave, but this only delivers good performance in very clear water, and requires tight alignment due to the demand for the sight and the limitation of very short transmission ranges [4]. The characteristics of optical link have made itself impractical for many underwater applications. On the other hand, radio propagation through water is very different from propagation through air because of the high permittivity and electrical conductivity of water medium. Following sections explore the underwater acoustic and radio signal propagation and recent advancements.

Acoustic Signals

Extensive research and development has been carried out in underwater acoustic networks. Acoustics is a proven technology for underwater sensor applications which offers long transmission ranges of up to 20 km despite its certain challenges and limitations [5]. Acoustic waves yield poor performance in shallow water where transmission can be affected by turbidity, ambient noise, salinity, and pressure gradients; in addition, acoustic technology can have an adverse impact on marine life [6].

Unlike RF propagation in terrestrial networks, underwater acoustic propagation possesses the following unique characteristics [7]

- Long propagation delay: Sound speed in water v can be theoretically obtained from the linear wave Eq. (1).

$$v = \sqrt{\gamma \frac{B_T}{\rho_0}} \tag{1}$$

where γ is the adiabatic index, B_T is the isothermal bulk modulus and ρ_0 is the equilibrium density.

The variations of these three parameters with temperature and depth are not easy to predict, so a number of empirical formulas were given in the last decades, for example Eq. (2). Since the speed of sound underwater is five orders of magnitude lower than RF propagation over the air, measurement errors due to node mobility may become significant. A typical speed of acoustic waves near the ocean surface is about 1500m/s, more than four times faster than the speed of sound in air but five orders of magnitude smaller than the speed of electromagnetic in air.

And the speed of sound v in water can be calculated according to the following Mackenzie [8] empirical formula:

$$\begin{aligned} v = {} & 1448.96 + 4.591T - 5.304 \times 10^{-2}\, T^2 + 2.374 \times 10\text{-}4\, T^3 \\ & + 1.340\,(S - 35) + 1.630 \times 10^{-2}\, D + 1.675 \\ & \times 10^{-7}\, D^2 - 1.025 \times 10^{-2}\, T\,(S - 35) - 7.139 \\ & \times 10^{-13}\, T\,D^3 \end{aligned} \tag{2}$$

where T, D and S are temperature, depth and salinity and constrains for these variables are 2-30˚C, 0-8000m and 25-40ppt respectively.

- Multipath fading and shadowing: The underwater acoustic channel is a frequency selective channel with a delay spread of the order of hundreds of taps (a tap refers to the extraction of the signal at a certain position within the channel's impulse response delay-line). Multipath models as well as actual measurements taken from sea trials show that the energy of the direct path of the channel's impulse response is not always the strongest [9]. As a result, multipath (indirect) signals can be mistaken if RSSI is considered in distance estimation.
- Sound speed variation: Unlike the speed of light which is constant, the speed of sound underwater varies with water temperature, pressure and salinity, giving rise to refraction. Without measuring the sound speed, the accuracy of distance measurements based on time-of-arrival approaches may be degraded. We propose few mechanisms to determine the speed of sound from the in-situ environmental variables, which does not require expensive devices that depends on bouncing technique.
- Highly unreliable and asymmetric signal-to-noise ratio: For a node pair (*i*, *j*), the signal attenuation in underwater acoustic channels is widely modelled as Eq. (3).

$$TL(d_{ij}) = 10\lambda \log_{10}\left(\frac{d_{ij}}{1m}\right) + \alpha d_{ij} \text{ dB} \tag{3}$$

where *TL* is the transmission loss, d_{ij} is the distance from node *i* to node *j*, λ is the propagation loss parameter and α is the absorption loss parameter. The parameter, λ depends on the structure of the underwater medium, such that in shallow water or when transmitting from one sound speed layer to another, it can exceed 2, which is a typical value for omnidirectional propagation in free-space. The parameter α increases with the carrier frequency and is affected by the salinity as well as water temperature, among other factors. Since the ambient noise level is depth dependent and decreases with frequency and can be modelled as 50 – log(*f*) dB, where *f is* carrier frequency [10], small variations in *f* can affect the SNR significantly. As a result, bandwidth is very limited in underwater acoustic channels and communications links are unreliable. Moreover, nodes *i* and *j* may be at different depths, the respective noise levels may be different, giving rise to asymmetric SNR.

- Asymmetric power consumption: Unlike RF modems, acoustic modems typically consume much more power (order of tens of watts) in transmit mode compared to receive mode (order of milliwatts). This asymmetry in power consumption makes it preferable for ordinary nodes to be localized through passive/silent listening.

Radio Signals

Underwater radio communications were investigated with fervent interest in the last century up until the 1970s. Because its range is restricted by fundamental attenuation and noise factors that must be considered as unchangeable environmental elements, significant breakthroughs were not to be expected in submarine radio communication [11]; hence, radio communication, although it has notable merits in the terrestrial wireless network field, has had very few practical underwater applications to date. Recent studies shows that radio signal can propagate up to 1.8-323m underwater and the propagation speed can reach up to 4.30x106m/s in MHz frequency [12]. Underwater communication research conducted at Liverpool John Moores University has shown that transmission at 5MHz frequency is feasible in seawater up to 90m giving a data rate of 500kbps that allows duplex video and data streams [13]. Abdou et.al in [14] has shown attenuation of high frequency radio signals in different types of water with various conductivity and they also have emphasized on many advantages of radio signal including bandwidth, data rate and transmission in cross boundaries with 3x107m/s speed.

As because radio signalling uses a different transmission mechanism than acoustic, it can extend the arena of application; radio signalling, coupled with digital technology and signal compression techniques, has many advantages that make it suitable for niche underwater applications. Even though RF can suffer from limited transmission range and electromagnetic interference (EMI), it also has some valuable features that can enable flexible deployment of UWSNs in coastal regions. Despite the limited underwater propagation distance of radio signal, it possesses some merits. First, both acoustic and optical waves cannot perform smooth transition through air-and-water interface. Radio signal can cross water-to-air or water-to-earth boundaries easily; its signal follows the path of least resistance, where both air and seabed paths can extend the transmission range. Second, radio transmissions are tolerant to turbulence that is caused by tidal waves or human activities, as opposed to the case of acoustic and optical waves. Third, radio can work in dirty water conditions, while optical waves are susceptible to particles and marine fouling [15]. Fourth, radio operation is also immune to acoustic noise, and it has no unknown effect on marine lives.

Radio signal propagation through water is very different from propagation through air because of the high permittivity and electrical conductivity of water. Propagating waves continually cycle energy between electric and magnetic fields; hence, high conduction leads to strong attenuation. Besides, plane wave attenuation also increases rapidly with frequency. An important consideration for underwater radio performance is its multi-path propagation feature caused by the effects of the water-to-air interface. Propagation loss and the refraction angle are such that a radio signal crosses the water-to-air boundary and appears to radiate from a patch of water directly above the transmitter. The large refraction angle produced by the high permittivity launches a signal almost parallel with the water surface [16]. This effect aids communication from a submerged station to the land and between shallow submerged stations without the need for surface repeater buoys. A similar effect can also be produced at the seabed. Since the conductivity of the seabed is much lower than water, it can provide an alternative low loss, low noise, covert communications path. In many deployments, the single propagation path with the least resistance will be dominant. Should the air path or the seabed path be chosen as the dominant data path, relatively longer transmission range can be achieved as compared to the water path. Hence the multi-path propagation of electromagnetic waves can be advantageous for signal transmission in shallow water conditions.

Magnetic coupled loop antennas are the most compact practical solution for duplex submerged systems. Loop antennas are directional in nature and this property can be exploited to allow selection of a single propagation path. Alternatively, Omni-directional antennas can be implemented by crossing two loops so their planes intersect at right angles. Larger loop area will always provide greater antenna gain but practical systems can be designed using relatively compact loops, for instance, a small area loop antenna has been demonstrated in [17]. Another option is to use an electric dipole antenna for lateral electromagnetic waves. In [18], implemented a system using a crossed uninsulated terminated dipole with a diameter of 2 cm and 1 m in length, which makes careful reciprocal orientation unnecessary, thus simplifying deployment.

Table 1 shows the variation of key parameters vs. frequency, which is based on the equations below.

$$\lambda = \frac{1}{\sqrt{(f\sigma \times 10^{-7})}} \tag{4}$$

$$v = \sqrt{\frac{f \times 10^{7}}{\sigma}} \tag{5}$$

$$\delta_{skin} = \frac{1}{(2\pi\sqrt{f\sigma \times 10^{-7}})} \tag{6}$$

here, λ is the wavelength, f is the frequency, σ is the conductivity, v is the propagation velocity, and δ_{skin} is the skin depth. Values have been acquired using representative conductivity value σ = 0.01 S/m which is typical for fresh water. As for sea water conductivity, σ is set to 3.2, 4.2 and 4.3 S/m [12] for the respective frequencies listed in the table. First part of the table shows how the velocity increases with the increase of frequency. At 1MHz, radio signal is more than 1000 times faster than acoustic signal in sea water, which has important advantages for command latency and networking protocols where many signals have to be exchanged.

Table 1. Radio Signal Characteristics in Underwater

		Frequencies		
		100(Hz)	1 x 10^3(Hz)	1 x 10^6(Hz)
Velocity (m/s)	Sea water	1.77 x10^4	4.88 x 10^4	1.52 x 10^6
	Fresh water	3.16 x 10^5	1.00 x 10^6	3.16 x 10^7
	Free space	3.00 x 10^8	3.00 x 10^8	3.00 x 10^8
Wavelength (m)	Sea water	1.76 x 10^2	4.88 x 10^1	1.52 x 10^0
	Fresh water	3.16 x 10^3	1.00 x 10^3	3.16 x 10^3
	Free space	3.00 x 10^6	3.00 x 10^5	3.00 x 10^2
Propagation distance (m) for 100 dB attenuation	Sea water	3.23 x 10^2	8.92 x 10^1	2.79 x 10^0
	Fresh water	5.78 x 10^3	1.83 x 10^3	5.78 x 10^1

The second part of table shows the impact on wavelength by increasing frequency, and highlights the degree to which a wavelength is shortened under water: for instance, at 100 Hz the free space wavelength is 3000 km while in sea water it is only 176 m. This effect has important implications for sensing and navigation applications where the frequency required for a specified dimensional resolution is much lower than in air. The third part of the table shows the range of propagation distance with the impact of increasing frequency. Recently in [19], very low frequency (VLF) has been used and achieved 40m in transmission range for 100bps data rate. By carefully choosing the frequency and associated communication protocol, it is possible to achieve greater ranges as depicted in Table 1.

MEASUREMENT TECHNIQUES

Measurement techniques in WSN localization can be broadly classified into three categories: distance related measurements, AOA measurements and RSS profiling techniques. Following sections explores those techniques as well as its scope and limitations.

Distance Related Measurement

Distance related measurements include propagation time based measurements, i.e., one-way and roundtrip propagation time measurements, time-difference-of-arrival (TDOA) measurements, and RSS measurements. Another interesting technique measuring distance, which does not fall into the above categories, is the lighthouse approach shown in [20]. Following paragraphs explores those.

Time of Arrival (ToA) Measurements

Distances between neighboring sensors can be estimated from one-way or roundtrip propagation time of the signals in between beacon and sensors. One-way propagation time measurements measure the difference between the sending time of a signal at the transmitter and the receiving time of the signal at the receiver. It requires the local time at the transmitter and the local time at the receiver to be accurately synchronized. This requirement may add to the cost of sensors by demanding a highly accurate clock and/or increase the complexity of the sensor network by demanding a sophisticated synchronization mechanism. This disadvantage makes one-way propagation time measurements a less attractive option than measuring roundtrip time in WSNs. Roundtrip propagation time measurements measure the difference between the time when a signal is sent by a sensor and the time when the signal returned by a second sensor is received at the original sensor. Since the same clock is used to compute the roundtrip propagation time, there is no synchronization problem. The major error source in roundtrip propagation time measurements is the delay required for handling the signal in the second sensor. This internal delay is either known via *a priori* calibration, or measured and sent to the first sensor to be subtracted.

Time delay measurement is a relatively mature field in the terrestrial localization. The most widely used method for obtaining time delay measurement is the generalized cross correlation method [21]. A recent trend in propagation time measurements is the use of ultra wide band (UWB) signals for accurate distance estimation [22]. A UWB signal is a signal whose bandwidth to center frequency ratio is larger than 0.2 or a signal with a total bandwidth of more than 500 MHz. UWB can achieve higher accuracy because its bandwidth is very large and therefore its pulse has a very short duration. This feature makes fine time resolution of UWB signals and easy separation of multipath signals possible. The feasibility of using UWB signal underwater not possible due to propagation distance. Besides, GPS uses the same technique with collaboration of atomic clock for synchronization; it gives pretty accurate result since the distance between the satellite and the sensors on the ground. For a short distance, using this technique is quite impossible due to complexity in time synchronization between sensors.

Time Difference of Arrival (TDoA) Measurements

Figure 1 shows a TDOA localization scenario with a group of four receivers at locations r_1, r_2, r_3, r_4 and a transmitter at r_t. The TDOA between a pair of receivers i and j is given by

$$\Delta t_{ij} \overset{\Delta}{=} t_i - t_j = \frac{1}{C}\left(\|r_i - r_t\| - \|r_j - r_t\|\right),\ i \neq j \tag{7}$$

where t_i and t_j are the time when a signal is received at receivers i and j, respectively, C is the propagation speed of the signal, and $\|...\|$ denotes the Euclidean norm. Measuring the TDOA of a signal at two receivers at separate locations is a relatively mature field. The most widely used method is the generalized cross-correlation method, where the cross-correlation function between two signals s_i and s_j received at receivers i and j is given by integrating the lag product of two received signals for a sufficiently long time period T as in Eq. (8).

$$\rho_{i,j}(\tau) = \frac{1}{T}\int_0^T s_i(t)s_j(t-\tau)dt \tag{8}$$

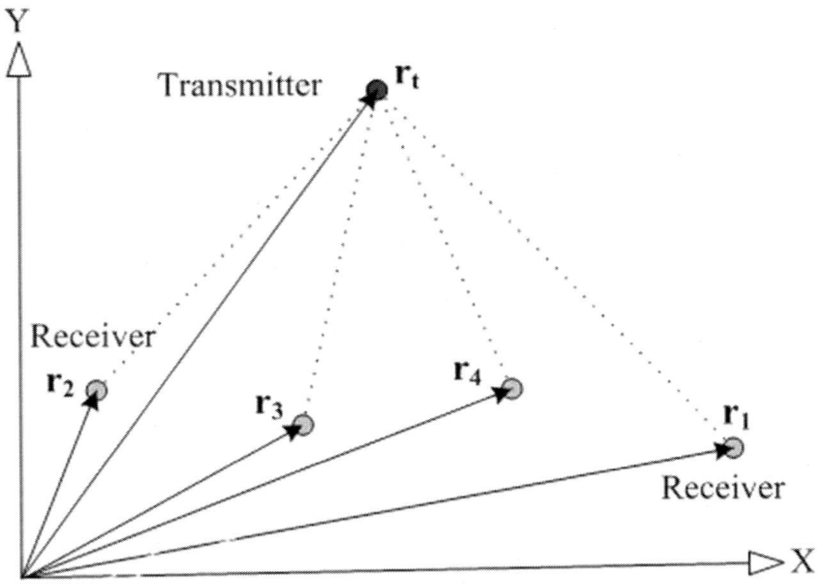

Figure 1. Localization using time difference of arrival measurements.

The cross-correlation function can also be obtained from an inverse Fourier transform of the estimated frequency domain cross-spectral density function. Frequency domain processing is often preferred because the signals can be filtered prior to computation of the cross-correlation function. The cross-correlation approach requires very accurate synchronization among receivers but does not impose any requirement on the signal transmitted by the transmitter. The accuracy and temporal resolution capabilities of TDOA measurements will improve when the separation between receivers increases because this increases differences between time-of-arrivals. Closely spaced multiple receivers may give rise to multiple received signals that cannot be separated. For example, TDOA of multiple signals that are not separated by more than the width of their cross-correlation peaks (whose location on the time-delay axis corresponds to TDOA) usually cannot be resolved by conventional TDOA measurement techniques [23]. Yet another factor affecting the accuracy of TDOA measurement is multipath. Overlapping cross-correlation peaks due to multipath often cannot be resolved. Even if distinct peaks can be resolved, a method must be designed for selecting the correct peak value, such as choosing the largest or the first peak [24]. It is worth noting that Gardner and Chen proposed an approach in [23] which exploits the cyclostationarity property of a certain signal to obtain substantial tolerance to noise and interference. The cyclostationarity property is a direct result of the underlying periodicities in the signal due to periodic sampling, scanning, modulating, multiplexing, and coding operations employed in the transmitter. Both the frequency-shifted and time-shifted cross-correlations are utilized to exploit the unique cyclostationarity property of the signal. Their method requires the signal of interest to have a known analog frequency or digital keying rate that is distinct from that of the interfering signal.

Received Signal Strength (RSS) Measurements

In this method each ordinary node determines its distance from a reference node by measuring the received signal strength and comparing it with a range dependent signal attenuation model [25].

These techniques are based on a standard feature found in most wireless devices, a received signal strength indicator (RSSI). They are attractive because they require no additional hardware, and are unlikely to significantly impact local power consumption, sensor size and thus cost. However, it is difficult to achieve accurate ranging when multipath and shadow fading effects exist.

In free space, other things being equal the RSS varies as the inverse square of the distance d between the transmitter and the receiver. Let us denote this received power by $P_r(d)$. The received power $P_r(d)$ is related to the distance d through Eq. (9) the Friis equation [26].

$$P_r(d) = \frac{P_t G_t P G_r \lambda^2}{(4\pi)^2 d^2} \tag{9}$$

where P_t is the transmitted power, G_t is the transmitter antenna gain, G_r is the receiver antenna gain and λ is the wavelength of the transmitter signal in meters.

The free-space model however is an over-idealization, and the propagation of a signal is affected by reflection, diffraction and scattering. Of course, these effects are environment (indoors, outdoors, rain, buildings, etc.) dependent. However, it is accepted on the basis of empirical evidence that it is reasonable to model the RSS by $P_r(d)$ at any value of d at a particular location as random and log-normally distributed random variable as in [27] as follows:

$$P_r(d)[dBm] = P_0(d_0)[dBm] - 10n_p \log_{10}\left(\frac{d}{d_0}\right) + x_\sigma \tag{10}$$

where $P_r(d)$[dBm] is a known reference power value in dB milliwatts at a reference distance d_0 from the transmitter, n_p is the path loss exponent that measures the rate at which the RSS decreases with distance and the value of n_p depends on the specific propagation environment, x_σ is a zero mean Gaussian distributed random variable with standard deviation σ and it accounts for the random effect of shadowing [26].

It is trivial to conclude from Eq. (10) that, given the RSS measurement P_{ij} between a transmitter i and a receiver j, a maximum likelihood estimate of the distance, d_{ij}, between the transmitter and the receiver is

$$\hat{d}_{ij} = d_0\left(\frac{P_{ij}}{P_0(d_0)}\right)^{1/n_p} \tag{11}$$

where P_{ij} and $P_0(d_0)$ are measured in milliwatts instead of dB milliwatts. Maximum likelihood estimate in Eq. (11) is a biased estimate of the true distance and an unbiased estimate is given by Eq. (12).

$$\hat{d}_{ij} = d_0\left(\frac{P_{ij}}{P_0(d_0)}\right)^{-1/n_p} e^{-\frac{\sigma^2}{2\eta^2 n_p^2}} \tag{12}$$

where $\eta = \dfrac{10}{\ln(10)}$. Since the path loss in underwater acoustic channels is usually time varying and multipath effect can result in significant energy fading, the RSSI method is not the primary choice for underwater localization.

Angle of Arrival (AoA) Measurements

The angle-of-arrival measurement techniques can be further divided into two subclasses: those making use of the receiver antenna's amplitude response and those making use of the receiver antenna's phase response. Beamforming is the name given to the use of anisotropy in the reception pattern of an antenna, and it is the basis of one category of AOA measurement techniques. The measurement unit can be of small size in comparison with the wavelength of the signals. The beam pattern of a typical anisotropic antenna is shown in Figure 2. One can imagine that the beam of the receiver antenna is rotated electronically or mechanically, and the direction corresponding to the maximum signal strength is taken as the direction of the transmitter. Relevant parameters are the sensitivity of the receiver and the beam width. A technical problem to be faced and overcome arises when the transmitted signal has varying signal strength. The receiver cannot differentiate the signal strength variation due to the varying amplitude of the transmitted signal and the signal strength variation caused by the anisotropy in the reception pattern. One approach to dealing with the problem is to use a second non-rotating and omnidirectional antenna at the receiver. By normalizing the signal strength received by the rotating anisotropic antenna with respect to the signal strength received by the non-rotating omnidirectional antenna, the impact of varying signal strength can be largely removed.

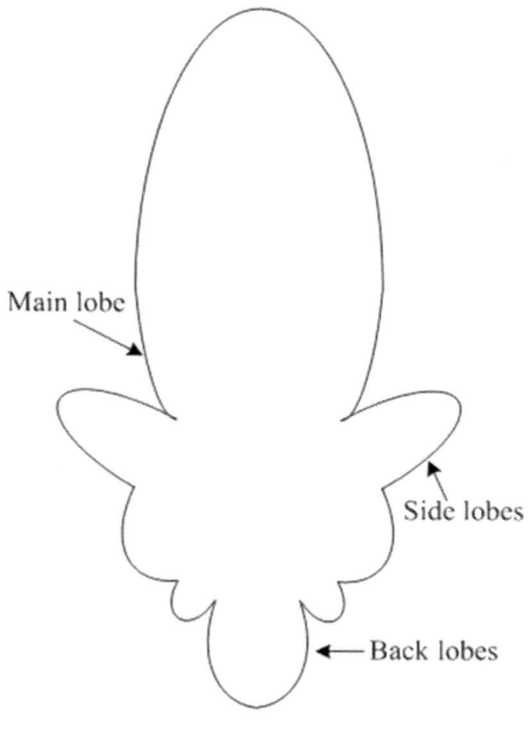

Figure 2. Horizontal pattern of a typical anisotropic antenna.

The second category of measurement techniques, known as phase interferometry [24] where it derives the AOA measurements from the measurements of the phase differences in the arrival of a wave front. It typically requires a large receiver antenna (relative to the wavelength of the transmitter signal) or an antenna array. Figure 3 shows an antenna array of N antenna elements. The adjacent antenna elements are separated by a uniform distance d. The distance between a transmitter far away from the antenna array and the ith antenna element can be approximated by

$$R_i \approx R_i - id\cos\theta \tag{13}$$

where R_0 is the distance between the transmitter and the 0th antenna element and θ is the bearing of the transmitter with respect to the antenna array. The transmitter signals received by adjacent antenna elements have a phase difference of $d2\pi\frac{d\cos\theta}{\lambda}$, which allows us to obtain the bearing of the transmitter from the measurement of the phase difference. This approach works quite well for high SNR but may fail in the presence of strong co-channel interference and/or multipath signals.

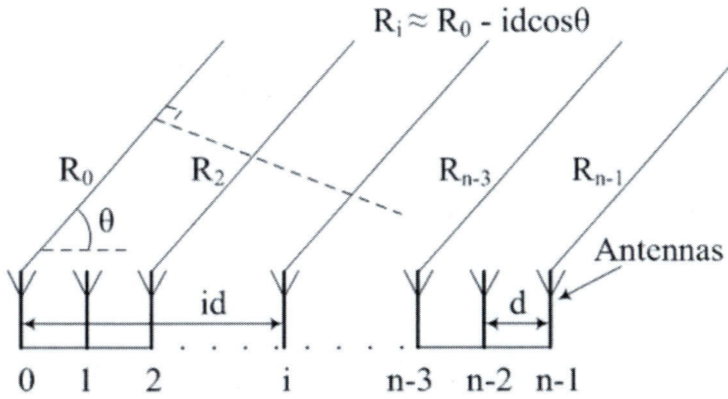

Figure 3. Antenna array with *n* antenna elements.

The accuracy of AOA measurements is limited by the directivity of the antenna, by shadowing and by multipath reflections. How to obtain accurate AOA measurements in the presence of multipath and shadowing errors has been a subject of intensive research. AOA measurements rely on a direct line-of-sight (LOS) path from the transmitter to the receiver. However a multipath component may appear as a signal arriving from an entirely different direction and can lead to very large errors in AOA measurements. Multipath problems in AOA measurements can be addressed by using the maximum likelihood (ML) algorithms [7]. Different ML algorithms have been proposed in the literature which make different assumptions about the statistical characteristics of the incident signals [28, 29]. They can be classified into deterministic and stochastic ML methods. Typically ML methods will estimate the AOA of each separate path in a multipath environment. The implementation of these methods is computationally intensive and requires complex multidimensional search. The dimensionality of the search is equal to the total number of paths taken by all the received signals.

The problem is further complicated by the fact that the total number of paths is not known a priori and must be estimated. Different from the earlier ML methods, which assume the incoming signal is an unknown stochastic process, another class of ML methods [30, 31] assume that the structure of the signal waveform is known to the receiver. This assumption is possible in some digital communication systems because the modulation format is known to the receiver and many systems are equipped with a known training sequence in the preamble. This extra information is exploited to improve the accuracy of AOA measurements or simplify computation.

Another class of AOA measurement methods is based on so-called subspace-based algorithms. The most well-known methods in this category are multiple signal classification (MUSIC) and estimation of signal parameters by rotational invariance techniques (ESPRIT). These eigenanalysis based direction finding algorithms utilize a vector space formulation, which takes advantage of the underlying parametric data model for the sensor array problem. They require a multi-array antenna in order to form a correlation matrix using signals received by the array. These eigenanalysis based algorithm works well in terrestrial environment but installing of multi-array of antenna in underwater environment is very difficult due to water current. Moreover, dynamic localization is quite impossible where previous infrastructure is absent.

Received Signal Strength (RSS) Profiling Measurement

The RSS profiling-based localization techniques are mainly performed by constructing a form of map of the signal strength behavior in the coverage area. The map is obtained either offline by *a priori* measurements or online using sniffing devices deployed at known locations. They have been mainly used for location estimation in WLANs, but they would appear to be attractive also for wireless sensor networks.

In this technique, in addition to anchor nodes (e.g., access points in WLANs) and non-anchor nodes, a large number of sample points (e.g., sniffing devices) are distributed throughout the coverage area of the sensor network. At each sample point, a vector of signal strengths is obtained, with the jth entry corresponding to the jth anchor's transmitted signal. Of course, many entries of the signal strength vector may be zero or very small, corresponding to anchor nodes at larger distances (relative to the transmission range or sensing radius) from the sample point. The collection of all these vectors provides a map of the whole region by extrapolation in the vicinity of the sample points. The collection constitutes the RSS model, and it is unique with respect to the anchor locations and the environment. The model is stored in a central location. By referring to the RSS model, a non-anchor node can estimate its location using the RSS measurements from anchors. RSS profiling measurement technique performs better job when the problem domain is predefined and does not change its specification so often; in case of underwater environment where the variables changes from one place to other. Besides, dynamic localization technique does not depend on previously measured specifications or infrastructure; hence this technique of measurement in localization is not suitable for underwater environment.

Localization Techniques

Localization has been widely explored for terrestrial wireless sensor networks, with many localization schemes being proposed so far. Generally speaking, these schemes can be classified into three categories: range-based, range-free and finger-printing schemes. The former covers the protocols that use absolute point-to-point distance (i.e., range) estimates or angle estimates to calculate locations, while the rest of them have no assumptions about the availability or validity of such range information. Although range-based protocols can provide more accurate position estimates, they need additional hardware for distance measures, which will increase the network cost. On the other hand, range-free schemes do not need additional hardware support, but can only provide coarse position estimates. As we are interested in accurate localization, thus range-based schemes are potentially good choice for

UWSNs. Following sections elaborates different schemes, focusing mainly on range-based localization.

Range-Based Localization

In range-based schemes, precise distance or angle measurements are made to estimate the location of nodes in the network. Range based schemes, which rely on range and/or bearing information, use Time of Arrival (ToA), Time Difference of Arrival (TDoA), Angle of Arrival (AoA) or Received Signal Strength Indicator (RSSI) to estimate their distances to other nodes in the system. GPS and Cricket are examples of schemes that use ToA or TDoA of acoustic or RF signals for localization in terrestrial sensor networks.

In the context of wireless sensor networks, range-based schemes can be divided into three categories: infrastructure-based schemes, distributed positioning schemes and schemes that use mobile beacons. Each category is discussed in detail followed by the challenges faced by this class of schemes.

Infrastructure-Based Positioning Schemes

Infrastructure-based (anchor-based) localization systems are similar to the GPS scheme. The GPS space segment consists of 24 satellites in the medium earth orbit at a nominal altitude of 20,200 km with an orbital inclination of 550. Each satellite carries several high accuracy atomic clocks and radiates a sequence of bits that starts at a precisely known time. The location of a GPS satellite at any particular time instant is known. A GPS receiver located on the earth derives its distance to a GPS satellite from the difference of the time a GPS signal is received at the receiver and the time the GPS signal is radiated by the GPS satellite. Ideally, distance measurements to three GPS satellites allow the GPS receiver to uniquely determine its position.

In reality, four satellites, rather than three, are required because of synchronization error in the receiver's clock.

The fourth distance measurement provides information from which the synchronization error of the receiver can be corrected and the receiver's clock can be synchronized to accuracy better than 100 ns.

Time of Arrival Based

Generally in a WSN, for a non-anchor node at unknown location x_t with noise-contaminated distance measurements $\tilde{d}_1, \ldots, \tilde{d}_N$ to N anchors at known locations $x_t, \ldots, x_N$, the location estimation problem can be formulated using a maximum likelihood approach as

$$\hat{x}_t = \arg\min \left[d(\hat{x}_t) - \tilde{d} \right]^T S^{-1} \left[d(\hat{x}_t) - \tilde{d} \right] \tag{14}$$

where $\tilde{d}$ is a $N \times 1$ distance measurement vector, $d(\hat{x}_t)$ is also a $N \times 1$ vector

$[\|\hat{x}_t - x_1\|, \ldots, \|\hat{x}_t - x_N\|]$ and S is the covariance matrix of the distance measurement errors. This minimization problem can be solved by conventional method.

An interesting development in the area is the use of the Cayley–Menger determinant [32] to reduce the impact of distance measurement errors on the location estimate. To illustrate the concept, consider a non-anchor node x_t having distance measurements to three anchors x_1, x_2, x_3 in $\mathcal{R}^2$ which is shown in Figure 4. The Cayley–Menger determinant of this quadrilateral is given by

$$D(x_1, x_2, x_3, x_t) = \begin{vmatrix} 0 & 1 & 1 & 1 & 1 \\ 1 & 0 & d_{12}^2 & d_{13}^2 & d_{1t}^2 \\ 1 & d_{12}^2 & 0 & d_{23}^2 & d_{2t}^2 \\ 1 & d_{13}^2 & d_{23}^2 & 0 & d_{3t}^2 \\ 1 & d_{1t}^2 & d_{2t}^2 & d_{3t}^2 & 0 \end{vmatrix} \tag{15}$$

According to the Eq. (15), in $\mathcal{R}^2$,

$$D(x_1, x_2, x_3, x_t) = 0 \tag{16}$$

The essence of using the Cayley-menger determinant to reduce the impact of distance measurement errors is: the six edges of a planar quadrilateral are not independent; instead they must satisfy the equality constraint in Eq. (15). This equality constraint can be exploited to reduce the impact of distance measurement errors. This idea may also extend to TDOA and AOA based localization.

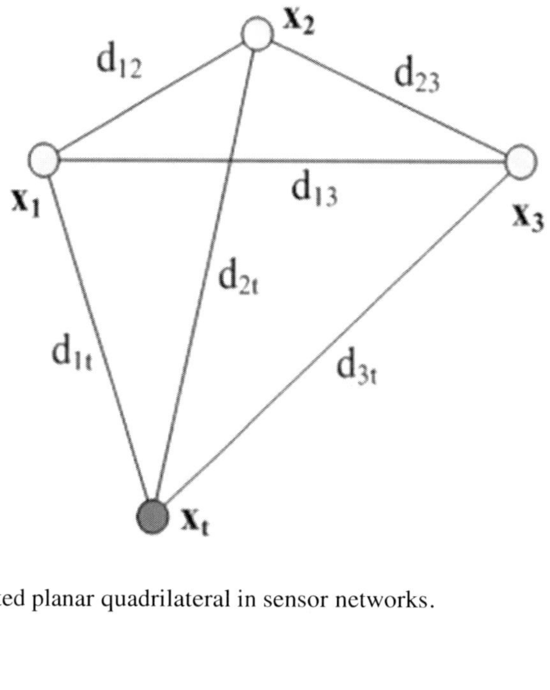

Figure 4. A fully connected planar quadrilateral in sensor networks.

In such a system underwater anchor nodes are deployed on the sea-bed at pre-determined locations. Surface buoys, whose locations are determined by GPS, might also serve as anchor nodes. The distance to multiple anchor nodes is computed by using the propagation time of the sound signals between the sensor or the AUV and the anchors. In many cases, the number of independent range measurements exceeds the number of unknown coordinates. In an over-determined system, the position estimate is made using least squares method. Such a scheme called Seaweb technology was implemented by the U. S. Navy and used to track AUVs [33]. The Seaweb technology was shown to track AUVs with an accuracy of 7-9 meters, in a roughly 3 km by 4 km area.

Prospector, a commercial system developed by Sonardyne, is also an infrastructure-based positioning system. Four acoustic transponders are deployed on the seabed at known locations, with surface or sub-surface floats. Each transponder is deployed at a corner of a 500m×500m area. The system can track divers equipped with transceivers or ROVs with a high degree of accuracy in water depths ranging from 5 meters to 500 meters. Sonardyne claims that it can track objects with an accuracy of 300 mm, in a 500m×500m grid under shallow water conditions. But the major limitation of infrastructure-based positioning schemes is that it is not dynamic as well as handy.

Angle of Arrival Based

In the absence of noise and interference, bearing lines from two or more receivers (anchors) will intersect to determine a unique location, i.e., the location estimate of the transmitter. In the presence of noise, more than two bearing lines will not intersect at a single point and statistical algorithms, sometimes called triangulation or fixing methods, are required in order to obtain the location estimate of the transmitter as shown in Figure 5.

Location estimation using bearing measurements is a well-researched problem. The pioneering work in the area is that of Stanfield [34]. His approach has been further generalized and has been implemented in many practical systems. Another well-known approach is the maximum likelihood estimator. The 2D localization problem using bearing measurements can be formulated as follows. Let $x_t = [x_t, y_t]^T$ be the true coordinate vector of the transmitter to be estimated from bearing measurements $\beta = [\beta_1, ..., \beta_N]^T$ where N is the total number of receivers. Let $x_i = [x_i, y_i]^T$ be the known location of the receiver associated with the ith bearing measurement. Denote by $\theta(x) = [\theta_1(x), ..., \theta_N(x)]^T$ the bearings of a transmitter located at $x = [x, y]^T$ at the receiver locations, where $\theta_i(x)$, $1 \le i \le N$ is related to x by

$$\tan\theta_i = \frac{y - y_i}{x - x_i} \tag{17}$$

The measured bearings of the transmitter consist of the true bearings corrupted by additive noises $\varepsilon = [\varepsilon_1, ..., \varepsilon_N]^T$ which are assumed to be zero-mean Gaussian noises with $N \times N$ covariance matrices $S = \text{diag}\{\sigma_1^2, ..., \sigma_N^2\}$, i.e.,

$$\beta = \theta(x_t) + \varepsilon \tag{18}$$

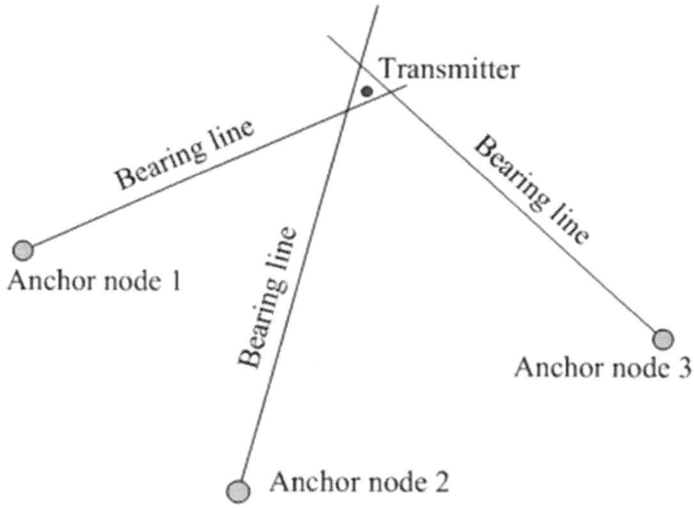

Figure 5. Bearing Line from Three Anchor Nodes with Noise.

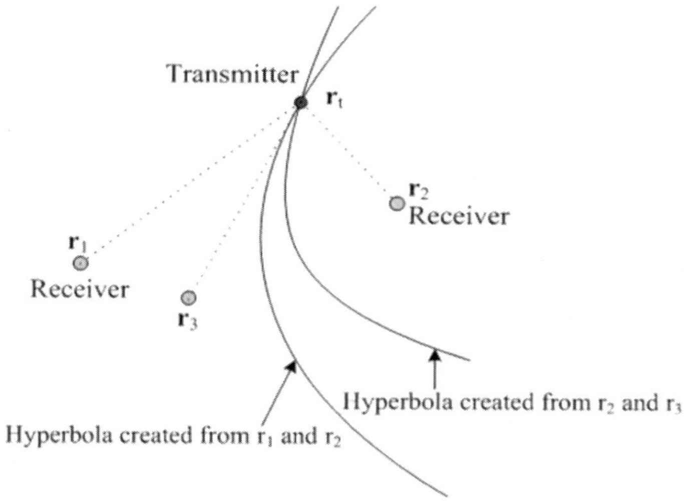

Figure 6. Intersecting hyperbolas from three receivers.

When the receivers are identical and much closer to each other than to the transmitter, the variances of bearing measurement errors are equal, i.e., $\sigma_1^2 = \sigma_N^2 = \sigma^2$. The ML estimator of the transmitter location x_t is given by

$$\hat{x}_t = \arg\frac{\min 1}{2}\left[\theta(\hat{x}_t) - \beta\right]^T S^{-1}\left[\theta(\hat{x}_t) - \beta\right] = \arg\frac{\min 1}{2}\sum_{i-1}^{N}\frac{\left(\theta_i(\hat{x}_t) - \beta_i\right)^2}{\sigma_i^2} \tag{19}$$

The nonlinear minimization problem in Eq. (19) can be solved by a Newton–Gauss iteration [35]

$$\hat{x}_{t,k+1} = \hat{x}_{t,k} + \left(\theta_x(\hat{x}_{t,k})^T S^{-1} \theta_x(\hat{x}_{t,k}) \right)^{-1} \theta_x(\hat{x}_{t,k})^T S^{-1} \left[\beta - \theta_x(\hat{x}_{t,k}) \right] \quad (20)$$

where $\theta_x(\hat{x}_{t,k})$ denotes the partial derivative of θ with respect to x evaluated at $\hat{x}_{t,k}$. The use of Eq. (20) requires an initial estimate close enough to the true minimum of the cost function. Such an initial estimate may be obtained from prior information, or using a suboptimal procedure. In underwater environment, determining angle of received signal is cumbersome. Moreover, at least three anchor node needs to be installed with prior location information makes this procedure not dynamic at all.

Time Difference of Arrival Based

Given the TDOA measurement Δt_{ij} and the coordinates of receivers i and j, Eq. (7) defines one branch of a hyperbola whose foci are at the locations of receivers i and j and on which the transmitter r_t must lie. In $\mathcal{R}^2$, measurements from a minimum of three receivers are required to uniquely determine the location of the transmitter. This is illustrated in Figure 6.

In a system of N receivers, there are N-1 linearly independent TDOA equations, which can be written compactly as

$$\begin{bmatrix} \|r_1 - r_t\| - \|r_N - r_t\| - c\Delta t_{1N} \\ \vdots \\ \vdots \\ \|r_{N-1} - r_t\| - \|r_N - r_t\| - c\Delta t_{N-1,N} \end{bmatrix} = 0 \quad (21)$$

In practice Δt_{ij} is not available; instead we have the noisy TDOA measurement $\Delta \tilde{t}_{ij}$ given by

$$\Delta \tilde{t}_{ij} = \Delta t_{ij} + n_{ij} \quad (22)$$

where n_{ij} denotes an additive noise, which is usually assumed to be an independent zero-mean Gaussian distributed random variable. Eq. (21) is a nonlinear equation that is difficult to solve, especially when the receivers are arranged in an arbitrary fashion. This method relies on a good initial guess of the transmitter location. Moreover, in some situations this method can result in significant location estimation errors due to geometric dilution of precision (GDOP) effects. GDOP describes a situation in which a relatively small ranging error can result in a large location estimation error because the transmitter is located on a portion of the hyperbola far away from both receivers [36]. In [37], an exact solution to the hyperbolic equations in Eq. (21) is given when the number of TDOA measurements are equal to the number of unknown transmitter coordinates. However his solution cannot make use of extra measurements. Chan and Ho [38] developed a closed form solution valid for an arbitrary number of TDOA measurements and arbitrarily distributed transmitters. The solution is an approximation of the maximum likelihood estimator when the TDOA measurement errors are small. The computational complexity of Chan's method is comparable to the spherical interpolation method but substantially less than the Taylor-series method.

Distributed Positioning Schemes

Distributed positioning schemes are employed in cases where a positioning infrastructure is not available, i.e., anchor-free. In distributed positioning schemes, nodes are able to communicate only with their one-hop neighbours and compute the distances to their one-hop neighbours. Multilateration techniques, which encompass atomic, collaborative and iterative multilateration, are then used in a distributed manner to estimate the location of each sensor node. Distributed positioning algorithms generally have three positioning phases: the distance estimation phase, where nodes estimate the distances to their neighbours, the position estimation phase, where a system of linear equations is generally solved using a least squares approach to estimate the position of the node, and finally a refinement phase, where the accuracy of the algorithm is improved by using an iterative algorithm. The NHop Multilateration Scheme, the Hop-TERRAIN and Refinement Scheme, Ad Hoc Localization System (AHLoS) and Ad Hoc Positioning System (APS) "Distance Propagation" and "Euclidian Propagation" Schemes fall under this category.

The N-Hop Multilateration Scheme discusses the requirements for location solution uniqueness in the one-hop, two-hop and *n*-hop case. In this scheme, initial estimates for all nodes are made using the conditions of position uniqueness, and the constraints obtained from distance measurements to neighbouring nodes. A refinement process is then carried out using Kalman filters. In [39], initial estimates are obtained using an algorithm similar to the range-free scheme DV-Hop. Then, a least squares method is used to refine nodes' locations based on local computations. The AHLoS scheme uses iterative multilateration where unknown nodes, which estimate their locations by triangulation, become beacon nodes. The problem with such a scheme is that the error propagates through the network as the number of hops as the anchor node increases.

In distributed positioning schemes, nodes estimate their distances to neighbours by making RSSI or ToA measurements. RSSI based schemes can only provide a ranging accuracy of a few meters, while ToA based schemes can achieve ranging accuracy of a few centimetres. In underwater sensor networks, ToA based ranging is the preferred option as acoustics is the mode of communication between nodes.

Distributed positioning algorithms generally assume anchor nodes to be randomly distributed throughout the network, and the percentage of anchor nodes in the network to be quite high too (5- 20%) [40]. In terrestrial sensor networks, deploying anchor nodes is not a challenge, as nodes equipped with GPS could act as anchor nodes. However, in the case of underwater sensor networks, setting up a backbone of randomly distributed anchor nodes, whose precise locations are known, is not a trivial problem.

Under distributed positioning schemes, not all the nodes in the system are localized, even though the network might be fully connected. For example, the nodes which do not satisfy the position uniqueness conditions might not be able to compute their locations.

Schemes with Mobile Beacons

Traditional range-based schemes have fixed anchor nodes whose locations are known. Schemes have been proposed which use mobile beacons whose locations are always known [41]. In this scheme, a mobile beacon traverses the sensor network while broadcasting beacon packets which contain the location coordinates of the beacon. Any node receiving the beacon packet will be able to infer that it must be somewhere near the mobile beacon with a certain probability. RSSI measurements of the received beacon packets are used for ranging purposes. After a number of packets have been received from the mobile beacon, Bayesian inference is used to determine the location of the node. In terrestrial networks, an autonomous vehicle installed with GPS could traverse the network and broadcast beacon packets. The challenge faced by an underwater network is that the location of the AUV itself might be unknown. The location of the AUV would have to be determined first using other means before it could be used for positioning nodes on the seabed.

A scheme that uses RSSI has to deal with problems caused by large variances in reading, multi-path fading, irregular signal propagation patterns and background interference. Such schemes may not be useful in the underwater scenario due to the large variances in RSSI. Alternatively, in the underwater domain, the ToA of the acoustic signals from the mobile beacon could be used for ranging purposes.

Commercial positioning solutions have been developed by Sonardyne for shallow and deep water applications. A ship equipped with GPS suspends a transponder into the water. The sensor nodes dropped on the seabed are also equipped with acoustic transponders. The position of a node on the seabed is then calibrated by sailing the vessel over the area in which the nodes are dropped. In [42] this scheme has been shown to work well in shallow waters. It has also been claimed that the nodes on the seabed are localized with an accuracy of within one meter, for water depths up to 500 meters. The acoustic range and bearing data from the moving ship is used to localize the nodes. In this case, the ship serves as a mobile anchor and the localization process is typically carried out in less than 20 minutes which is the biggest drawback of the scheme.

Very recently in [43] proposed a localization solution with a single mobile beacon (i.e., boat/buoy) where the beacon takes distance measurements between itselfs and deployed the sensors. Once the measurements are done, Cayley-menger determinant is used followed by linearization to solve for sensors' coordinates. Figure 7 shows the configuration of at least three sensors and a beacon for coordinate determination.

Schemes without Reference Point

The fourth class of schemes is different from the first three in that it does not require anchor nodes or beacon signals. In [44], a central server models the network as a series of equations representing proximity constraints between nodes, and then uses sophisticated optimization techniques to estimate the location of every node in the network.

Range-Free Localization

Range-free localization schemes do not use range or bearing information; that is, they do not make use of any of the techniques mentioned above (ToA, TDoA and AoA) to estimate distances to other nodes. The accuracy of range-based localization depends on the accuracy of range measurement, which could suffer from large errors due to node mobility as well as harsh underwater acoustic propagation environment. Hence, range-free schemes have been proposed that do not rely on range measurement for localization. It is worth noting, range free schemes only provide a coarse estimate of a node's location.

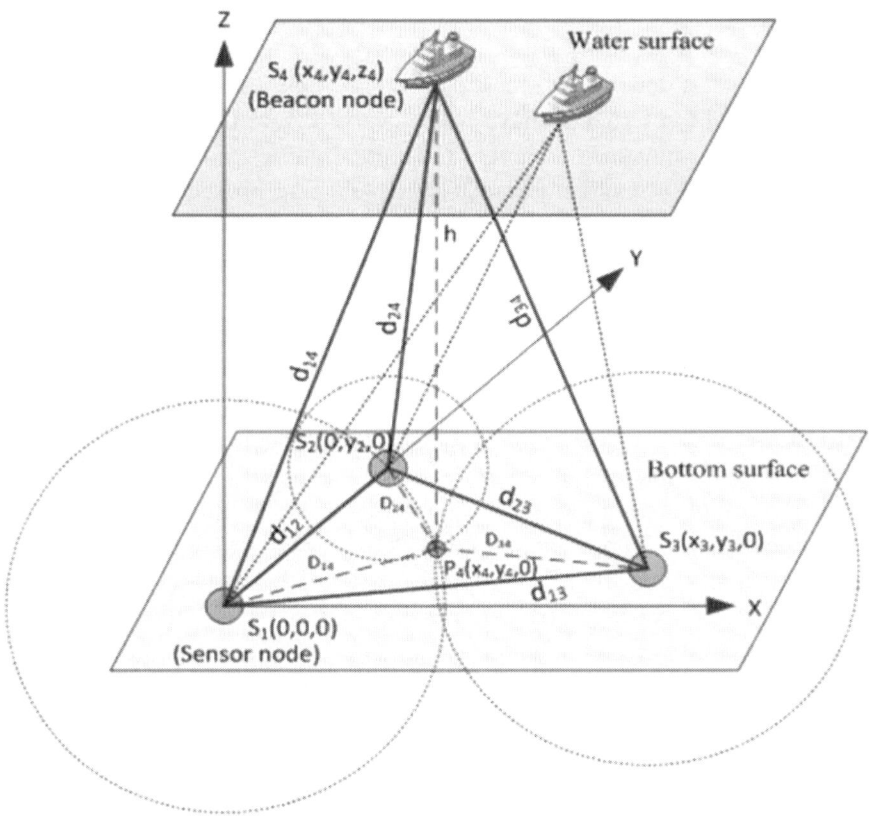

Figure 7. Subset of sensors and coordinates determination.

Hop Count Based Schemes

DV-Hop is one of the most basic range-free schemes, and it first employs a classical distance vector exchange so that all nodes in the network get distances, in number of hops, to the anchor nodes. Each node maintains a table and exchanges updates only with its neighbours. Once a landmark (i.e., an anchor) gets distances to other landmarks, it estimates an average distance for one hop, which is then propagated as a correction to the entire network. Upon receiving the correction, an arbitrary node then estimates its distances to the landmarks, in meters, which can be used to perform triangulation. The DV-Hop algorithm performs well only in networks that have uniform and dense node distributions.

For actual deployments where the node distribution is more likely to be non-uniform and sparse in certain regions, schemes like Density-aware Hop-count Localization (DHL) [45] have been proposed to improve the accuracy of location estimation when the node distribution in the network is not uniform. This scheme takes into account both the density of a node's neighbourhood when computing the average hop distance, as well as, the fact that error in distance estimation tends to accumulate with the increase of path length.

Iterative multilateration, the process where unknown nodes which have estimated their locations become anchor nodes, must be carefully employed in range free hopcount based schemes. For example, in a network with anchor nodes placed at the corners of a square grid, it is observed that the error is higher along the boundaries and lower in the middle of the region. Based on this observation, a Selective Iterative Multilateration (SIM) algorithm [46] is proposed where new anchor nodes are selected judiciously such that their initial position estimates are sufficiently accurate.

Centroid Based Scheme

In this scheme, anchor nodes are placed to form a rectangular mesh. The anchor nodes send out beacon signals at periodic intervals with their respective locations. From the beacon signals received, a receiver node infers proximity to a collection of anchor nodes. The location of the node is then estimated to be the centroid of the anchor nodes that it can receive beacon packets from. A high concentration of anchor nodes is required for this scheme to work well. Also, such a scheme would be hard to implement in the underwater context as it would require setting up a rectangular mesh of anchor nodes on the seabed.

Area Based Schemes

Chandrasekhar and Seah in [47] proposed a 2D area localization scheme, Area-based Localization Schemes (ALS), to estimate a node's position within a certain area rather than its exact location. The propagation of acoustic signals underwater is subject to losses due to spreading, absorption, dispersion, multipath fading and Doppler effects.

Assuming a spherical attenuation model, and neglecting losses due to multipath fading and Doppler effects, when each reference node transmits at power P_i, an ordinary node can receive the transmission as long as it falls within a circular region centered at the reference node whose radius $r(P_i)$ depends on the transmission power. Hence, by deploying several reference nodes that transmit beacons at multiple power levels, the plane is divided into many small sub-regions defined by intersecting circles. Each ordinary node listens and reports the ID and minimum transmit power at which it received the respective node's beacon to a central sink, which can then estimate its location.

Zhou et al. [48] proposed a scheme, 3D multistage area localization scheme(3D-MALS) that combines the concepts of ALS and LSL-DET. It considers a hierarchical network architecture that comprises surface buoys with "detachable elevator transceivers" (DET), ordinary nodes and sink nodes, and extends ALS to 3D. Simulation results demonstrate its performance gain over ALS in terms of localization accuracy. However, as with ASL, it is a model-based, centralized scheme that provides coarse localization and does not consider node mobility.

Directional Beaconing Based Schemes

While the above schemes rely on static references, Luo et al. in [49] proposed a 2D and 3D underwater localization scheme (UDB and LDB respectively) using a single AUV with directional beacons. Here, the AUV traverses a preprogramed route and performs directional (vertical) beaconing periodically. The scheme assumes that the AUV moves with constant and known speed and knows its position underwater accurately using integrated GPS and INS, and that the vertical channel used in UDB is characterized by little or no time dispersion.

Figure 8 gives an illustration of how ordinary sensor node, equipped with a pressure sensor, localizes itself with LDB.

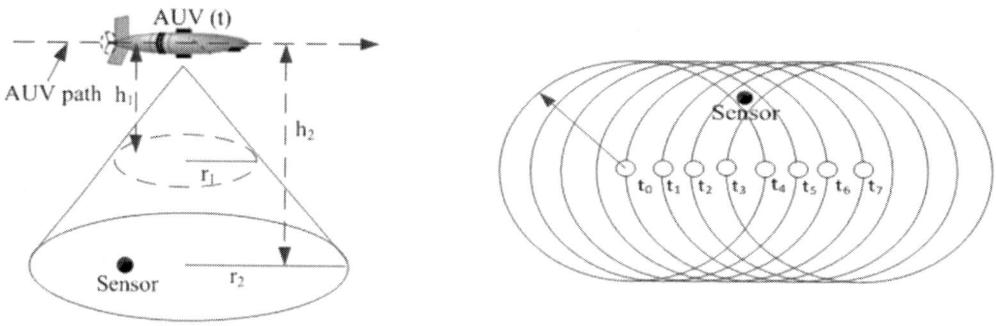

Figure 8. Localization with Directional Beaconing (LDB).

Assuming a beamwidth of α, the radius of the circle formed by the intersection of the beam with the horizontal plane for which sensor resides, r_2 is given as

$$r_2 = \tan\left(\frac{\alpha}{2}\right) \times h_2 \tag{23}$$

where h_2 is the difference in depth between the AUV and node S.

Assuming that the AUV traverses a straight line path and broadcasts its own location periodically, at times $t_0, t_1, \ldots, t_n$ at instant t_i, node sensor would record the AUV's coordinates (x_i, y_i), if it can hear them, i.e., if it lies within the circle of radius r_2 centered at (x_i, y_i). According to Figure 8, node sensor first hears the AUV's beacons when it transmits at (x_i, y_i) at time t_1 and last hears them when it transmits at (x_i, y_i) at time t_5. Accordingly, it estimates its position, $(\bar{x}_i, \bar{y}_i)$ as follows:

$$\bar{x} = \frac{x_1 + x_2}{2} \tag{24}$$

$$\bar{y} = y_1 + \frac{\sqrt{r_2^2 - \frac{x_5 - x_1 + 2d^2}{2}} + \sqrt{r_2^2 - \frac{x_5 - x_1^2}{2}}}{2} \tag{25}$$

where d is the distance traversed by the AUV between successive beaconing instances.

Finger Printing-Based Localization

A different variant of range-free localization schemes based on finger-printing (PM, PCA, PF) have recently been proposed.

Such schemes involve an offline (or training) stage prior to the online (or prediction) stage. The setup comprises an acoustic signal source capable of transmitting at M different frequencies, and L reference locations with known positions and a node (receiver) to be localized.

During the offline stage, the receiver is placed at each reference location (with known position), collects N samples of acoustic communication signals at each frequency to constitute an $M \times N$ acoustic signal map. All the signals are projected onto the eigenspace for principal component analysis, where M' signals corresponding to the largest eigenvalues are extracted in order to reduce the complexity and noise effects. This is repeated at the L reference locations.

In the online stage, the receiver is placed at an unknown location (within the reference location space) and collects acoustic communication signals from M different frequencies to establish a signal vector, from which M_0 principal components are extracted as in the offline stage.

A likelihood function is used to express the probability that the unknown location corresponds to a reference one, and the unknown location can then be estimated by the ''probabilistic weighted'' summation of different reference locations. The efficacy of the proposed scheme is verified in actual experiments in a water tank. However, the practical use of this scheme is limited since the actual underwater acoustic channel in the sea is highly time varying.

PROBLEMS AND LIMITATIONS

Most of the localization algorithms that are suitable for terrestrial environment possesses difficultly and in some cases almost impossible to use in underwater localization due to harsh environment. Moreover the variable nature of underwater environment and limitations in using signals made it more difficult in localization arena; whereas localization in underwater is as important as terrestrial. Any scheme that relies on ToA or TDoA requires tight time synchronization between the transmitter and the receiver clocks. Moreover, TDoA schemes determine the time difference of received signal between multiple receivers, where to localize one sensor node multiple receiver nodes are necessary. One simple way to achieve synchronization between the receivers as well as between transmitter and receivers in terrestrial networks is to use a radio signal. The luxury of using RF signals for time synchronization is not readily available in the underwater scenario as RF waves do not propagate well underwater. But, with the advancement of sensors' capability in measuring received signal strength and choosing the right frequency shows the possibility of using radio signal underwater. However, the propagation distance of radio signal is confined within few hundred meters. If problem domain is out of this scope, it would be practical to use acoustic signal for measurement purposes. The speed of sound is assumed to be constant in many schemes, while the speed of sound is a function of temperature, salinity and depth. It is conspicuous that schemes that take into account the variation in the speed of sound are expected to perform better than those that just assume a uniform speed of 1500 m/s.

Multipath fading is one of the major influencing factors while determining distance between transmitters and receivers with the help of RSSI. There are other environmental as well as physical factors that affect the signal strength. Like acoustic signal is affected by reflection and refraction due to sea surface and seabed. Typical frequencies associated with underwater acoustics are between 10Hz and 1MHz. The propagation of sound in the ocean at frequencies lower than 10Hz is usually not possible without penetrating deep into the seabed, whereas frequencies above 1MHz are rarely used because they are absorbed very quickly. So for any appropriate acoustic frequency that is used in underwater to measure the propagation loss is affected by multipath fading. Experiments reported in [50] have shown that multipath effects can be modelled as Rayleigh fading in shallow water environments. Acoustic signals, apart from undergoing large scale spherical or cylindrical losses under water, also undergo attenuation losses and losses due to air bubbles, and are subjected to external sources of noise like ship and shrimp noise.

Several range-based localization schemes for terrestrial sensor networks are based on AoA, where sensor nodes calculate the relative angles between neighboring nodes. However, schemes that use AoA entail sensors and anchor nodes to be equipped with special antenna configurations which may not be feasible to embed on each sensor, let alone underwater sensors where mobility and external force in some case is inevitable. Such schemes also involve solving complex non-linear equations.

Range-free schemes offer a less precise estimate of location compared to range-based schemes. Range-free schemes are useful in the context of terrestrial sensor networks, where sensor nodes might not be capable of sending acoustic signals for ranging purposes. In the case of underwater sensor networks, acoustic signals can be used for fairly accurate ranging. However, there are scenarios where a coarse estimate of the node's location might suffice. For example, geographical routing protocols could use the coarse location information obtained from range-free schemes for establishing source-destination paths. On the other hand, finger printing based schemes are suitable for a static environment; not suitable at all for dynamic underwater environment.

REFERENCES

[1] Cui, J. H., Kong, J., Gerla, M., S. Zhou, 2006. The challenges of building mobile underwater wireless networks for aquatic applications. *Journal of Network*. 20, 12-18.

[2] Tan, H. P., Diamant, R., Seah, W. K. G., Waldmeyer, M., 2011. A survey of techniques and challenges in underwater localization. *Ocean Engineering*. 38, 1663-1676.

[3] Burdic, W. S., (2002). *Underwater Acoustic System Analysis*. 113, Peninsula Publishing.

[4] Schill, F., Zimmer, U. R., J. Trumpf, 2004. Visible spectrum optical communication and distance sensing for underwater applications. *Proceedings of ACRA*. 1-6.

[5] Sozer, E. M., Stojanovic, Proakis, M., J. G., 2000. Underwater acoustic networks. *IEEE Journal of Oceanic Engineering*. 25, 72-83.

[6] Au, W. W. L., Nachtigall, P. E., Pawloski, J. L., 1997. Acoustic effects of the ATOC signal (75 Hz, 195 dB) on dolphins and whales. *The Journal of the Acoustical Society of America*. 101, 2973-2978.

[7] Etter, P. C., (2003). *Underwater Acoustics Modelling and Simulation: Principles, Techniques and Applications*, Taylor & Francis.

[8] Mackenzie, K. V., 1981. Nine term equation for sound speed in the oceans. *The Journal of the Acoustical Society of America*, 70, 807-812.

[9] Diamant, R., Chorev, L., 2005. Emulation system for underwater acoustic channel. *Proceedings of the Undersea Defence Technologies Europe Conference (UDT).*163-171.

[10] Stojanovic, M., 2007. On the relationship between capacity and distance in an underwater acoustic communication channel. *ACM SIGMOBILE Mobile Computing and Communications Review*. 11, 34-43.

[11] Moore, R. K., 1967. Radio communication in the sea. *IEEE Spectrum*. 4, 42-51.

[12] Che, X., Wells, I., Dickers, G., Kear, P., Gong, X., 2010. Re-evaluation of RF electromagnetic communication in underwater sensor networks. *IEEE Communications Magazine*. 48, 143-151.

[13] Shaw, A., Al-Shamma'a, A., Wylie, S., Toal, D., 2006. Experimental investigations of electromagnetic wave propagation in seawater. *36th European Microwave Conference*. 572-575.

[14] Abdou, A., Shaw, A., Mason, A., Al-Shamma'a, A., Cullen, J., Wylie, S., 2011. Electromagnetic (EM) wave propagation for the development of an Underwater Wireless Sensor Network (WSN). *IEEE Sensors*. 1571-1574.

[15] Kerr, A., Smith, M., Cowling, M., 2003. Optimising optical port size on underwater marine instruments to maximise biofouling resistance. *Materials & design*, 24, 247-253.

[16] White, D. W., 1978. *Investigation of an underwater electromagnetic communications channel*. MIT Press.

[17] Smith, P., 2008. Measurement and analysis of transmit antenna configurations for underwater RF communications. *Proceeding of 3rd SEAS DTC Technical Conference.*

[18] Cella, U. M., Johnstone, R., Shuley, N., 2009. Electromagnetic wave wireless communication in shallow water coastal environment: theoretical analysis and experimental results. *Proceedings of the Fourth ACM International Workshop on UnderWater Networks*.

[19] Che, X., Wells, I., Dickers, G., Kear, P., 2012. TDMA frame design for a prototype underwater RF communication network. *Ad Hoc Networks*. 10, 317-327.

[20] Römer, K., 2003. The lighthouse location system for smart dust. *Proceedings of the 1st international conference on Mobile systems, applications and services*. 15-30.

[21] Knapp, C., Carter, G., 1976. The generalized correlation method for estimation of time delay. *IEEE Transactions on Acoustics, Speech and Signal Processing*. 24, 320-327.

[22] Gezici, S., Tian, Z., Giannakis, G. B., Kobayashi, H., Molisch, A. F., Poor, H. V., Sahinoglu, Z., 2005. Localization via ultra-wideband radios: a look at positioning aspects for future sensor networks. *IEEE Signal Processing Magazine*. 22, 70-84.

[23] Gardner, W. A., Chen, C. K., 1992. Signal-selective time-difference-of-arrival estimation for passive location of man-made signal sources in highly corruptive environments. I. Theory and method. *IEEE Transactions on Signal Processing*. 40, 1168-1184.

[24] Rappaport, T. S., Reed, J. H., Woerner, B. D., 1996. Position location using wireless communications on highways of the future. *IEEE Communications Magazine*. 34, 33-41.

[25] Patwari, N., Hero III, A. O., Perkins, M., Correal, N. S., O'dea, R. J., 2003. Relative location estimation in wireless sensor networks. *IEEE Transactions on Signal Processing*. 51, 2137-2148.

[26] Rappaport, T. S., (2001). *Wireless communications: principles and practice*, Second ed.: Prentice Hall PTR New Jersey.

[27] Bernhardt, R., 1987. Macroscopic diversity in frequency reuse radio systems. *IEEE Journal on Selected Areas in Communications*. 5, 862-870.

[28] Bliss, D. W., Forsythe, K. W., 2000. Angle of arrival estimation in the presence of multiple access interference for CDMA cellular phone systems. *Proceedings of the 2000 IEEE Sensor Array and Multichannel Signal Processing*. 408-412.

[29] Ziskind, I., Wax, M., 1998. Maximum likelihood localization of multiple sources by alternating projection. *IEEE Transactions on Acoustics, Speech and Signal Processing*. 36, 1553-1560.

[30] Li, J., Halder, B., Stoica, P., Viberg, M., 1995. Computationally efficient angle estimation for signals with known waveforms. *IEEE Transactions on Signal Processing*. 43, 2154-2163.

[31] Halder, B., Viberg, M., Kailath, T., 1993. An efficient non-iterative method for estimating the angles of arrival of known signals. *Twenty-Seventh Asilomar Conference on Signals, Systems and Computers*. 1396-1400.

[32] Crippen, G. M., Havel, T. F., (1988). *Distance geometry and molecular conformation*, John Wiley and Sons Inc., New York.

[33] Hahn, M. J., (2005). *Undersea navigation via a distributed acoustic communications network*, DTIC Document.

[34] Stansfield, R., 1947. Statistical theory of DF fixing. *Journal of the Institution of Electrical Engineers-Part IIIA: Radiocommunication*. 94, 762-770.

[35] Gavish,M., Weiss, A. J., 1992. Performance analysis of bearing-only target location algorithms. *IEEE Transactions on Aerospace and Electronic Systems*. 28, 817-828.

[36] Bancroft, S., 1985. An algebraic solution of the GPS equations. *IEEE Transactions on Aerospace and Electronic Systems*. 56-59.

[37] Fang, B. T., 1990. Simple solutions for hyperbolic and related position fixes. *IEEE Transactions on Aerospace and Electronic Systems*. 26, 748-753.

[38] Chan, Y., Ho, K., 1994. A simple and efficient estimator for hyperbolic location. *IEEE Transactions on Signal Processing*. 42, 1905-1915.

[39] Rabaey, C. S. J., Langendoen, K., 2002. Robust positioning algorithms for distributed ad-hoc wireless sensor networks. *USENIX technical annual conference*.

[40] Savvides, A., Park, H., Srivastava, M. B., 2002. The bits and flops of the n-hop multilateration primitive for node localization problems. *Proceedings of the 1st ACM international workshop on Wireless sensor networks and applications*. 112-121.

[41] Sichitiu, M. L., Ramadurai, V., 2004. Localization of wireless sensor networks with a mobile beacon. *IEEE International Conference on Mobile Ad-hoc and Sensor Systems*. 174-183.

[42] Vickery, K., 1998. Acoustic positioning systems. A practical overview of current systems. *Proceedings of the Autonomous Underwater Vehicles*. 5-17.

[43] Rahman, A., Muthukkumarasamy, V., and Sithirasenan, E., 2013. Localization of Submerged Sensors Using Radio and Acoustic Signals with Single Beacon. Ad-hoc, Mobile, and Wireless Network. *Lecture Notes in Computer Science*. 7960, 293-304.

[44] Doherty, L., L. Ghaoui, El, 2001. Convex position estimation in wireless sensor networks. *Proceedings of the IEEE Computer and Communications Societies*. 1655-1663.

[45] Wong, S. Y., Lim, J. G., Rao, S., Seah, W. K. G., 2005. Multihop localization with density and path length awareness in non-uniform wireless sensor networks. IEEE 61st *Vehicular Technology Conference*. 2551-2555.

[46] Tay, J. H. S., Chandrasekhar, V. R., Seah, W. K. G., 2006. Selective Iterative Multilateration for Hop Count-Based Localization in Wireless Sensor Networks. *7th International Conference on Mobile Data Management*. 152-155.

[47] Chandrasekhar, V., Seah, W., 2007. An area localization scheme for underwater sensor networks. *OCEANS*. 1-8.

[48] Zhou, Y., He, J., Chen, K., Chen, J., Liang, A., 2009. An area localization scheme for large scale underwater wireless sensor networks. *WRI International Conference on Communications and Mobile Computing*. 543-547.

[49] Luo, H., Guo, Z., Dong, W., Hong, F., Zhao, Y., 2010. LDB: Localization with directional beacons for sparse 3D underwater acoustic sensor networks. *Journal of Networks*. 5, 28-38.

[50] Chitre M., Potter, J., Heng, O. S., 2004. Underwater acoustic channel characterisation for medium-range shallow water communications. *OCEANS*. 40-45.

In: Recent Advances in Ad Hoc Networks Research
Editor: Natarajan Meghanathan
ISBN: 978-1-63321-337-1

Chapter 9

ASYMPTOTIC ANALYSIS OF NETWORK TOPOLOGIES

András Faragó*
The University of Texas at Dallas, TX, US

ABSTRACT

Modern networks are often too large to allow a fully detailed description. We review some models and methods that aim at capturing the network topology of large, random, or random-like networks.

The goal of this chapter is to survey a number of existing models that aim at describing these large, random network topologies. We also exhibit common generalizations of various sets of models that cover a number of known constructions as special cases.

Keywords: Network Topology, Random Graph, Asymptotic Analysis

INTRODUCTION

Enormously large, complex network topologies are encountered in numerous settings. Well known examples are the Internet and its logical overlay networks, such as the World Wide Web, and online social networks.

At the same time, extensive and rapidly growing wireless ad hoc and sensor networks also lead to hard topology modeling questions. The goal of this chapter is to survey a number of existing models that aim at describing these large, random network topologies. We also exhibit common generalizations of various sets of models that cover a number of known constructions as special cases. Our survey is based on the extensive literature, as well as the author's own earlier work on the subject, e.g., [24-29].

* Erik Jonsson School of Engineering and Computer Science, The University of Texas at Dallas, US. Email: farago@utdallas.edu

Emergence of Random Network Models

Internet and Web Topology Models

The first major wave of work in the considered direction was the statistical analysis of the Web graph, in which the nodes are web pages and the edges are the hyperlinks. Similar investigations were made regarding the physical Internet topology, as well. Below we review some of the main directions.

Experimental Statistical Analysis

The power law degree distribution means that if n_k denotes the number of nodes with degree k, and $n = \Sigma\, n_k$, then

$$\frac{nk}{n} \sim k^{-\beta}$$

where ~ denotes asymptotic proportionality, and β is called the *power law exponent*. The typical measured values of β are between 2 and 3. All this was in sharp contrast with traditional random graph models that have independent edges, and exhibit (asymptotically) Poisson node degree distributions. The latter models are known as Erdős-Rényi random graphs.

To describe the observed network structure, Barabási and Albert [6] coined the term "scale-free network", based on the observation that in a power law distribution the rescaling of the considered quantity preserves the same power law, changing it only with a constant factor. This quickly became very popular, and triggered the statistical analysis of "scale-freeness" of network topologies not only in (physical or logical) communication networks, but also in networks that arise in biology, genetics, epidemiology, linguistics, electric power distribution, social sciences and in many other areas; see, e.g., the books [11, 12, 14, 15, 55], and hundreds of further references therein.

In retrospect, one may say that "scale-free networks" generated somewhat more hype than substance. It was rightfully pointed out, e.g., by Li et al. [52] and Alderson et al. [4] that the power law degree distribution alone can easily fall short from adequately modeling the Internet topology, if no other domain specific knowledge is applied.

Generative Models

A parallel major wave of research was to create generative models. In contrast to experimental statistical analysis, generative models aim at explaining the observed network structures, and provide algorithmic approaches to generate them, also offering the opportunity for in-depth mathematical analysis. The first such model that became well known was the Preferential Attachment model of Barabási and Albert [6]. This model generates a graph such that new nodes are more likely to get connected to those that already have a higher degree. Although the authors did not provide a rigorous analysis, only an approximate reasoning, based on the mean-field approach of physics, the model certainly had intuitive appeal ("the rich get richer" principle). This model had an explanatory power and generated scale-free graphs, so it triggered many follow-up investigations. The first truly rigorous formulation and deep analysis of a preferential attachment model, called Linearized Chord Diagram model, was provided by Bollobás at al. [10].

Since then, numerous static and evolving graph models of networks have been proposed and analyzed, both experimentally and with serious mathematical rigor, primarily focusing on asymptotic properties. A few examples are: the ACL model of Aiello, Chung and Lu [3]; the copying model of Kleinberg et al. [44]; the growth-deletion model of Chung and Lu [16]; the self-similar Kronecker-graph model of Leskovec et al. [49]; the compressible Web model of Chierichetti et al. [18]; the forest fire model of Leskovec, Kleinberg and Faloutsos [50]; the geometric preferential attachment model of Flaxman, Frieze and Vera [31]; the spatial preferential attachment model of Aiello et al. [2]; the random perturbation model of Flaxman [30]; as well as a large number of other models and variants, with a lot of intellectual power in their analysis.

As an example of such models, consider the following, which is due to Chung and Lu [17]. It is motivated by the fact that since the degree distribution may vary, and it appears a significant issue in characterizing a random graph model, therefore, it is important that *any* feasible degree distribution can be efficiently generated. This is accomplished by the model of Chung and Lu [17], which is a static (i.e., not evolving) random graph model, having the advantage of high flexibility, in the sense that it can exhibit any possible degree distribution (including power law with any exponent) in the expected node degrees. The model is built as detailed below.

Let $\mathbf{d} = (d_1, ..., d_n)$ be any degree sequence. For example, it may be chosen to exhibit power law with exponent β. In that case, the number k is included in the sequence nk times, such that $n_k/n \sim k^{-\beta}$. Then, between any two nodes i and j, an dedge is drawn independently with probability

$$p_{ij} = \frac{d_i d_j}{\sum_{k=1}^{n} d_k}$$

It is not hard to show that in the arising random graph, the expected degree of node i will indeed be d_i. In this sense, any possible degree distribution can be represented. Note that in this model the degree values are pre-selected, only the edges are random. The random edges are drawn such that the arising *expected* degrees obey the given degree sequence.

As a highly non-trivial feature of this model, Chung and Lu [17] prove, among other things, the following property. Let G be the arising random graph, and let $L(G)$ denote the *average hop distance* between two randomly chosen nodes. Then (under some minor technical conditions for which we refer to the original article [17]), the following holds:

If the expected node degrees are distributed by a power law distribution with exponent $2 < \beta < 3$, *then the average hop distance is bounded as*

$$L(G) \le (2 + o(1)) \frac{\log \log n}{\log(1/(\beta - 2))}$$

where $o(1)$ *means a function of n that tends to* 0, as $n \to \infty$.

This is a useful result, as it provides a nontrivial upper bound on expected hop distances that otherwise would be hard to obtain. For example, assume we consider a piece of the Web graph with 10 million web pages, and we measured that it has a power law degree distribution with exponent $\beta = 2.5$. From this information alone, can we say something about the average hop distances between web pages? By the cited result (assuming that with n = 107 we can approximately take $o(1) = 0$), we have:

$$L(G) \leq 2\frac{\log\log 10^7}{\log(1/(2.5-2))} \approx 8$$

which is a reasonably low specific bound on the average hop distance. It would clearly be much harder to obtain the same via direct computations on a graph of 10 million nodes.

Scalability of Large Wireless Networks

About the same time when the Web and Internet topology investigations began, another independent wave of asymptotic network modeling was initiated by Gupta and Kumar [37]. This direction focused on analyzing the scalability of large wireless networks, primarily ad hoc and sensor networks, from the viewpoint of fundamental limits for transport capacity and related properties. This line of research also attracted much attention. Interestingly, and unfortunately, most of the results are negative. Specifically, they show under various conditions, that the achievable per node throughput tends to 0 with growing network size, which we call the *vanishing throughput effect*. Even maintaining global network connectivity is impossible under rather general conditions, if we want to apply nodes with finite processing capacity, see Faragó [25].

The Vanishing Throughput Effect

To explain this phenomenon, let us review some fundamental results in this direction. The most important result in the paper of Gupta and Kumar [37] considers the achievable throughput per source-destination (S-D) pair in a large random network, where n nodes are placed independently and uniformly at random in a planar disk of unit area. Thus, the network topology is random, but static. The nodes have the same transmission radius which can be chosen arbitrarily. They can transmit with a fixed maximum rate (bit/sec), but they are allowed to divide the channel into sub channels without any constraint, in any domain (e.g., frequency, time, code). The nodes communicate using arbitrary protocols for channel access and routing, with the only restriction that there is a minimal requirement of interference avoidance in the same (sub)channel to ensure successful receptions. The considered traffic pattern is that each node has a randomly chosen destination in the network. The authors prove that in this general model the achievable throughput per S-D pair is

$$\Theta\left(\frac{1}{\sqrt{n\log n}}\right).$$

Regarding scalability, the key message of this result is that the achievable throughput per S-D pair tends to zero as the network size grows to infinity. This is what we call the vanishing throughput effect. It means, the network is fundamentally not scalable, since it becomes unable to usefully operate when it grows extremely large.

It is then a natural question to investigate how robust is the vanishing throughput effect under changing the model. Is it merely an artifact due to some special modeling assumptions, or is it a fundamental phenomenon that remains true in any reasonable model?

Already in their original paper [37] Gupta and Kumar point out that if the area where the nodes are located is the surface of a sphere rather than a planar disk, the results still remain in effect. They also show that no essential change results even if instead of random node placement, the nodes are located optimally and their transmission radiuses are also chosen optimally. For 3-dimensional network topology (random node placement in a unit cube) Toumpis and Goldsmidth [67] show that, although the rate of vanishing is different, the per node throughput still tends to zero. Similar results are obtained by Gupta and Kumar in [39].

Various other static network scenarios were also analyzed by different authors. For example, Yi, Pei and Kalyanamaran [71] show that the use of directional antennas, although can increase the capacity, still does not invalidate the vanishing throughput effect. Peraki and Servetto [62] prove that even if the nodes can generate multiple beams in parallel, aimed at multiple receivers, the achievable improvement is still insufficient to sustain positive per node throughput in the limit. Kozat and Tassiulas [45] consider the scenario when the ad hoc network has infrastructure support, i.e., besides the ad hoc operation, it can also use a cellular-like infrastructure. They show that although this support can bring an exponential improvement in the capacity yet, the per node throughput still asymptotically vanishes, although at a much slower rate. Infrastructure based hybrid scenarios were also considered by Liu, Liu and Towsley [53] and Toumpis [66], all pointing in the direction that vanishing throughput remains in effect, given that the infrastructure size is not overwhelming compared to the ad hoc network size.

Escapes from the Vanishing Throughput Effect

At this point one may wonder: has any model been found at all for large random ad hoc networks in which constant (i.e., non-vanishing) per node throughput can be maintained in the asymptotic regime? The answer is yes, but, unfortunately, with serious reservations.

One possibility is to consider the effect of mobility, since all the above results refer to random, but static networks. Grossglauser and Tse [36] analyze the mobile version of the Gupta-Kumar [37] model, assuming that the nodes move randomly and independently with uniform stationary distribution over the unit disk. The key advantage of mobility in this setting is that either a source node can get close to its destination and send the data directly, or it can spread the packets among other nodes, which relay the data to the destination whenever they get close to it. A typical general state of this network is that each node buffers many packets destined to different destinations and whenever a node gets close to another node, it sends the data, if any, waiting for that destination. Grossglauser and Tse [36] prove that in this setting it is possible to maintain asymptotically constant per session throughput. The problem is, however, that it comes at the price of infinitely growing delay. Gamal et al. [34] analyzed the trade-off between throughput and delay and found that with bounded node movement speed (it is certainly bounded at least by the speed of light) the average delay grows to infinity with the network size. Note that each packet travels at most 2 hops in this network (either directly to the destination or through a single relay node), so the delay is due to waiting for getting close to the destination. Another problem is that mobility in the Grossglauser-Tse model is not an *option*, it is an *obligation*: essentially, the nodes must be on the move all the time to make the solution workable.

Another possible escape from the vanishing throughput effect is to restrict the traffic pattern in the random static network. Li et al. [52] argue that the random destination scenario in Gupta-Kumar model can be regarded as a worst case traffic distribution. The authors find that if the traffic tends to be local, in the sense that the expected route hop-length is bounded, then constant throughput can be maintained in the static random network. This is still not sufficiently reassuring, however, since it would be desirable that the network can handle any traffic pattern, rather than only a small subset of the possibilities. Furthermore, if we do not want to replace the network with a multitude of small local networks that are disconnected from each other, then the problem of the infinitely growing node degrees still remains there.

Another approach to improve the asymptotic throughput scaling is to apply more sophisticated physical layer techniques such as MIMO. A paper of Özgür, Lévéque and Tse [56] shows that with intelligent, hierarchical node cooperation and MIMO techniques it is possible to achieve an aggregate throughput of $\Omega(n^{1-\varepsilon})$ for n randomly placed nodes, where $\varepsilon > 0$ is an arbitrarily small, but positive, constant. This translates into a per S-D pair throughput of $\Omega(1/n^{\varepsilon})$. If ε is chosen small enough, then it is close to the ideally sought constant throughput per node. Nevertheless, since ε must be a fixed positive constant, therefore, no matter how small it is, the per node throughput will still vanish as $n \to \infty$.

Why Does the Throughput Vanish?

To better understand a fundamental reason for the vanishing throughput, let us briefly discuss what causes it and how in the Gupta-Kumar model [37].

One may observe that the transmission radius r of nodes has two opposite effects. If r is small, then more hops are needed to deliver a packet to its destination, since in each hop the packet can advance at most a distance of r towards its destination. Therefore, small r causes a growing burden of nodes to serve as relays, which decreases the end-to-end throughput. This would justify choosing r as large as possible. On the other hand, large transmission radius increases the interference which causes the throughput to decrease again, so interference reduction would require choosing r as small as possible.

The detailed analysis of the above conflicting tendencies in [37] shows that the forwarding burden is proportional to $1/r$, since the average route hop-length is proportional to $1/r$. On the other hand, the interference increases quadratically with the radius, due to the area involved, which is proportional to r^2: Balancing the two effects yields the conclusion that has to be chosen as small as possible, as the interference reduction, due to its quadratic nature, brings more benefit than what is lost by longer routes. Specifically, the joint effect results in the formula

$$\lambda(n) = O\left(\frac{1}{n * r(n)}\right) \tag{1}$$

where n is the number of nodes, $\lambda(n)$ is the throughput in bit/sec for each S-D pair and $r(n)$ is the transmission radius (as a function of n). It is clear from (1) that if we want to avoid $\lambda(n) \to 0$, then $r(n)$ has to tend to 0 at least as fast as $1/n$, so that $n^*r(n)$ does not grow to infinity.

There is, however, an effect that does not allow to choose the transmission radius arbitrarily small. This is the requirement that the network topology must be connected, since otherwise communication between certain endpoints becomes impossible. The discussed model uses an earlier result of the same authors [38] about the needed transmission radius for asymptotic connectivity. They show that if the nodes are placed uniformly at random in a unit disk, then the network is connected with probability approaching 1 if and only if the transmission radius satisfies

$$\pi r^2 = \frac{\ln n + c(n)}{n}$$

with $c(n) \to \infty$. According to this, it is necessary for connectivity that

$$r > \sqrt{\frac{\ln n}{\pi n}}$$

holds for all large enough values of n. Combining it with (1), we obtain:

$$\lambda(n) = O\left(\frac{1}{n\sqrt{\frac{\ln n}{n}}} \right) = O\left(\frac{1}{\sqrt{n \ln n}} \right)$$

clearly showing the vanishing throughput effect.

Nevertheless, as we have already mentioned earlier, there are notable exceptions, utilizing various effects, such as mobility (Grossglauser and Tse [36]), restricted traffic pattern (Li et al. [51]), using infrastructure (Liu, Liu and Towsley [53]), or relaxing the condition of full connectivity (Dousse, Franceschetti and Thiran [22], Faragó [28]), to recall only a few examples. Therefore, the issue of wireless network scalability is still under further research.

It is worth mentioning, that the graph models that are used in the wireless network investigations are very different from the Internet and Web models. The random graphs in wireless network analysis are based on geometric considerations, and termed geometric random graphs. They also have a rich set of analytical results, see, e.g., the books of Franceschetti and Meester [32], and Penrose [58]. In a sense, geometric random graphs are between the classical Erdős-Rényi model and those graph models that are used to describe the Internet and Web topologies. Specifically, geometric random graphs have (asymptotically) Poisson node degree distributions, just like the Erdős-Rényi random graphs. That is, geometric random graphs (modeling wireless network topologies) do not exhibit scale-free behavior. On the other hand, their edges are not independent, just like in the Internet/Web models, so they have many properties that are distinctively different from the Erdós-Rényi random graphs.

GRAPH MODELS FOR LARGE, MULTI-HOP WIRELESS NETWORKS

Wireless networks of large size, random topology and no supporting infrastructure, such as ad hoc and sensor networks, are expected to play an important role in the future. The random network topology of these systems is frequently described by various random graph models, most often by some variant of *geometric random graphs*. First we review some of the typical classes of graphs that are used in this context.

Frequently Used Graph Classes

An important class is the *Unit Disk Graph* (*UDG*) [19] model of the network topology. A UDG is a graph that is defined by the (planar) geometry of node positions. It is assumed that each node has the same transmission radius r, and two nodes are connected by a link if and only if they are within distance r (which is often normalized to $r = 1$, hence the name). In other words, the radio range of each node is just a circular disk. As a critical difference from the physical model, in a UDG it does not matter where the rest of the nodes are located and how much interference they generate.

A clear advantage of UDGs is that a number of important algorithmic problems that are NP-complete for general graphs become solvable in polynomial time for this special class [65], thus allowing much more efficient protocols.

Unfortunately, the UDG model is quite simplistic, it is rather far from accurately reflecting the actual radio network topology. A refinement is the Quasi-Unit Disk Graph (Q-UDG) model [46], in which a shrink factor ρ is added, with $0 < \rho < 1$, for describing the radio range of a node by two concentric circular disks, the outer one with radius r, and the inner one shrunk by the factor ρ, yielding radius ρr. If two nodes are at most ρr distance apart, then they are always connected by a link. If they are more than r apart, then they are never connected. Finally, if the distance is between ρr and r, then the link may or may not exist. Geometrically this means that the radio range of a node can have arbitrary shape, but moderated by the requirement that it should be between a circumscribed circle of radius r and an inscribed circle of radius ρr.

A nice feature of Q-UDGs is that, while providing a more general network topology model, they still preserve the algorithmic advantages of UDGs, at the price of an additional $1/\rho^2$ factor in complexity [46]. Thus, if the shrink factor □□is a not too small constant, then most of the UDG advantages carry over, with only a constant factor penalty in complexity.

Another natural issue is that different nodes may transmit with different power, or have different spectrum-dependent attenuation of the transmission signal. This leads to the concept of *Disk Graph (DG)*, which differs from the UDG in that each node i has its own, possibly different, transmission radius r_i, and two nodes are connected by an undirected link if they are mutually in each other's range. DGs are somewhat less friendly from the algorithmic point of view than UDGs and Q-UDGs, but still better than general graphs and still allow efficient solutions or approximations for a number of algorithmic problems, as we investigated in [68].

Similarly to the generalization that leads to the Q-UDG concept, one can also introduce *Quasi-Disk Graphs (Q-DG)*, by adding a shrink factor ρ that allows to refine the radio range description as for Q-UDG.

All the above graph models can naturally be extended to higher dimensions, replacing the disks by balls in the appropriate space.

A common nontrivial generalization of all these graphs, the Bounded Independence Graph (BIG) model is also worth mentioning [65]. (It is also referred to as Bounded Growth Graph [47].) This class is defined by the requirement that the maximum number of independent nodes (a set of nodes in a graph is called independent if there is no edge between them) within the k-hop neighborhood $N_k(v)$ of any node v is bounded by a polynomial of k. Although this definition is based purely on the graph structure and does not have a direct geometric meaning, it can still be related to geometry through the concept of doubling metric spaces [65]. These are metric spaces in which any ball of radius r can be covered by a finite number of balls of radius $r/2$. This property does not hold for all metric spaces, although it holds for Euclidean spaces of any finite dimension (Radio propagation properties may lead to a *ratio distance* that is quite different from Euclidean). It can be shown that if a geometric graph is defined in a doubling metric space, in analogy with UDG or DG, then it is always a Bounded Independence Graph [65]. A nice feature of this class is that a number of hard algorithmic problems become efficiently solvable in it [47].

So far we have described these classes deterministically, ignoring randomness. Of course, from each graph class one can generate random members, according to various probability distributions. These are usually defined indirectly, through some generating mechanism. For example, if we pick the node positions uniformly at random in a planar domain, e.g., a square, and then construct a UDG over these nodes, then we get a Random Unit Disk Graph.

All these graph classes are related to some kind of geometric insight. It is not surprising, since geometry and distance play a key role in forming the radio network topology. On the other hand, radio propagation (with possible obstacles and other irregularities) can induce much more complicated distances that may not satisfy the mathematical distance axioms, primarily the triangle inequality. Nevertheless, even in this more complicated situation, it is still possible to meaningfully analyze geometric-like graphs and prove nontrivial results about important properties.

Some Results on Geometric Random Graphs

In our context, the typical model in the literature is the following: n nodes are placed randomly and independently in a regularly shaped domain, which is most often a square or a disk in the Euclidean plane. Each node has a transmission radius of r, and two nodes are connected with a link if and only if their distance is at most r. The radius is typically a function of n in the asymptotic analysis. Note that this geometric random graph model is different from the more traditional independent-edge random graph model (often called Erdős-Rényi random graphs), since in the geometric setting the edges are correlated. While many deep results are available for the traditional model (see, e.g., [10]), they are not directly applicable to ad hoc networks.

As one of the early results on ad hoc network connectivity, Philips, Panwar and Tantawi [63] proved the following. Assume the nodes are chosen in a square of area A from a planar Poisson process of constant density D. (This is asymptotically equivalent to choosing the points independently at random from the uniform distribution over the domain.) The area A of the square grows to infinity, while the density remains constant, so the number of nodes also grows to infinity. A result of [63] is that for any $\varepsilon > 0$, if

$$r \le \sqrt{(1-\varepsilon)\ln A/\pi D}$$

then the network gets disconnected with probability approaching 1, as $A \to \infty$. It implies that the transmission radius r cannot remain bounded if we want connectivity with a growing number of nodes that are placed with constant density in a growing area. If we want to keep the entire domain constant, it can be achieved by normalizing the quantities with the domain size.

Gupta and Kumar [38] analyzed the situation when the nodes are placed uniformly at random in a unit disk in the plane. They investigated the *critical transmission range*, that is, the minimum transmission radius needed for connectivity. They obtained that the network is asymptotically connected with probability 1 if and only if the transmission radius satisfies

$$\pi r^2 = \frac{\ln n + c(n)}{n}$$

with $c(n) \to \infty$. Wan and Yi [73] extended the results to k-connectivity on a unit disk and square.

The above result of Gupta and Kumar [38] can also be deduced from Penrose's formula [59, 61] on the asymptotic distribution of the longest edge of a minimum spanning tree in a random geometric graph, since the longest edge length in a minimum spanning tree is known to be equal to the critical transmission range [61]. Penrose analyzes a rather general setting, including a large class of probability density functions, allowing that the nodes are placed in an irregularly shaped area, in a (possibly) high dimensional space. It is assumed, however, that it is a normal space, thus the considered distance is not arbitrary. It is derived from a norm, which does not apply to every distance metric.

The node degree required for connectivity was analyzed by Xue and Kumar [69] in a somewhat different model. They place n nodes uniformly at random in a unit square in the plane, but the edges are not defined via a transmission radius. They consider the graph that arises if each node is connected to its φ_n nearest neighbors. That is, an edge between nodes i, j exists, if either i is among the φ_n nearest neighbors of j or j is among the φ_n nearest neighbors of i. The arising graph is denoted by $G(n, \varphi_n)$. Note that this model is somewhat different from the transmission radius based geometric random graph model. For example, in the latter it may happen with positive probability that a node is isolated. On the other hand, by definition, no node can be isolated in $G(n, \varphi_n)$ for $\varphi_n > 0$. This captures the situation when each node adjusts its transmission radius individually until it has the desired number of neighbors. It is shown in [69] that $G(n, \varphi_n)$ is asymptotically almost surely connected (i.e., the probability that it is connected tends to 1 as $n \to \infty$, if n, $\varphi_n > 5.1774 \ln n$. On the other hand, if n, $\varphi_n < 0.074 \ln n$, then the graph will be asymptotically almost surely disconnected. Thus, the critical number of neighbors is on the order of $\ln n$, but the gap between the upper and lower bounds is significant, their ratio is close to two orders of magnitude. The upper bound was improved by Wan and Yi [73] to $\alpha e \ln n$, where $e \approx 2.718$ is the base of the natural logarithm and $\alpha > 1$ is any real constant.

The issue of connectivity is closely related to the minimum degree in geometric random graphs. Penrose [60] shows that if the points are chosen uniformly at random in a d-dimensional unit cube ($d \geq 2$) and the edges are added one by one in the order of increasing length, then the graph becomes k-connected almost surely whenever all nodes reach degree $\geq k$. This can be interpreted that for large geometric random graphs, almost surely, the sole reason for not being k-connected is the trivial reason that at least one node does not have sufficient degree. For simple connectivity it means that the graph is connected asymptotically almost surely if and only if the transmission radius is chosen large enough so that there are no isolated nodes. All this holds not only with the Euclidean distance, but also for all l_p; $1 < p \leq \infty$, distances.

For the l_∞ distance Appel and Russo [5] determined the exact asymptotics of the minimum transmission radius r_n needed to eliminate isolated nodes. They obtain

$$r_n \sim \left(\frac{\ln n}{2dn}\right)^{1/d}$$

where $d \geq 1$ is the dimension of the space in which the nodes are chosen uniformly at random from the unit cube. The combination of this with the above mentioned results of Penrose on the degrees yields precise asymptotics for the needed transmission radius for k-connectivity, if the nodes are placed uniformly at random in a d-dimensional unit cube ($d \geq 2$) and the distance is based on the maximum norm (l_∞ distance). For Euclidean distance in the plane the asymptotics for the needed transmission radius for simple connectivity ($k = 1$) was derived earlier by Dette and Henze [21].

Generalizations of Geometric Random Graphs

Pre-Metric Random Graphs

In real networks the radio coverage area is often more complicated than a simple disk, since signal propagation may depend on various factors, such as terrain, foliage, weather and atmospheric conditions etc. Therefore, the range can be direction and location dependent. In other words, the existence of a link between two nodes is not necessarily determined by their distance alone. Moreover, the status of a node can possibly be characterized not only by its random spatial coordinates, it may include other random variables, as well. For example, one may also include the traffic load, processor load, queue length, jamming level, battery level or any other parameter. If the condition of link existence is expressed such that a distance function based on the variables does not exceed a threshold, then it is not surprising that this (abstract) distance will not be a metric in the traditional sense. To capture this complexity, a generalized model was proposed in [27]. It is based on a space that is much more general than what is used in other models.

Definition 1 (Pre-metric Space) A pre-metric space is a pair M = (S, ρ), where S is a set and $\rho : S \times S \rightarrow R$ is a real-valued function, such that for every x, y ∈ S the following hold:

(i) $\rho(x, y) \geq 0$
(ii) $\rho(x, y) = 0$ if and only if x = y
(iii) $\rho(x, y) = \rho(y, x)$

The difference between a pre-metric space and the usual concept of a metric space is that in the pre-metric space the well known triangle inequality $\rho(x, y) \leq \rho(x, z) + \rho(z, y)$ does not have to hold. Thus, ρ(x, y) is not necessarily a distance in the usual sense. Still, to help visualization, we refer to it as distance, keeping in mind that it can be a more general function.

The nodes in this model are chosen randomly and independently from a pre-metric space. Their common probability distribution, however, does not have to be uniform at all. In principle, it can be arbitrary. A totally arbitrary distribution over an abstract set, however, can have pathological mathematical properties. Therefore, to avoid unnecessary technical difficulties, it is assumed that all considered sets are measurable with respect to the probability measure and all considered expected values exist. Otherwise the distribution is arbitrary. Note that while it is mathematically possible to create pathological examples that do not satisfy these conventions, they never occur in practically meaningful cases.

Let us now define the pre-metric random graph model. In the definition N and R_+ denote the set of natural numbers and positive real numbers, respectively.

Definition 2 (Pre-Metric Random Graph Model) The model is given by a triple G = (M, r, P), where M = (S, ρ) is a pre-metric space, $r : N \rightarrow R_+$ is a function and P is a probability measure on M. A random graph is generated by the model in the following way. For some n ∈ N random points X_1, ..., X_n are drawn from the pre-metric space independently at random, according to the probability measure P. These points are the nodes of the graph. The edges of the graph are defined by connecting any two different points X_i, X_j if and only if

$$\rho(X_i, X_j) \leq r(n).$$

In the above definition the function r(n) represents the transmission radius, which may depend on the number of nodes for normalization purposes, as it is typical in most models. The arising grap, intends to capture the network topology in a general setting. The interesting thing is that even in this general model one can prove highly nontrivial properties. Since the details are rather technical, we skip them here, and refer to the article Faragó [27].

Abstract Geometric Random Graphs

We have analyzed an even more general model, called Abstract Geometric Random Graph. This model includes many others as special cases, including all geometric and pre-metric random graphs, yet the model still allows proving surprising nontrivial results, despite the high level of generality. Due to space limitations, we only elaborate here on the model description and showing how it includes other models as special cases. Regarding theorems and proofs, we refer the reader to Faragó [28].

Building the Model

Let us now introduce a very general model class that reflects a typical feature of geometric random graph models. This feature is that in geometric random graphs the primary random choice is picking random nodes from some domain and then the edges are already determined by some geometric property (typically some kind of distance) of the random nodes. We elevate this approach to an abstract level that includes many special cases of interest. The most general version of our abstract geometric model is built using the components detailed below.

Representing the Nodes: Node Variables. The nodes are represented by an infinite sequence X_1, X_2, ... of random variables, called *node variables*. They take their values in an arbitrary (nonempty) set S, which is called the *domain* of the model. In most practical cases the domain is a simple subset of the Euclidean plane or of the 3-dimensional space. In general, however, S can be any abstract set from which we can choose random elements. When we want to generate a random graph on n nodes, then we use the first n entries of the sequence, that is, X_1, X_2, ... X_n represent the nodes in G_n. It is important to note that we do not require the node variables to be independent.

Representing the Links: Edge Functions. We denote by $Y_{ij}^{(n)} \in \{0,1\}$ the indicator of the edge between nodes X_i, X_j in the random graph G_n. Since loops are not allowed, we always assume $i \neq j$, without repeating this condition each time. The (abstract) geometric nature of the model is expressed by the requirement that the random variables $Y_{ij}^{(n)} \in \{0,1\}$ are determined by the nodes X_1, X_2, ... X_n, possibly with additional independent randomization. Specifically, we assume that there exist functions $f_{ij}^{(n)}$ such that

$$Y_{ij}^{(n)} = f_{ij}^{(n)}(X_1,\dots,X_n,\xi_{ij})$$

where ξ_{ij} is a random variable that is uniformly distributed on $[0,1]$ and is independent of all the other defining random variables of the model (i.e., the node variables and all the other ξ_{kl} variables). Henceforth the role of ξ_{ij} is referred to as *independent randomization*. (Note that the specified distribution of xi j does not impose a restriction, since the functions $f_{ij}^{(n)}$ are arbitrary.)

The undirected nature of the graph is expressed by the requirement $Y_{ij}^{(n)} = Y_{ji}^{(n)}$, which can simply be enforced by computing all values for $i < j$ only and defining the $i > j$ case by exchanging i and j. Another condition that we use in the examples is locality. It means that the edge indicators $Y_{ij}^{(n)}$ depend only on the nodes that are the endpoints of the edge, but not on the other node variables. In formula:

$$Y_{ij}^{(n)} = f_{ij}^{(n)}(X_i,X_j,\xi_{ij})$$

Most of the frequently used wireless network topology models naturally satisfy the condition of locality.

Subclasses of Abstract Geometric Random Graphs

We present some examples to show the comprehensiveness of the generalization provided by our abstract geometric random graphs. These examples illustrate that most practically relevant models for wireless network topologies fit in our common generalization.

1. Geometric Random Graphs. All the usual geometric random graph models fit naturally in our general framework. For example, the base set S can be chosen as a unit disk or square in the plane or a unit ball or cube (or any other domain) in higher dimension. Let us choose i.i.d. points $X_1, X_2, \ldots$ from S, according to some probability distribution. Let $\rho(x,y)$ denote the distance of the points $x,y \in S$, it can be any distance function. Finally, let $r > 0$ be a radius (possibly depending on n). Then the edge function

$$f^{(n)}\left(X_i, X_j, \xi_{ij}\right) = \begin{cases} 1 & \text{if} \quad \rho(X_i, X_j) \le r \\ 0 & \text{if} \quad \rho(X_i, X_j) > r \end{cases} \tag{2}$$

defines a geometric random graph in the usual sense. (The independent randomization is not used here, so the edge function does not depend on ξ_{ij}.) It is clear that this includes all the usual geometric random graph models, allowing any metric space as the basis. Moreover, we can also use non-independent points, such as the "clustered uniform" example in the previous section, as long as the distribution is exchangeable.

2. Erdös-Rényi Random Graphs. The by now classical random graph model of Erdös and Rényi (see, e.g., [8, 43]), where each possible edge is included independently with some probability p is also included as a direct special case. We can set $S = \{1, \ldots, n\}$ and for $X_i, X_j \in S$

$$f^{(n)}\left(X_i, X_j, \xi_{ij}\right) = \begin{cases} 1 & \text{if} \quad \xi_{ij} \le p \\ 0 & \text{if} \quad \xi_{ij} > p \end{cases}$$

Note that now the edge function depends only on the independent randomization, so indeed each edge is included independently with probability p.

3. A Geometric But Non-Metric Example: Battery Levels. In geometric random graph models ρ satisfies the triangle inequality. This, however, cannot capture all situations that occur in ad hoc or sensor networks. As an example, assume the nodes are located in the plane. Let x_i, y_i be the coordinates of the ith node. Furthermore, we also characterize a node with its battery level $E_i > 0$. E_i represents the remaining energy, assuming the node is not fully out of energy. Thus, a node is represented by a triple $X_i = (x_i, y_i, E_i)$. Let $d(E_i)$ be the distance over which a node can communicate, given its energy level E_i. (The function $d(E_i)$ can be derived from the physical characteristics of the node and from radio propagation conditions.) Now, a possible example of such a "distance" function is

$$\rho_1(X_i, X_j) = \frac{\sqrt{(x_i - x_j)^2 + (y_i - y_j)^2}}{\min\{d(E_i), d(E_j)\}}$$

If we take $r = 1$ and use the above ρ_1 function in (2), then it expresses the condition that a link exists if and only if its end nodes are at most at a distance that can be bridged by the energy levels of both nodes. Note that the above function ρ does not satisfy the triangle inequality, so it does not lead to a geometric random graph model in the usual sense. On the other hand, it still fits in our framework, as in (2) we did not require the triangle inequality to hold for ρ.

4. Another Non-Metric Example: Link Blocking. We can capture some features of traffic dependent network characteristics, as well. Let each node i be characterized by a triple $Xi = (x_i, y_i, \lambda_i)$, where x_i, y_i are planar coordinates and λ_i is the traffic demand of the node. Let B_{ij} be the blocking probability of the link (i, j), given that the link exists. We may compute B_{ij} as a function of λ_i, λ_j from some traffic model. For example, if we use Erlang's well known formula, assuming a capacity of C units on the link and its load is taken as the sum of its end nodes' traffic load $\lambda_i + \lambda_j$, then we obtain

$$B_{ij} = \frac{(\lambda_i + \lambda_j)^C / C!}{\sum_{i=0}^{C} (\lambda_i + \lambda_j)^i / i!}$$

(Of course, we may use other traffic models, as well, this is just an example.) Now we can take the "distance" function

$$\rho_2(X_i, X_j) = \frac{1}{1 - B_{ij}} \sqrt{(x_i - x_j)^2 + (y_i - y_j)^2}$$

and use it in (2) with some radius r. We can observe that for small blocking probability ($B_{ij} \ll 1$) $\rho_2(X_i, X_j)$ will be approximately the same as the Euclidean distance. On the other hand, as B_{ij} approaches 1, the factor $\frac{1}{1 - B_{ij}}$ tends to infinity and, therefore, high blocking probability makes the existence of the link in the model less likely, even if the physical distance is small. This example also violates the triangle inequality, so it is not a geometric random graph.

5. Log-Normal Shadowing. A typical phenomenon in the radio environment is *fading*. An example of fading is a relatively slow random fluctuation in the signal strength, which occurs even if the locations are fixed. Measurements show that this random variation can be accurately modeled by a log-normal distribution (see, e.g., [57]). Hence the name *lognormal shadowing*, which is widely used for this phenomenon. A way to capture it in our model is this. Let us characterize a node i by a triple $X_i = (x_i, y_i, \eta_i)$, where x_i, y_i represent a random position in the plane and each η_i is an infinite sequence of independent, lognormally distributed random variables:

$$\eta_i = (\eta_j^{(i)}; j = i, i+1, i+2, \ldots).$$

The "distance" is defined as

$$\rho_3(X_i,X_j)=\eta_b^{(a)}\sqrt{\left((x_i-x_j)^2+(y_i-y_j)^2\right)}$$

where $a = \min\{i, j\}$ and $b = \max\{i, j\}$. (The reason for we need an infinite sequence of log-normal random variables is that this way we can have independent log-normal shadowing for every link.) This distance can express the fact that from the radio communication point of view we really perceive an "effective distance", which is a log-normally modulated random variant of the physical distance. Using this ρ_3 in (2) leads again to a random graph that is not geometric, as ρ does not satisfy the distance axioms.

6. Directional Antennas. We can also represent directional antennas in the model. As a simple example, let Y_i be the position of a node in the Euclidean plane, α_i be the angle (with respect to some fixed coordinate axis) at which its antenna is directed, and δ_i be the angular width of the beam (assuming an idealized directional antenna). Let us represent the node by the variable Xi = $(Y_i, \alpha_i, \delta_i)$: Let $S(X, \alpha, \delta)$ denote the planar angular sector pointed at X, with its axis of symmetry directed at α and of angular width δ. Further, let ||.|| denote the Euclidean norm. Then we can introduce the following "distance":

$$\rho_4(X_i,X_j)=\begin{cases}\| Y_i-Y_j \| \ \ \mathit{if} & X_i\in S(X_j,\alpha_j,\delta_j)\ \ \mathit{and} \\ & Xj\in S(X_i,\alpha_i,\delta_i) \\ \infty \qquad \mathit{otherwise} & \end{cases}$$

If we use this function $\rho_4(X_i, X_j)$ in (2), then we get a model of a random ad hoc network topology with directional antennas.

7. Terrain Variations, Obstacles. Another example is to take into account uneven radio propagation characteristics due to terrain variations or propagation obstacles. For example, let us assume that the nodes operate in a frequency band in which only line of sight communication is possible (such as infrared). Then two nodes can only communicate if there is no obstacle covering them from each other. This feature can also be built into the model. Let X_i be the plane position of a node. Assume there exists a set $R = \{R_1, R_2, ...\}$ of random obstacles in the area. Let $s(X_i, X_j)$ be the line segment connecting the points X_i, X_j, and let $L(X_i, X_j, R)$ be the "line of sight" function:

$$L(X_i,X_j,R)=\begin{cases}1 \ \ \mathit{if} & s(X_i,X_j)\cap R_k=\phi(\forall k) \\ \infty \ \ \mathit{otherwise} & \end{cases}$$

To express that only those nodes can communicate that are in line of sight of each other, let us introduce the "distance"

$$\rho_5(X_i,X_j)=\| X_i-X_j \| \, L(X_i,X_j,R).$$

If this is used in (2), then we get a network topology model that can deal with radio propagation obstacles.

8. Combinations. The various conditions in the preceding examples can be combined into more complex models. For example, if we want that all the conditions expressed by the $\rho_1,\ldots,\rho_5$ functions are satisfied, then we can use

$$\rho(X_i, X_j) = \max\{\rho_1(X_i, X_j), \ldots, \rho_5(X_i, X_j)\}$$

in (2).

Why are Abstract Geometric Random Graphs Useful?

As we have seen, all the above listed specific models, as well as many others, are special cases of the Abstract Geometric Random Graph model. Interestingly, despite this high level of generality, the Abstract Geometric Random Graph model still allows proving nontrivial results, especially about connectivity properties. This means, the theorems then immediately apply to all the incorporated special model classes. In this way we can derive useful results for many relevant types of models at once, without having to develop a special proof for each class with different methods. For further details, as well as specific theorems and proofs, we refer the reader to, e.g., Faragó [28].

CONCLUSION

We have reviewed a number of models that can describe large, random network topologies. We have also demonstrated that it is possible to find interesting common generalizations of various sets of models. As a closing statement, let us emphasize that the modeling of very large networks with various random mathematical structures is a fruitful, vibrant and promising research area, which will likely attract further research interest in the future.

ACKNOWLEDGMENTS

The author gratefully acknowledges the support of NSF Grant CNS-1018760.

REFERENCES

[1] Agarwal, A., Kumar, P. R., 2004. Improved Capacity Bounds for Wireless Networks. *Wireless Communications and Mobile Computing*. 4, *3*, 251-261.

[2] Aiello, W., Bonato, A., Cooper, C., Janssen, J., Pralat, P., 2009. A Spatial Web Graph Model with Local Influence. *Internet Mathematics*. 5, *2*, 175-196.

[3] Aiello, W., Chung, F., Lu, L., 2002. Random Evolution in Massive Graphs. *Handbook on Massive Data Sets* (Eds. Abello et. al). 97-122.

[4] Alderson, D., Li, L., Willinger, W., Doyle, J. C., 2005. Understanding Internet Topology: Principles, Models, and Validation. *IEEE/ACM Transactions on Networking*. 13, *6*, 1205-1218.

[5] Appel, M. J. B., Russo, R. P., 1997. The Minimum Vertex Degree of a Graph on Uniform Points in $[0, 1]^d$. *Advanced Applied Probability*. 29, 582-594.

[6] Barabási, A. L., Albert, L., 1999. Emergence of Scaling in Random Networks. *Science*. 286, *5493*, 509-512.

[7] Barabási, A. L., Albert, L., Jeong, H., 2000. Scale-Free Characteristics of Random Networks: The Topology of the World-Wide Web. *Physics A: Statistical Mechanics and its Applications*. 281, *1-4*, 69-77.

[8] Bollobás, B., (2001). *Random Graphs*. 1st ed., Cambridge University Press.

[9] Bollobás, B., Riordan, O., 2003. Mathematical Results on Scale-Free Random Graphs. *Handbook of Graphs and Networks*. 1-37.

[10] Bollobás, B., Riordan, O., Spencer, J., Tusnády, G., 2001. The Degree Sequence of a Scale-Free Random Graph Process. *Random Structures and Algorithms*. 18, *3*, 279-290.

[11] Bonato, A., (2008). *A Course on the Web Graph*. American Mathematics Society.

[12] Bornholdt, S., Schuster, H. G., (2003). *Handbook of Graphs and Networks*. 1st ed., Wiley.

[13] Broder, A., Kumar, R., Maghoul, F., Raghavan, P., Rajagopalan, S., Stata, R., Tomkins, A., Wiener, J., 2000. Graph Structure in the Web. *The International Journal of Computer and Telecommunications Networking*, 33, *1-6*, 309-320.

[14] Caldarelli, G., (2007). *Scale-Free Networks*. 1st ed., Oxford University Press.

[15] Chung, F., Lu, L., (2006). *Complex Graphs and Networks*. American Mathematics Society.

[16] Chung, F., Lu, L., 2003. Coupling Online and Offline Analyses for Random Power Law Graphs. *Internet Mathematics*. 1, *4*, 409-461.

[17] Chung, F., Lu, L., 2003. The Average Distance in a Random Graph with Given Expected Degrees. *Internet Mathematics*. 1, *1*, 91-114.

[18] Cheirichetti, F., Kumar, R., Lattanzi, S., Panconesi, A., Raghavan, P., 2009. Models for the Compressible Web. *Proceedings of the 50th Annual IEEE Symposium on Foundations of Computer Science*. 331-340.

[19] Clark, B. N., Colbourn, C. J., Johnson, D. S., 1990. Unit Disk Graphs. *Discrete Mathematics - Topics on Domination*. 86, *1-3*, 165-177.

[20] Cooper, C., Frieze, A., 1996. On the Connectivity of Random Kth Nearest Neighbor Graphs. *Combinatorics, Probability and Computing*. 4, *4*, 343-362.

[21] Dette, H., Henze, N., 1989. The Limit Distribution of the Largest Nearest Neighbor Link in the Unit *d*-Cube. *Journal of Applied Probability*. 26, 67-80.

[22] Douse, O., Franceschetti, M., Thiran, P., 2006. On the Throughput Scaling of Wireless Relay Networks. *IEEE Transactions on Information Theory*. 52, *6*, 2756-2761.

[23] Faloutsos, M., Faloutsos, P., Faloutsos, C., 1999. On Power-Law Relationships of the Internet Topology. *Proceedings of the ACM Conference on Applications, Technologies, Architectures, and Protocols for Computer Communication*. 29, *4*, 251-262.

[24] Faragó, A., 2012. Network Topology Models for Multihop Wireless Networks. *ISRN Communications and Networking*. Article ID 362603, 23 pages.

[25] Faragó, A., 2009. Scalability of Node Degrees in Random Wireless Network Topologies. *IEEE Journal on Selected Areas in Communications*, 27, *7*, 1238-1244.

[26] Faragó, A., 2009. Quantifying the Trade-off between the Level of Connectivity and Local Complexity in Random Wireless Network Topologies. *Proceedings of the 6th International Conference on the Quantitative Evaluation of Systems*, 237-246.

[27] Faragó, A., 2007. On the Fundamental Limits of Topology Control in Ad Hoc Networks. *Algorithmica*, 49, *4*, 337-356.

[28] Faragó, A., 2011, Asymptotically Optimal Tradeoff between Local and Global Connectivity in Wireless Networks. *Performance Evaluation*. 68, *2*, 142-156.

[29] Faragó, A., 2008. Random Graph Models and the Limits of Scalability in Ad hoc and Sensor Networks. *Sensor and Ad hoc Networks, Theoretical and Algorithmic Aspects* (Eds. Makki, S. K., et. al). 19-42.

[30] Flaxman, A. D., 2006. Expansion and Lack Thereof in Randomly Perturbed Graphs. *Microsoft Research Technical Report* TR-2006-118.

[31] Flaxman, A. D., Frieze, A., Vera, J., 2004. A Geometric Preferential Attachment Model of Networks. *Proceedings of the International Workshop on Algorithms and Models for the Web-Graph*. 44-55.

[32] Franceschetti, M., and Meester, R., 2007. *Random Networks for Communication.* 1st ed., Cambridge University Press.

[33] Frieze, A. M., and Luczak, T., 1990. Edge Disjoint Spanning Trees in Random Graphs. *Periodica Mathematica Hungarica*, 21, *1*, 35-37.

[34] Gamal, A. E., Mammen, J., Prabhakar, B., Shah, D., Throughput-Delay Tradeoff in Wireless Networks. *Proceedings of the IEEE International Conference on Computers and Communications*.

[35] Gowaikar, R., Hochwald, B., Hassibi, B., 2006. Communication over a Wireless Network with Random Connections. *IEEE Transactions on Information Theory*. 52, *7*, 2857-2871.

[36] Grossglauser, M., Tse, D., 2002. Mobility Increases the Capacity of Ad hoc Wireless Networks. *IEEE/ACM Transactions on Networking*. 10, *4*, 477-486.

[37] Gupta, P., Kumar, P. R., 2000. The Capacity of Wireless Networks. *IEEE Transactions on Information Theory*. 46, *2*, 388-404.

[38] Gupta, P., Kumar, P. R., 1998. Critical Power for Asymptotic Connectivity in Wireless Networks. *Stochastic Analysis, Control, Optimization and Applications*: *A Volume in Honor of W. H. Fleming* (Eds. McEneany, W. M., Yin, G., Zhang, Q). 547-566.

[39] Gupta, P., Kumar, P. R., 2000. Internets in the Sky: Capacity of 3D Wireless Networks. *Proceedings of the 39th IEEE Conference on Decision and Control*. 3, 2290-2295.

[40] Hemkat, R., Van Mieghem, P., 2006. Study of Connectivity in Wireless Ad hoc Networks with an Improved Radio Model. *Mobile Networks and Applications*. 11, 351-360.

[41] Hirate, Y., Kato, S., Yamana, H., 2006. Web Structure in 2005. *Proceedings of Algorithms and Models for the Web Graph*. 36-46.

[42] Jacquet, P., Laouti, A., 1999. Analysis of Mobile Ad hoc Network Routing Protocols in Random Graph Models. *INRIA Technical Report No.* 3835.

[43] Janson, S., Luczak, T., Rucinksi, A., 2000. *Random Graphs*. 1st ed., Wiley.

[44] Kleinberg, J. M., Kumar, R., Raghavan, P., Rajagopalan, S., Tomkins, A. S., 1999. The Web as a Graph: Measurements, Models and Methods. *Lecture Notes in Computer Science*. 1627, 1-17.

[45] Kozat, U. C., Tassiulas, L., 2003. Throughput Capacity of Random Ad hoc Networks with Infrastructure Support. *Proceedings of the 9th Annual International Conference on Mobile Computing and Networking*. 55-65.

[46] Kuhn, F., Wattenhofer, R., Zollinger, A., 2008. Ad hoc Networks beyond Unit Disk Graphs. *Wireless Networks*. 14, *5*, 715-729.

[47] Kuhn, F., Moscibroda, T., Wattenhofer, R., 2005. On the Locality of Bounded Growth. *Proceedings of the 24th Annual ACM Symposium on Principles of Distributed Computing*. 60-68.

[48] Kumar, R., Raghavan, P., Rahagopalan, S., Romkins, A., 1999. Traveling the Web for Emerging Cyber-Communities. *Proceedings of the 8th International Conference on World Wide Web*. 1481-1493.

[49] Leskovec, J., Kleinberg, J., Faloutsos, C., 2005. Realistic Mathematically Tractable Graph Generation and Evolution, Using Kronecker Multiplication. *Lecture Notes in Computer Science*. 3721, 133-145.

[50] Leskovec, J., Kleinberg, J., Faloutsos, C., 2005. Graphs Over Time: Densification Laws, Shrinking Diameters and Possible Explanations. *Proceedings of the ACM International Conference on Knowledge Discovery in Data Mining*. 177-187.

[51] Li, J., Blake, C., De Couto, D. S. J., Lee, H. I., Morris, R., 2001. Capacity of Ad Hoc Wireless Networks. *Proceedings of the ACM International Conference on Mobile Computing and Networking*. 61-69.

[52] Li, L., Alderson, D., Doyle, J. C., Willinger, W., 2005. Towards a Theory of Scale-Free Graphs: Definition, Properties and Implications. *Internet Mathematics*. 2, *4*, 431-523.

[53] Liu, B., Liu, Z., Towsley, D., 2003. On the Capacity of Hybrid Wireless Networks. *Proceedings of the International Conference on Computers and Communications*. 1543-1552.

[54] Lloyd, E. L., Liu, R., Marathe, M. V., Ramanathan, R., Ravi, S. S., 2005. Algorithmic Aspects of Topology Control Problems for Ad hoc Networks. *Mobile Networks and Applications*. 10, *1-2*, 19-34.

[55] Newman, M., Barabási, A. L., Watts, D. J., (2006). *The Structure and Dynamics of Networks*. 1st ed., Princeton University Press.

[56] Özgür, A., Lévéque, O., Tse, D., 2007. Hierarchical Cooperation Achieves Optimal Capacity Scaling in Ad Hoc Networks. *IEEE Transactions on Information Theory*. 53, *10*, 3549-3572.

[57] Pahlavan, K., Krishnamurthy, P., 2002. *Principles of Wireless Networks*. 1st ed., Prentice Hall.

[58] Penrose, M., 2003. *Random Geometric Graphs*. 1st ed., Oxford University Press.

[59] Penrose, M. D., 1997. The Longest Edge of the Random Minimal Spanning Tree. *annals of Applied Probability*. 7, *2*, 340-361.

[60] Penrose, M. D., 1999. On *k*-Connectivity for a Geometric Random Graph. *Random Structures and Algorithms*. 15, *2*, 145-164.

[61] Penrose, M. D., 1999. A Strong Law for the Longest Edge of the Minimal Spanning Tree. *Annals of Applied Probability*. 27, *1*, 246-260.

[62] Peraki, C., Servetto, S. D., 2003. On the Maximum Stable Throughput Problem in Random Networks with Directional Antennas. *Proceedings of the 4th ACM International Symposium on Mobile Ad hoc Networking and Computing*. 76-87.

[63] Philips, T. K., Panwar, S. S., Tantawi, A. N., Connectivity Properties of a Packet Radio Network Model. *IEEE Transactions on Information Theory*. 35, *5*, 1044-1047.

[64] Ramanathan, R., Rosales-Hain, R., 2000. Topology Control of Multihop Wireless Networks using Transmit Power Adjustment. *Proceedings of the IEEE International Conference on Computers and Communications*. 404-413.

[65] Schmid, S., Wattenhofer, R., 2008. Modeling Sensor Networks. *Algorithms and Protocols for Wireless Sensor Networks* (Ed., Boukerche, A). 1st ed., Wiley.

[66] Toumpis, S., 2004. Capacity Bounds for Three Classes of Wireless Networks: Asymmetric, Cluster and Hybrid. *Proceedings of the 5th ACM International Conference on Mobile Ad hoc Networking and Computing*. 133-144.

[67] Toumpis, S., Goldsmith, A., 2000. Ad Hoc Network Capacity. *Proceedings of the Asilomar Conference on Signals, Systems and Computers*.

[68] Wang, C., Park, M-A., Willson, J., Cheng, Y., Faragó, A., Wu, W., 2008. On Approximate Optimal Dual Power Assignment for Biconnectivity and Edge-Biconnectivity. *Theoretical Computer Science*, 396, *1-3*, 180-190.

[69] Xue, F., Kumar, P. R., 2004. The Number of Neighbors Needed for Connectivity of Wireless Networks. *Wireless Networks*. 10, *2*, 169-181.

[70] Yan, C., Xiang, Y., Dragan, F. F., 2009. Compact and Low Delay Routing Labeling Scheme for Unit Disk Graphs. *Lecture Notes in Computer Science*. 5664, 566-577.

[71] Yi, S., Pei, Y., Kalyanamaran, S., 2003. On the Capacity Improvement of Ad hoc Wireless Networks using Directional Antennas. *Proceedings of the 4th ACM International Conference on Mobile Ad hoc Networking and Computing*. 108-116.

[72] Yukich, J. E., 1998. Probability Theory of Classical Euclidean Optimization Problems. *Lecture Notes in Mathematics* 1675.

[73] Wan, P-J., Yi, C-W., 2004. Asymptotic Critical Transmission Radius and Critical Neighbor Number for *k*-Connectivity in Wireless Ad hoc Networks. *Proceedings of the 4th ACM International Conference on Mobile Ad hoc Networking and Computing*. 1-8.

In: Recent Advances in Ad Hoc Networks Research
Editor: Natarajan Meghanathan
ISBN: 978-1-63321-337-1

Chapter 10

CLOUD ENVIRONMENT ON COGNITIVE RADIO NETWORK FOR EFFICIENT RESOURCE ALLOCATION

Yenumula B. Reddy*
Grambling State University, Grambling, LA, US

ABSTRACT

Cognitive radio is a promising technology for efficient utilization of an unused spectrum. The primary function of cognitive radio networks is their ability to scan the entire spectrum band to detect the presence/absence of primary (licensed) users. The detection of the primary user is called the spectrum sensing. The detection and analysis help to identify the spectrum holes to utilize by secondary users. The basic characteristics to determine the appropriate band is the signal-to-noise ratio, link error rate, delays, interference, and holding time. The processing of this information takes a lot of computational resources including hardware and energy consumption. If we can create a virtual environment called cloud for signal sensing, network management, efficient utilization of spectrum holes, the mobile devices will be benefited in eliminating the overheads for packet transfer and improving the battery life. Cloud environment on cognitive radio is a combination of cloud and mobile technologies. The goal is to support mobile applications more efficient way to utilize bandwidth, energy consumption, hardware utilization, and cost. Cloud is a virtualization concept (borrowed from the virtual machine environment introduced in 1970's) in wireless communications to utilize the resources efficiently and provide the quality of service. The new cloud architecture for Cognitive radio solves the 4G bottlenecks including current spectrum shortage, improving the data storage capacity and processing power, better network management, and minimizes the energy consumption. The objective of the chapter is to provide cognitive virtualization platform, network architecture, performance analysis, and management issues.

Keywords: Cognitive Radio Networks, Cloud Computing, Cloud Security, Bandwidth, Virtualization, Cloud Test-bed, Packet Transfer

---

* Department of Computer Science, Grambling State University, Grambling, LA, US. Email: ybreddy@gram.edu

Introduction

In conventional radio system, each group is assigned a fixed frequency or set of frequencies. The user operates by selecting a channel using channel selector. In 1985, Federal Communication Commission (FCC) allocated three frequency bands (military, civilian and Technology) for a radio transmission technique known as spread spectrum communications. Spread spectrum takes a narrow band and spreads it over a broader portion of the radio frequency band. The spread spectrum is interference resistant. In conventional radios, there is no requirement to change the parameters dynamically in response to interferences. These radios require pristine and dedicated (i.e., licensed) spectrum to operate.

Unlike traditional radio, the cognitive radios (CR) can view their environment in a great detail to identify the unused spectrum and quickly tune to that frequency to transmit or receive the signals. It has the capability of detecting the interference through sampling and transmits/receives signals within the acceptable interference levels. The CR understands the network conditions, interference levels and switches the channels in unacceptable interference levels. The CR takes real-time decisions, intelligently share spectrum, and dynamically change the frequencies to improve the transmission. The CR sensing technology can be used to power radios in any frequency band. Incorporating the CR technology helps the unused spectrum opportunistically.

Cognitive radio in the cloud is a combination of cognitive mobile communication technologies and cloud applications with the goal of supporting mobile applications in a more efficient way in terms of cost, bandwidth, hardware utilization, and energy consumption. The technology associated CR with cloud includes the centralization of application, automation of tasks, dynamic movement of resources, low cost, and smooth transmission of data on the network. The cognitive mobile application happens outside of mobile device by moving the computing power and data storage away from cognitive nodes. Shifting mobile applications to cloud alleviates CR capabilities in situation awareness, command, control, intelligence, surveillance, and reconnaissance. Robust network connectivity allows CR to guarantee persistent data communications in dynamic and hostile environment.

CR requires to perform various functions and some of them will drain the battery quickly. The radio environment dynamics functions namely jamming, electromagnetic pulse, multipath, and interference require less energy can be done internally. Signal detection, classification, and decoding needs complex computations can be performed on cloud using high performance computers. Vision and learning functions require computations and may move to the cloud to improve the efficiency. To enhance the performance, CR network performs offline learning by collecting data from various nodes. These functions are useful for long term planning and will be performed using multicore systems (or GPU based high performance computers) through cloud based technology.

The cognitive radio cloud network (CRCN) requires real-time performance. The existing MapReduce package may not guarantee the real-time operations for sensitive operations including defense. Therefore, it is suggested to create a private cloud architecture where real-time performance is required. The general architecture includes connection of base stations (networking nodes) connected through local area or internet. The services are delivered through cloud via Internet. The cloud controllers process the requests to provide mobile users the uninterrupted services through cloud. The basic challenge involves the connection of heterogeneous nodes, protocol design, signal detection hardware, software support, and updating the data on the real-time basis. The cloud test-bed is provided in Figure 1. The Test-bed contains various mobile computers, building with local area network, mobile vehicles, and corporate headquarters. The devices are connected through a wired and wireless facility. The facility includes file transfer, voice, and multi-way communications. The transmission of packets may jam, channel may not be available to mobile devices, and various communication problems may arise. The cloud architecture will help to solve all the problems with affordable cost.

The cloud test-bed has many service functions including performance, linking of high speed centers, data storage, building the network platform to customer needs, testing the customer applications, and reliability. The cloud facility meets the unpredictable user demands without advanced reservation of resources. These facilities are provided on pay per usage. The performance and security are not guaranteed for specific applications. Due to the global mobile market the cloud applications are available in various fields.

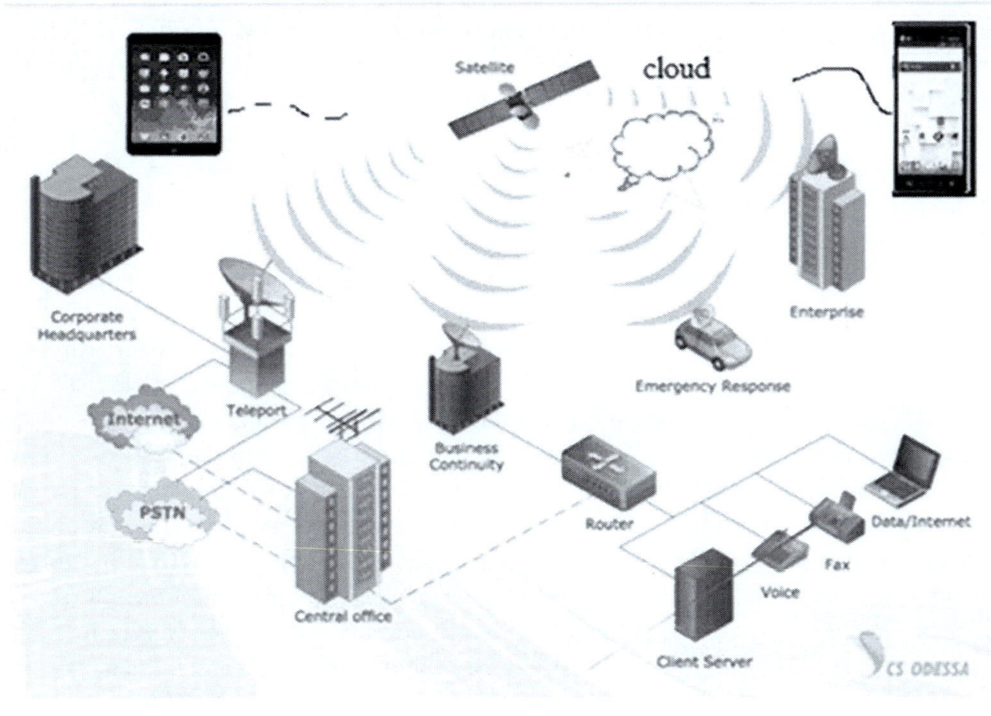

Figure 1. Cloud Testbed.

Mobile commerce uses the cloud services to fulfil the finance, advertising, and shopping demand. Mobile commerce applications are integrated with encryption and authentication to meet the various challenges of bandwidth, complex device configuration and security. Mobile learning provides the rich services between teachers and students. Mobile medical services minimize the limitations of traditional medical treatment. The medical services monitor the patients in and outside medical facilities. The mobile device monitors detect pulse rate, blood pressure, level of alcohol, and current status of the patient. The potential market generating revenues is mobile gaming. Social networks tag the photos, capture the video shots, information searching using tags, keywords, and voice.

Bandwidth is one of the main issues in the mobile cloud computing (MCC) and will be solved using CR technology. Traffic congestion is another issue in MCC. The congestion will be solved in cognitive radio networks in cloud (CRNC) by maintaining the network channel table as part of the cloud. The CRNC is a heterogeneous network and issues of wireless network and on demand scalability of connectivity and energy efficiency will be taken care. Security and privacy are main issues in CRNC due to the cloud environment.

CURRENT AND FUTURE OF COGNITIVE RADIO WITH CLOUD COMPUTING

Cloud can provide the robust network connectivity in spite of security breaches for cognitive users. The cloud environment can collect data from users, process the data and distribute the results to users. These functions help the cognitive network to manage efficient resource allocation. Feng et al. [3] introduced the prototype system that explores the opportunities of cloud that overcomes the intensive computations, storage and jamming problems.

Integrating cloud computing into a mobile environment overcomes the obstacles that affect the performance. The main obstacles include battery life, storage, and bandwidth. The authors [5] presented the overview of the cloud architecture, existing issues, possible solutions, and future directions of cloud integration. The applications including mobile learning, mobile commerce, mobile health care, mobile gaming, and mobile searching were outlined. The article highlights the privacy and security issues of cloud integration in mobile applications as well as enhancing the data access with an increasing number of cloud services.

Chun-Hsien et al. [4] proposed the cooperative spectrum sensing algorithm to improve the processing speed using cloud. Kranthi et al. [8] discussed the work lead to ultra-low power cloud computing system. The gain in power reduction lead to design methods for cloud architecture optimized around low latency, lower power, and energy dissipation proportional to workload. Cloud computing design was simulated to solve the hidden terminal problem [15,16, 17]and efficient data transfer. The work presents the transmission of data in real-time using cloud integration and switching the channel automatically whenever primary user presence is detected. The simulations illustrate the relationship between cloud database table and node table that resembles the channel status and switching the free channels during the sudden entry of the primary user. Such arrangement in real-time helps the continuous service to the cognitive user.

Thanapal et al. [11] discussed the analysis of energy savings and increasing the battery life. A modified medium access protocol was used [13] to collect sensing reports that includes the mean squared errors and cognitive radio channel vacating delay. Antonios [7] presented a cooperative review of two prominent access control models for the cloud (Role-based Access Control model and the Usage Control model). Sachin and Rawat [9] discussed the overview of the performance of spectrum sensing and spectrum management in the cloud computing platforms. They further discussed the Hadoop and Storm models that are currently used in distributed cloud platforms.

Cloud customers required the trust and privacy environment in cloud integration in cognitive networks. Kekkonen et al. [12] discussed the general trust between customer and provider. The work discussed the possible methods to strengthen the trust in the cloud environment. Frank [6] designed a platform for privacy integrated queries (PINQ). PINQ provides the differential privacy for most of the plat forms. It provides the privacy preserving algorithm across the data sets and domain. In addition to privacy the trust and integrity are required to ensure the security of the user information. The authentication and user access control helps the authorized users to access the data in the system. The attribute based access control mechanism was discussed by Abdul Raouf Khan [1].

The access control issues in cloud computing and Hadoop distributed systems were discussed by Young-Gi et al. and Yenumula [18, 16]. Young-Gi et al. discussed the security issues at the client level, application level, platform level, and infrastructure level. The security requirements, cloud attacks, and authentication are part of the discussions. Yenumula introduced the security mechanisms currently available in Hadoop systems, requirements of access control mechanisms, and change of access control depending upon the sensitivity of data. The paper further introduces the game model with access limitations in Hadoop distributed file systems.

Temporal access control in cloud computing is discussed by Yan Zhu et al. [14]. They proposed the integer comparison scheme and compared with bitwise comparison scheme. The results show the positive effectiveness. Shucheng [10] uniquely combining the techniques of attribute-based encryption, proxy re-encryption, and lazy re-encryption to achieve highly efficient model. They claim that their scheme is better than standard encrypted models.

The current state of the cloud computing is in its infant stage. It is understood that to access information the user need not be at a specific place and need not own the equipment. The principle is pay for usage of resources, which means the user can retrieve or perform the function as long as the user can have access to the appropriate electronic devices. The cloud helps to upgrade software more quickly than before. The Hadoop distributed file system (HDFS) is most commonly used for large scale cloud development. Hadoop is known for batch processing. It has two phases called Mapping and Reducing. The Map phase performs operations such as filtering, transforming and sorting. The Reduce phase takes that output and aggregates it. There are several advantages of the Hadoop systems. They are inexpensive, have storage flexibility, easy to add more nodes (scalability), inherent data redundancy, and use more processing power (parallel processing).

The smart collection, analysis and visualization of massive data in real-time are done by HStreaming [19]. HStreaming technology helps to process the structured and the unstructured geographically generated data. HStreaming merged with Adello, a leading European programmatic media-buying platform for mobile advertising in August 2013. Adello fulfills the highest brand safety requirements and serves industries including telcos, automotive, and consumer goods. Customers include large agency networks such as GroupM and leading mobile SSP's such as Smaato.

Storm, a Hadoop alternative that was built on real-time aggregation ETL (extract, transform, load) was developed by Nathan Marz in 2011 [20]. The functions of Storm architectures are read the stream of logs from the ad-servers, aggregate them on the fly, and store the aggregated data directly in the data warehouse as soon as they are available. Figure 2 illustrates a simple real-time aggregation of data. The streaming data has fields including time-stamp, publisher, advertiser, bid, website, cookies, and geological location. The data provides the number of impressions per minute and number of unique visitors per minute (using cookies).

The main functions of Storm are spout and bolt. Spout gets the input stream to the Storm cluster. The input may be from any blogs (twitter, Facebook, database, etc.). The output of spout will be the input to bolt. After processing, it will either store in a database or pass it to in a stream of other bolts. Each time it checks the impression type to count unique impressions. The counting will continue to maintain the number of unique impressions received and the total number of impressions received. Figure 3 illustrates the information collected by sprout and sending to bolt, where bolt is connected to the database to store the output as needed. The storm application will basically build the topology and run in local mode. In brief, the sprout receives log impressions from ad-servers and sends the logs to the bolt in streaming.

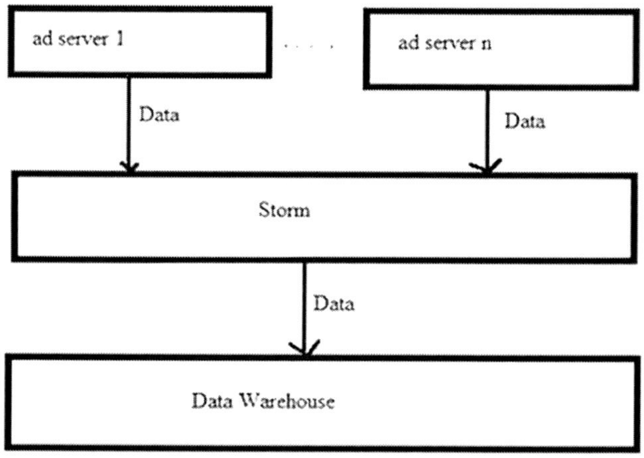

Figure 2. Real-time aggregation of data through streaming pipeline.

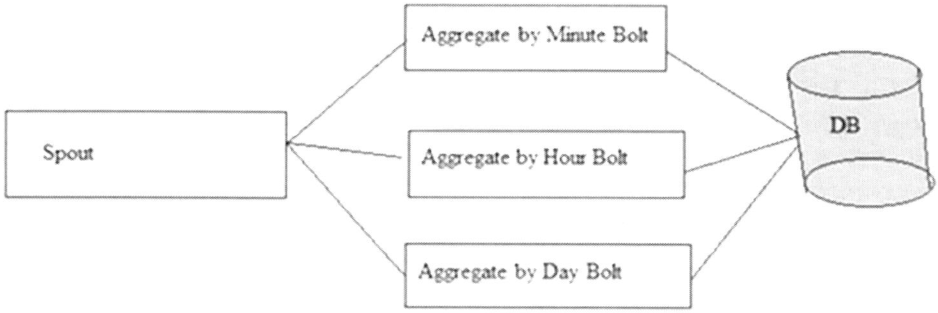

Figure 3. Sending Information from Sprout to Bolt (simultaneous).

PROPOSED MODEL OF COGNITIVE RADIO NETWORK WITH CLOUD (CRNC)

Cognitive radio network forms by connecting cognitive radios nodes (movable and immovable). The cognitive radio uses the unused spectrum efficiently by detecting, analyzing and allocating to cognitive users. The fundamental problem arises in movable devices. The movable devices have limited battery power. The cognitive radio functions require complex computations and many times they require computation help beyond the device level. These activities drain the battery quickly. To avoid the complexity and dependability, a third party called cloud is introduced to take care of the complex computations, needed package access, software, and hardware dependability functions. Therefore, we proposed cognitive radio network with cloud (CRNC) that connects the CRN network with cloud and move most of the complex activities to cloud. Our design requires the status of each node in the network must be stored on cloud database. Since the cloud knows the status of each node in the network, allocation of the communication path is easy to transfer the information.

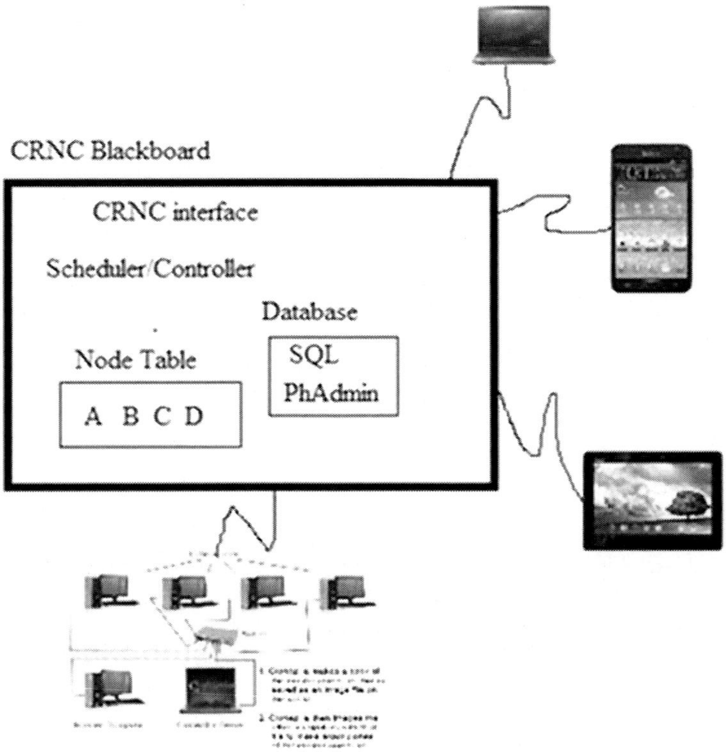

Figure 4. CRNC architecture.

In CRNC, the channels are controlled at cloud. This process eliminates the RTS/CTS problem and delay time. Furthermore, the model avoids the loss of information due to sudden entry of primary user or lack of spectrum availability. The functionalities of the CRNC model defined by Y. Reddy [15] are modified, since the machine learning part is not incorporated in the current model. The modified model of the cloud by [15] is shown in Figure 4.

The CRNC blackboard contains the scheduler, controller, node table and database. The node table is the reflection of the current status of all nodes in the CRN. The table is modified on the real-time basis. It is controlled and managed by the database administrator. The channel allocation and updates are done by the scheduler. In the paper [15] movable and immovable devises were discussed. In the current problem, the heterogeneous devices and heterogeneous activity (movable and immovable) is assumed. For database creation, we used

Python 2.7 since the PhAdmin, and MySql support is only for Python 2.7. The XAMPP package was used to facilitate and monitor the real-time activity. The details are discussed in simulations.

SIMULATIONS

The proposed CRNC model helps to maintain the reliable transmission and eliminated the following requirements:

- Eliminates the RTS/CTS before start the transmission to the next node
- Eliminates the radios for controlling and receiving/transferring
- Eliminates the unavailable of channel at any node during transmission
- Eliminates the problems of sudden entry of primary signal

To manage these requirements, a parallel table should be maintained at cloud. The cloud table maintains the status of all nodes in the network on the real-time basis. Once the simulations started, the database initializes status of all nodes in the table by storing the node's ID, location, and status of all channels of each node. The process is created using Python MySql database.

The XAMPP package was used to facilitate the real-time activity. For experimental purpose, we used ten nodes in the network and three channels in each node. We did many experiments, but due to space limitations, we included Four different experimental results. These graphs are compacted to adjust within the column.

In the first experiment, the channels are available in each node. Therefore, the channel path is set and transfer of packets takes place (Figure 5). The experiment was conducted to send the packets random source to destination. The sample screenshot is shown in Figure 5. If the channels in one of the nodes in the communication path are not available, the transmission will be delayed. The cloud will wait to lock the channel. As soon as the channels on the communication path are identified, the cloud mechanism locks the channels and gives the signal to transfer. Once the channel is notified as free, the updates will carry-out at node level as well as cloud table. This part is not shown in the current discussion.

In the next simulation experiment, we programmed the sudden entrance of the primary user (PU). If the PU suddenly enter in the scene two cases arise. The alternate channels are available to assign to the cognitive user and channels not available to assign. These two cases are discussed in Figures 6, 7, and 8.

If the PU enters and no channel is available in one or more nodes of the communication path, the packets will be temporarily stored in cloud buffer and released as soon as the channels are available. This problem is special case in mobile devices (particularly voice based) and difficult to solve. The case occurs when two users are in the middle of the communication. This particular case is not discussed in this paper and left for future research. Further, if the alternative channels are available, the cloud controller locks the new path and continues the transfer. We have packets travel to cloud or from cloud, node to node, primary user entrance, node color, and cloud color. Figure 6 shows the current status of the packet transfer, node status, and tables at cloud and node.

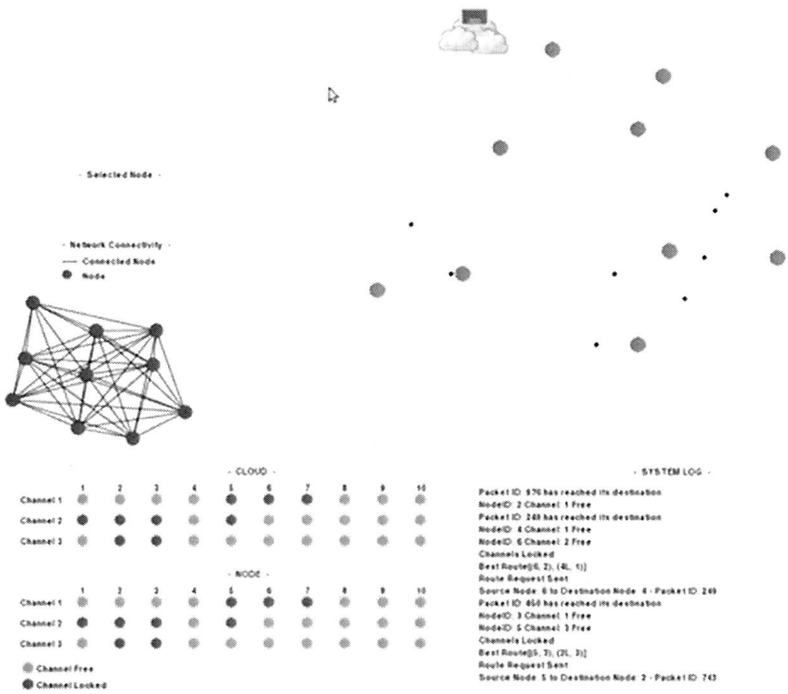

Figure 5. Network Nodes, Packet Transfer and Channel Status of Cloud Application.

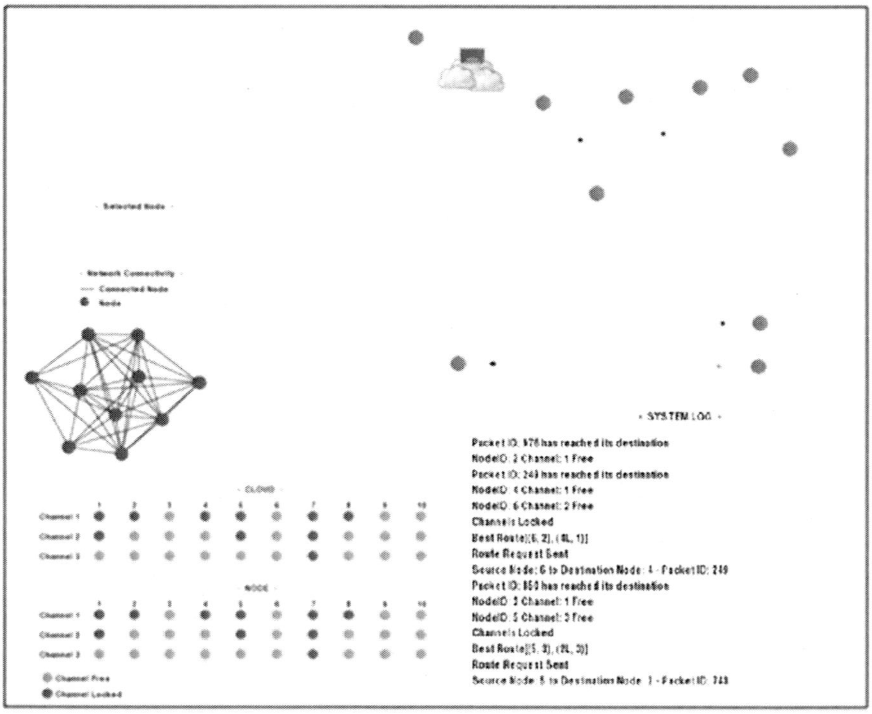

Figure 6. A screenshot of the simulated environment (Primary user with Nodes 1, 5 and 7; Secondary user with Channels 1 and 2).

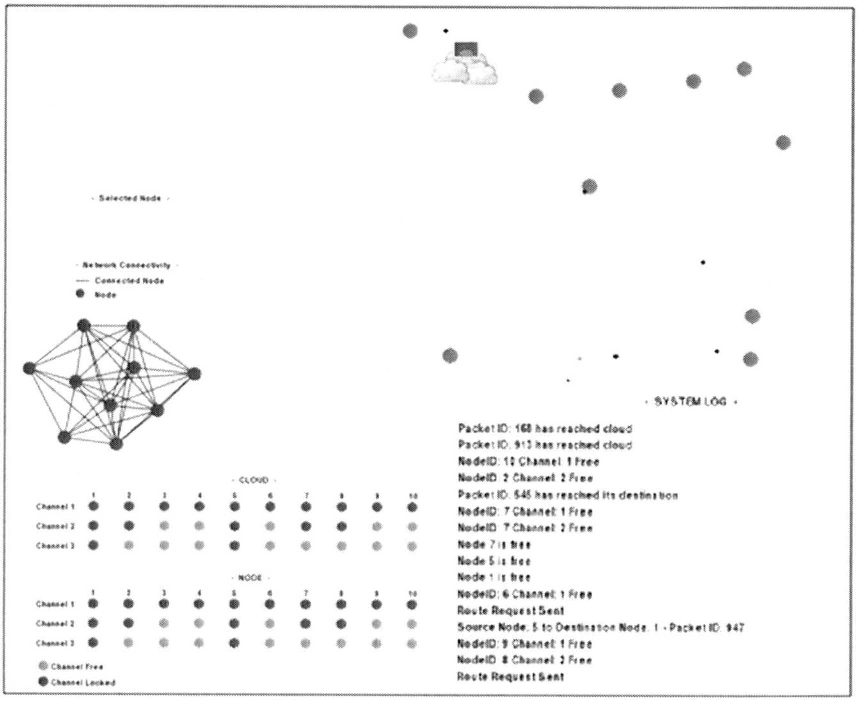

Figure 7. A Screenshot of the simulated environment (Packets avoid the Primary user; No Available Channels).

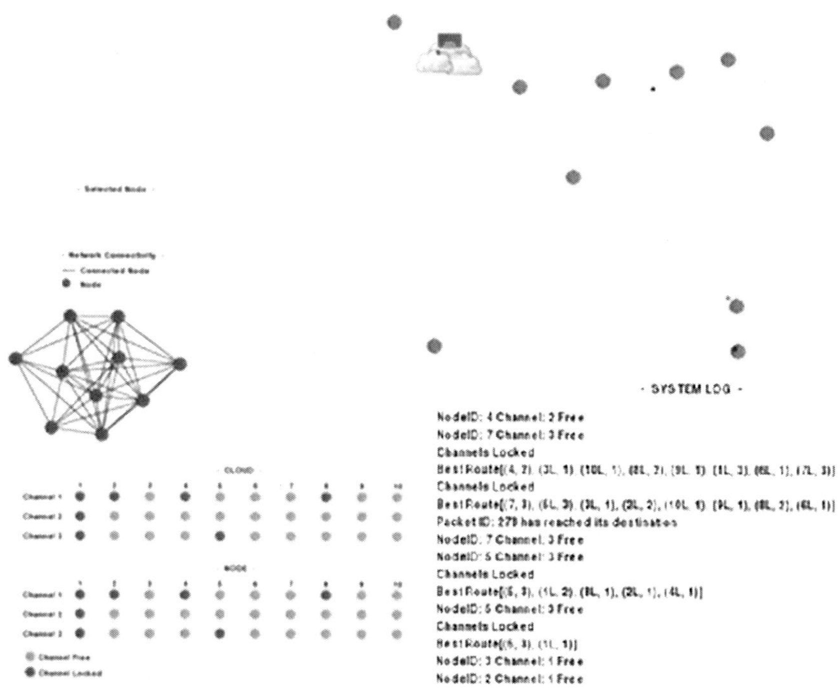

Figure 8. A Screenshot of the simulated environment (Packets Buffered at the Current Node in the Cloud).

The system status is the status of CRNC and is given in Figures 5 and 6. It shows the channels locked status, Node ID, channel available status (free channels) at each node, and the possible best route. Best rout calculation is part of the simulations. The optimum path selection is calculated using the greedy algorithm [2]. A screenshot of the simulated environment is shown in Figure 6 wherein a primary agent has entered the network and has taken nodes 1, 5 and 7.

The Secondary user takes channels 1 and 2 to prevent disruption from any other node receiving or transfer activity. Figures 7 and 8 shows the sudden entry of primary user and all channels were busy. The special case of unavailable spectrum is very important. The packet were buffered at current node of the cloud and transmitted as soon as the channels (spectrum) are free.

CONCLUSION

The paper "Cognitive radios rides on the cloud" presented in 2010 military communications opens many research ideas. Since 2010, many papers were published and presented in related areas that use cloud technology for communications. CRNC was coined in Feng et al. [3] and cloud simulations were presented in the current chapter. The simulations in many cases included the free channels, sudden entry of the primary user and reallocate the alternative channels during the presence of primary user, available/unavailable channels for sudden entry of the primary user were discussed.

The simulations were designed using Python 2.7. The following software was used to implement the simulations: Ubuntu 12.04 Linux operating system; XAMPP 1.8.1; Eclipse & PyDev; Python 2.7.3 package that includes: MySQLLdb, Pygame, NetyworkX, and Numpy.

The CRNC depends upon the best and most available route before sending a packet. The simulations illustrate a relationship between cloud database and nodes, channel verses node status, activity of network on real time, and presence and absence of the primary user. The selection and locking of packet route shows the saving in time (efficiency) because the transmission will not spend time on poling request for send and clear for send (RTS/CTS) at each node.

The future research includes the security issues and node failures. What happens if the cloud fails? It is a big question.

ACKNOWLEDGMENTS

The research work was supported by the Air Force Research Consortium program through contract number GRAM 13-S7700-02-C2. The author wishes to express appreciation to Dr. Connie Walton, Provost and Vice President, Academic Affairs, GSU for her continuous support. The author also wishes to express appreciation to Mr. Darien Lambert and Ms. Shatay Holmes of Department of Computer Science, GSU, for proof reading.

REFERENCES

[1] Khan, A., 2012. Access Control in Cloud Computing Environment. *APRN Journal of Engineering and Applied Sciences*. 7, *5*, 613-615.

[2] Cormen, T. H., Leiserson, C. E., Rivest, R. L., Stein, C., (2001). *Introduction to Algorithms*, 2nd ed., MIT Press.

[3] Ge, F., Lin, H., Khajeh, A., Chiang, C. J., Eltawil, A. M., Bostian, C. W., Feng, W., Chadha, R., 2010. Cognitive Radio Rides on the Cloud. *Proceedings of the 20th Military Communications Conference: Networking Protocols and Performance*. 1448-1453.

[4] Ko, C-H., Huang D., Wu, S-H., 2011. Cooperative Spectrum Sensing in TV White Spaces: When Cognitive Radio Meets Cloud. *Proceedings of the IEEE International Conference on Computer Communications*: *Workshop on Cloud Computing*. 683-688.

[5] Dinh, H. T., Lee, C., Niyato, D., Wang, P., 2013. A Survey of Mobile Cloud Computing: Architecture, Applications and Approaches. *Wireless Communication and Mobile Computing*, 13, *18*, 1587-1611.

[6] McSherry, F. D., 2009. Privacy Integrated Queries: An Extensible Platform for Privacy-Preserving Data Analysis. *Proceedings of the ACM SIGMOD International Conference on Management of Data*. 19-30.

[7] Gouglidis, A., Mavridis, I., 2011. Towards New Access Control Models for Cloud Computing Systems. *Presented at the IT Security for the Next Generation, Conference for Young Professionals, European Cup*.

[8] Manoj, K., Kelley, B., Prevost, J., 2010. Low Power Wireless Cloud Network Convergence Protocol for Next Generation Smart Micro-grids. *Proceedings of the World Automation Congress* (*WAC*).

[9] Shetty, S., Rawat, D. B., 2013. Cloud Computing based Cognitive Radio Networking. *Cognitive Radio Technology Applications for Wireless and Mobile Ad hoc Networks*, edited by: Meghanathan N., and Reddy, Y. B., *8*, 153-164.

[10] Yu, S., Wang, C., Ren, K., Len, W., 2010. Achieving Secure, Scalable, and Fine-Grained Data Access Control in Cloud Computing. *Proceedings of the 29th IEEE International Conference on Information Communications*. 534-542.

[11] Thanapal, P., Varshney, A., Saleem Durai, M. A., 2012. A Survey on Cloud Computing for Mobile Users: Making Smartphones Last Longer with Computation Offload. *International Journal of Computer Applications*, 56, *18*, 1-4.

[12] Kekkonen, T., Kanstren, T., Hatonen, K., 2014. Towards Trusted Environment in Cloud Monitoring. *Proceedings of the 11th International Conference on Information Technology*: *New Generations* (*ITNG*).

[13] Wu, S-H., Chao, H-L., Ko, C-H., Mo, S-R., Jaing, C-T., Li, T-L., Cheng, C-C., Liang, C-F., 2012. A Cloud Model and Concept Prototype for Cognitive Radio Networks. *IEEE Wireless Communications*, 19, *4*, 49-58.

[14] Zhu, Y., Hu, H., Ahn, G-J., Huang, D., 2012. Towards Temporal Access Control in Cloud Computing. *Proceedings of the IEEE International Conference on Communications*. 2576-2580.

[15] Reddy, Y. B., 2012. Solving Hidden Terminal Problem in Cognitive Networks using Cloud Applications. *Proceedings of the 6th International Conference on Sensor Technologies and Applications*. 235-240.

[16] Reddy, Y. B., Ellis, S., 2013. Modeling Cognitive Radio Networks for Efficient Data Transfer using Cloud Link. *Proceedings of the 10th International Conference on Information Technology: New Generations (ITNG)*. 525-530.

[17] Reddy, Y. B., 2013. Access Control for Sensitive Data in Hadoop Distributed File Systems. *Proceedings of the 3rd International Conference on Advanced Communications and Computation.*

[18] Min, Y-G., Shin, H-J., Bang, Y-H., 2012. Cloud Computing Security Issues and Access Control Solutions. *Journal of Security Engineering*, 9, 2, 135-141.

[19] Hstreaming, http://sourceforge.net/projects/hstream/files/stats/timeline, last accessed on: May 1, 2014.

[20] Storm, Preview of storm: The Hadoop Real-time Processing, https://github.com/nathanmarz/storm/wiki/Tutorial, last accessed on: May 1, 2014.

Index

A

B

C

D

E

N

O

P

Q

R

S

T

U

V

W

Y

Z